P9-DZZ-367

THE INTERDISCIPLINARY
TEACHER'S HANDBOOK

THE INTERDISCIPLINARY TEACHER'S HANDBOOK
Integrated Teaching Across the Curriculum

Stephen Tchudi
Stephen Lafer

NO LONGER
the property of
Whitaker Library

Boynton/Cook Publishers
HEINEMANN
Portsmouth, NH

111377

Boynton/Cook Publishers, Inc.
A subsidiary of Reed Elsevier Inc.
361 Hanover Street
Portsmouth, NH 03801–3912
Offices and agents throughout the world

Copyright © 1996 by Stephen Tchudi and Stephen Lafer. All rights reserved. No part of this book may be reproduced in any form or by any electronic or mechanical means, including information storage and retrieval systems, without permission in writing from the publisher, except by a reviewer, who may quote brief passages in a review.

The authors and publisher thank those who have given permission to reprint borrowed material.

Excerpt from *Zen and the Art of Motorcycle Maintenance* by Robert Pirsig. Copyright © 1974 by Robert Pirsig. By permission of William Morrow Company, Inc.

The authors are interested in on-going discussion of the concepts developed in this book. A web site is under construction. Readers wishing to participate can send a note indicating interest to either Stephen Tchudi at **stuchu@powernet.net** or Stephen Lafer at **lafer@unr.edu**.

Library of Congress Cataloging-in-Publication Data
Tchudi, Stephen, 1942–
    The interdisciplinary teacher's handbook : a guide to integrated
teaching across the curriculum / Stephen Tchudi, Stephen Lafer.
      p. c.m
    Includes bibliographical references and index.
    ISBN 0-86709-398-6 (alk. paper)
    1. Interdisciplinary approach in education--United States.
2. Teaching--United States. I. Lafer, Stephen. II. Title.
    LB1570.T297 1996
    375--dc20
                                              95-47264
                                              CIP

Editor: *Peter R. Stillman*
Production: *Melissa L. Inglis*
Cover design: *Jenny Jensen Greenleaf*
Manufacturing: *Louise Richardson*

Printed in the United States of America on acid-free paper
99 98 97 96   EB   1 2 3 4 5 6 7 8 9

CONTENTS

INTRODUCTION

e believe that interdisciplinary teaching is the way of the future in education.

There. We've said it.

And we'll restate it as plainly as we can: Interdisciplinary, integrated teaching has the most promise of any movement to revolutionize the schools during the reader's and our teaching lifetimes.

As an educational reform movement, interdisciplinary education (which we'll define and illustrate in more detail in Chapter 1) is gaining strength as we write in the late twentieth century, and it encompasses the kinds of educational aims that we think will prevail in the twenty-first.

It's tempting to call this a "new" approach, but the underlying concepts and values of interdisciplinary teaching have been implied and tacitly recognized from the very beginnings of school instruction. From the Greeks to the present, educators have called for teaching and learning that integrates disciplines and fields. Too, there are many examples and models of interdisciplinary learning throughout educational history: the Greek ideal of a "sound mind in a sound body"; the European inquiry-oriented traditions of Comenius, Pestalozzi, and Montessori; C.P. Snow's call for bridging the "two cultures" gap between science and humanities; the American progressive education movement of the first half of this century; the British infant schools of the mid-century; and the open and alternative schools of the second half century.

Until recently, interdisciplinary teaching has not made a significant impact on the curriculum of schools and colleges. The disciplinary model—centering instruction in the sciences, mathematics, history, and English—has dominated the educational system, even in the self-contained classrooms of the elementary schools, and manifestly in the courses of the high schools and universities.

However, recent trends in schools encourage us to assert that the times are a-changin' for interdisciplinary education. The general unhappiness of the public, politicians, teachers, and students with the achievements of education has led to the questioning of our educational traditions. Although some reformers have argued for a heightened emphasis on discipline (both behavioral and intellectual), many have recognized that discipline-centered learning often ignores or neglects the needs and interests of the learners themselves. The structures of the disciplines that prove helpful to scholars at the cutting edge of their fields may not be the best way to bring youngsters into the fold.

The challenge to disciplinary learning implies dramatic changes in everything from the organization of the classroom to the nature of assessment and testing, from teacher training to the role of students in their own learning.

We assume that many of our readers, whether veteran teachers or students preparing to come into the profession of teaching, have not fully experienced the richness of interdisciplinary teaching themselves. That is, we assume that you were reared (as we were) within the disciplinary model. Oh, there may have been the occasional cross-disciplinary course where, say, the history professor and the art professor teamed up to lecture on common topics, or one may have taken a hyphenated science course like bio-physics, but on the whole, we've all been a part of the intellectual system that this book rejects (or, more accurately, places in a larger context).

At first, then, interdisciplinary teaching can be a scary proposition for teachers. Having been disciplinary "majors" and "minors," we may have become isolated from significant learning in other fields, particularly across the "two cultures" gap of science and humanities.

However, if you have ever learned to do something on your own, without formal schooling, you have probably experienced and mastered interdisciplinary learning skills. Can you speak your native language? Can you read and select from the offerings in *TV Guide*? Have you raised a child or a pet, learned an art or craft by yourself, learned how to change a toilet bobber, found significance for your life in the comic page in the newspaper (or the news, weather, business, or editorials)? If so, you have employed skills and knowledge that cut across the disciplines. You are probably like Molière's *bourgeois gentilhomme*, who was astonished to discover that he had been speaking prose all his life! You have been *living* interdisciplinarily, even if you have never studied or taught that way.

Still, within school and college settings, the teacher who wants to operate from an interdisciplinary perspective often has to go it alone, creating materials as he or she goes, relying on libraries and media centers rather than on textbooks, developing classroom strategies that allow for unusual diversity of student activity, and designing assessment tools that measure broadly-based learning. All this while convincing parents, administrators, and even students that traditional subject matter is being covered.

We have found that once teachers overcome their initial caution about this philosophy toward teaching and plunge in, they find it extraordinarily enriching and liberating, both for themselves and for their students. However, they also describe it as a voyage of self-discovery, where there have, to date, been few maps, often just rough sketches by other explorers.

To some extent, we think the voyage of self-discovery is necessary and appropriate. That is, interdisciplinary teaching is not a simplistic method that can be reduced to a series of steps or an ACRONYM for a surefire strategy. (We tried to work out a formula for teaching based on the letters in INTERDISCIPLINARY: " 'I' is for 'Inquiry', 'N' is for, uhm, 'Nowledge' . . . ." No luck. The complexity of the word itself reflects the nonformulaic nature of the teaching.)

Thus all interdisciplinary teachers undertake voyages every time they choose (or have students choose) a new theme, a fresh direction, or a novel question for exploration.

This book is intended to be a companion for your voyage. We will explore issues and problems in interdisciplinary teaching to offer a theoretical and philosophical framework, coupled with practical classroom strategies, for teachers of a wide range of interests and experiences.

Because of the growing interest in this area, there is newfound knowledge and methods to this business of teaching across the disciplines. Through practical classroom experience as well as contemplating theoretical and research issues, teachers have found ways to set reasonable goals for interdisciplinary teaching within conventional as well as experimental school curricula; to find resources without spending all their waking hours in the library; to teach in disciplines where they haven't earned a college degree; to get thirty-five learners pursuing separate tracks of study while still maintaining classroom order and discipline; and to show growth and development that accurately reflects myriad knowledge, skills, and processes developed in good interdisciplinary teaching. We'll take up those ideas, projects, and strategies, chapter by chapter.

After our introductory discussion of definitions and issues (Chapter 1), we'll describe transitional structures, ways of beginning interdisciplinary work from within a traditional, discipline-centered structure (Chapter 2). Our alternative to the structure provided by the disciplines is thematic, or topical, teaching, with subjects for study growing from student (and disciplinary) interests (Chapter 3), leading to carefully articulated aims and goals that grow from the questions young learners have about their world (Chapter 4). Where to go for teaching resources is taken up next, including a discussion of classroom management structures to launch students on self-directed learning ventures (Chapter 5). We then take up ways of moving from idea to action (Chapter 6), and of assessing what has been learned (Chapter 7). Finally, lest we have overemphasized the role of the *independent* interdisciplinary teacher, we discuss interdisciplinary curriculum design, pointing toward what we see as the potential for fully integrated curricula in the coming decades (Chapter 8).

Each of those chapters contains many ideas for classroom implementation of interdisciplinary teaching, mixing pedagogical theory with practice. You'll also find boxed material from time to time that invites you to contemplate ideas we have presented, or to explore interdisciplinary teaching ideas with students and to reflect on the results. We call these "InterMusings"—"inter" meaning "between" or "among"; "musings" used as in the poetic "muse" or simply "a-musing." Some will suggest ideas for classroom activities and contemplation of the results. Others will accompany issues and topics covered by the book, inviting you to muse on, mull over, or act out interdisciplinary principles. For example:

InterMusing

Think about one of those life skills you have mastered on your own. How did you learn to tie your shoes or to wrap a package? Or change a tire or play a tune on a harmonica? Or file your income tax forms? What were the interdisciplinary aspects to your learning? How was it shaped by "science"? How did history enter in? math? language? the arts? You may attribute some of this learning to common sense, but with a little reflection, you'll see that it, too, is a distinctly interdisciplinary form of knowledge.

In Part 2 you will find some "Interdisciplinary Jumpstarters": ideas, resources, and activities for several interdisciplinary units. Some of these units may be the sort of thing you can implement directly in your classroom. More likely, we think, you will borrow from these ideas, take them as models, and move out to develop teaching units of your own.

We began this introduction with the bold claim that interdisciplinary teaching will be the direction of school education in the twenty-first century. We hope our prophecy will not fall victim to the fickle winds of educational change. It's possible that time and conditions may take the wind out of the sails of the interdisciplinary movement.

So we'll close with another bold claim, one that is a little less dependent upon outside conditions: If you try interdisciplinary or integrated teaching, you'll never go back to the kind of schooling you experienced. We know this to be true because it has happened to us. We began our careers as English/language arts teachers, and that is still our home base at the university. But as a result of our interdisciplinary teaching, our whole philosophy of education has changed, and we're not able to teach confined to the disciplinary cages in which we were raised. As a result of our work, we've found ourselves taking students to the planetarium and to agricultural irrigation projects; we've had them read about nuclear wastes, Darwin's finches, and the nature of Galileo's discovery process; we've presided over student projects that cover global economic conditions and global warming. We predict the same sort of thing will happen to you, and we are pleased to offer this book in support of your interdisciplinary future.

Stephen Tchudi
Stephen Lafer

The Theory and Practice of Interdisciplinary Teaching

1 *Redefining the Disciplines*
The Rationale for Interdisciplinary Teaching

> The influence of the academic discipline is pervasive. Colleges are organized by departments of separate disciplines; faculty are trained, hired, and promoted by colleagues within the discipline; the identity, professional development, and career paths of faculty are provided by disciplinary guilds and national associations; and students are expected to specialize in a discipline as well as sample from other specializations in order to graduate from college.
> GAFF 1989, 57

Jerry Gaff accurately describes the dominant role of "disciplinary" learning in higher education. Probably every reader of this book has experienced (or is in the process of experiencing) the disciplinary structure of higher education, what Gaff describes as "an efficient bureaucratic device for organizing academic life" (57). Majors, minors, core requirements, faculties, departments, publications—all are organized, some more neatly than others, around a standard collection of about one hundred disciplines and fields, from Astronomy to Zoology.

Disciplinary Learning and the Schools

One can easily see the influence of this structure on the high schools and elementary schools of the United States (and most other western countries). Although there may not be departments of Astronomy or Zoology, high schools have structured themselves around what we identify as the Big Four of disciplines: science, mathematics, history, and English. These are augmented by peripheral academic subjects such as art and music, "peripheral" not because they are unimportant or not valued, but because the schools have not figured out how to integrate them and support them financially. High schools also show additional fragmentation into what we might call the "applied" or "practical disciplines": shop, physical education, and journalism. All this dividing and subdividing is centered on a *disciplinary* model of learning.

If you peer into the desk of almost any elementary school child, beneath the arithmetic papers and gum wrappers, you'll likely find at least four plump textbooks teaching separately the Big Four disciplines. Although most elementary teachers are in a self-contained classroom and are, in principle, free to spend lesson time any way they want, the elementary school day is likewise and typically fragmented. There may not be bells ringing every fifty minutes signaling students to march to their next class, but there is, nonetheless, a progression through the traditional fields: "OK, children, put away your math books, it's time for social studies." In our area of the English/language arts, there has been a movement away from the fragmented day, to what's called "whole language" or "integrated" or "generative curriculum," but even here one often finds teachers inserting traditional materials—spelling lists, math drills, social studies chapters—in ways that pay allegiance to disciplinarity.

InterMusing

Figure 1–1 shows a curriculum overview from a fifth grade elementary school class. What influences do you see of the Big Four disciplines? (That's easy.) What rationale can you imagine for the curricular content of each component? (More difficult.) Why would a science unit on oceans appear the same year as a unit on American history and one on long division? Why would an educator suppose that students who are developmentally ready for historical fiction should also have units on cursive writing and the universe at the same time? Intermusing, think about some ways in which you could bring coherence to this program by linking ideas and topics across the disciplines. Alternatively, think about better ways of organizing the elementary school curriculum than by centering on the Big Four.

Middle and junior high schools are, characteristically, caught in a "middle" position, in part because they have often been created as schools of convenience: a place to store those difficult "transescent" kids, the ones who are too old for childish ways, too young for mature intellectual experiences—"Let's put them in a 'junior' or 'middle' school!" Happily, there is today a strong movement in the middle school curriculum toward interdisciplinarity, and many of the models we discuss in this book will be found operating successfully at that level. Some educators even argue that the middle school is the natural home of interdisciplinarity (Beane 1991). However, if you look at the telltale textbooks that many junior high and middle school kids lug around, or heave into lockers, you'll find evidence of the omnipresent Big Four disciplines. Above all, parents and many teachers and school board members seem to want middle school kids grounded in the fundamentals of disciplinary learning so they can go on to "high" school, where serious disciplinary study still carries the day.

Social Studies	Math
United States history	Long division
	Multiplication
Writing	Fractions
Writing workshop	Manipulatives
	Mental math
Science	Problem solving
Oceans	
Sound	**Reading**
Sensing and moving: human body	Literature based
Electricty/magnetisim	Novels
Living organism: plants and animals	Biography
The universe	Historical fiction
	Content reading
Spelling	Accelerated reading
Cursive writing	
Spelling tests	

FIG. 1–1 *A Fifth Grade Curriculum Overview*

Defining the "Disciplines"

What is a "discipline" anyway, and why should we even be questioning the concept as an approach to schooling?

The *New Lexicon Webster's* offers this intriguing (and chilling) definition:

> the training of the mind and character / a branch of learning / a mode of life in accordance with rules / self-control / control, order, obedience to rules / *eccles[iastical]* a system of practical rules for the members of a Church or an order / punishment, esp. mortification of the flesh by way of penance / a scourge for religious penance.

This dictionary goes on to point out that the past participle, *disciplined*, means "to bring under control / to train / to punish."

Those are definitions fraught with implications for education, most of them unpleasant. But let's *discipline* ourselves to discuss them!

We're not opposed to order, self-control, knowledge, and like concepts. Yet the links between discipline as knowledge and discipline as submission seem to us significant. The definitions echo of the Middle Ages when the central disciplines of the *trivium* (grammar, rhetoric, and logic) and the *quadrivium* (arithmetic, geometry, astronomy, and music) formed a curriculum that was both rigorous and self-denyingly academic and monastic. Further, the link to punishment must be examined in its various contexts. How often is it that school *discipline* (as punishment) has been linked to failure to master *disciplinary knowledge*? How often do *disciplinary* "problems" in school come from students' rebellion against the rigors of school *academic disciplines*? How often is mastery of those *disciplines* linked to moral or ethical or behavioral goodness? Why does Bart Simpson have to write the following on the chalkboard five hundred times?: "This punishment is not boring and pointless."

We confess that we've been a bit melodramatic here in showing the links between disciplinary learning and medievalism. We've stereotyped schools as dungeons and torture chambers (not that they haven't been called both by many students, possibly including the reader). We admit to somewhat overstating the definitional case against discipline.

The fact is, the Dark Ages aside, disciplinary learning *does* have a great many victories to its credit, and the people who have insisted on its primacy in schools and colleges are not fools. From the earliest days of civilization, humankind has recognized the need to codify and systematize its learning. It's no coincidence that the first parts of the world to create writing and mathematical systems were also leaders in commerce and culture, the first to create libraries, the first to create schools, the first to question the magical powers of the gods and goddesses, the first to treat medicine as science rather than superstition (Gaur 1984).

In our own time, the triumphs of disciplinary knowledge are enormous, giving us fairly certain knowledge of elements so small we can barely imagine them, offering understanding of intergalactic distances so huge they boggle the mind. The disciplines have led to spinoffs that equip us with everything from microwave ovens and cable TV to understanding the mysteries of our bodies and minds. So we'd certainly have to disagree somewhat with Jerry Gaff and state that the disciplines offer far more than a convenient bureaucracy for organizing schools and universities. The disciplines not only store knowledge in useful ways; they set guidelines for the generation of new knowledge, creating scholarly communities where fresh ideas are proposed, tested, rejected, and accepted. The disciplines bring order to our understanding. They have helped shape our ideas and have made life better for us all.

InterMusing

In *A History of Writing*, Albertine Gaur reflects on the connections between literacy and information storage. She presents evidence that complex societies develop literacy and mathematics as tools in their social and economic evolution. Obviously, the way we "store" information in the computer age differs greatly from that of the early days of literacy. What role does information storage play in the creation and maintenance of knowledge in *our* time? Visit a library and talk with a librarian about the current problem of knowledge storage and access. What does this tell us about the successes of the knowledge makers who have shaped our civilization?

The Challenges to Disciplinary Learning

The question thus comes up again: Why challenge the old order? Why fix it if it ain't broke? Why knock the disciplines if they are, in fact, so useful?

There are two ways of responding to that question, the first having to do with the nature of disciplinary learning itself. As it happens, scholars on the cutting edge of knowledge are increasingly finding disciplines to be barriers or confinements rather than administrative or intellectual conveniences. The disciplines sometimes serve as blinders rather than lenses, limiting vision rather than enhancing it. Paul DeHart Hurd (1991) notes that the proliferation of scientific knowledge has led to some 25,000 to 30,000 different research fields *within* the science disciplines, spawning some 70,000 journals, 29,000 of them established since 1978. Such proliferation demonstrates the problems of overspecialization, where a scholar becomes an expert in his or her unique corner of the universe, but can speak to few others. Hurd also shows that in science, the growing practice is toward interdisciplinarity and integration. He argues that schools need to be concerned with educating scientists who can see the big picture, rather than simply knowing the depths and details of their tiny corner of the universe.

Further, there is concern for integration across the traditional "two cultures" gap of science and humanities. In a speech before the American Academy of Science, Rep. George Brown, chair of the House Science, Space, and Technology Committee, chided scientists for the narrowness of their research: "Neither technology nor economics can answer questions of values. Is our path into the future to be defined by the literally mindless process of technological evolution and economic expansion, or by a conscious adoption of guiding moral precepts?" (Cordes 1993). He told the scientists, in essence, that specialized knowledge alone won't suffice for the future, despite the obvious success of science and technology in accomplishing apparent miracles.

InterMusing

One area of concern for science educators is the link between science, technology, and society. Echoing the concern of people like George Brown, they worry that students in our nation's schools aren't getting the kind of scientific understanding they need to make informed decisions. Reflect on a current issue of importance in your region that requires scientific or technological solutions: nuclear waste disposal, water supplies, air quality. Has your science education equipped you to make informed decisions, or do you, like many folks, tend to defer decisions on such matters to the experts, because they're in a better position to know?

In arguing for interdisciplinary programs on college campuses, Margaret Miller and Anne-Marie McCartan (1990) have pointed out that not only is the number of "amalgamated" fields increasing—for example, bio-technology, ethno-history—but "the most advanced research in these fields is occurring at the crossings between them" (33). Gaff, again, observes that "ideas from any field are enriched by theories, concepts, and knowledge from other fields. Problems of the world are not organized according to the categories of scholars; solutions to problems as diverse as pollution, defense, communications, and health require knowledge and perspectives from several disciplines" (57).

In other words, there is evidence that many disciplines have already rejected their specialized functions and there is good reason to suppose that the sacredness of the disciplines for scholars themselves will increasingly be challenged. Although universities are sometimes tortoise-like in their rate of change, we think it is reasonable to imagine that universities (and other scholarly institutions) will, in coming decades, see a major rearranging of their structures, leading away from disciplinarity and toward interdisciplinary points of view.

The second argument against the dominance of the disciplinary model is educational. We question the traditional assumption that the best way to present young or novice learners with knowledge is to categorize that knowledge along the lines of disciplinary structures. Traditionally, curriculum makers have looked at the structures of adult or scholarly knowledge, broken that knowledge down into component parts, and presented those parts to the young in sequential, hierarchical order. The final aim is to bring students up to speed with adult knowledge and performance. Educators have taught the sum of parts in order to reach a whole.

As logical as it may seem, this building-block approach doesn't seem to have worked to anyone's satisfaction. In the broadest sense of generally accepted goals for education, disciplinary teaching has not met *its own* best goals and aims.

Of science, for example, Paul DeHart Hurd says quite baldly: "There is agreement that the present curriculum is indefensible" (33). Echoing the kinds of remarks made by Representative Brown, Hurd adds that "science courses must [come to] reflect the ethos of modern science and technology; that instructional goals should focus on the welfare of individuals and societal needs . . ." (33).

This kind of shortcoming is not confined to science. The educational press documents the failures in mathematics education: "Students Fall Short on 'Extended' Math Questions" (Viadero 1993). It seems that kids are competent enough at answering multiple choice math problems on the National Assessment of Educational Progress, but when faced with "story problems," or problems that require exploration of mathematical implications, they do less well. "We teach math OK," goes the cliché, "but the students just don't use the math we teach."

So it is in other disciplines. In the English/language arts, teachers attempt to instill a joy of reading and a fluency and confidence in writing, but all too many graduates of schools and colleges regard their last English course as the end of their disciplined approach to literacy, books, and writing. Although many of the statistics on adult literacy are skewed or exaggerated, a number of studies have shown that, as with the extended math problems, perhaps one-third to one-half of

Americans have difficulty with any kind of literacy beyond the functional level of instructions, lists, and cereal boxes; perhaps one-third have trouble with even those skills. History/social studies, the other member of the Big Four, has its own stack of press clippings where reports snicker at the silly answers given by students on history exams—students who think Abe Lincoln and George Washington were college roommates, or students who don't know the difference between Europe and the countries in Europe, or even those who believe that Sir Francis Drake circumcised the world with a giant clipper.

Not all of these problems can be blamed on disciplinary teaching, of course. Television has changed our nation's literacy habits; modern packaging and electronics have cut out the need for many mathematical applications; science has grown so complex that many people have a phobia about it; map reading doesn't seem to be such an essential skill when rental cars advertise electronic satellite tracking in case you are lost.

However, we think it is important to point out that disciplinary learning has *not* been able to solve these fundamental problems of learning either, and there is precious little evidence to suggest that it will be able to solve them in the future. One still hears occasional cries for a return to the tough disciplinary curricula of the past. (Which curriculum of the past, we wonder—that of the nineteenth century, or the eighteenth? Should we convert schools to monasteries and have kids learn the *trivium* and *quadrivium*?) There is simply no reason to suppose that success lies with the older curricula that have dominated schools for the past centuries. As Hurd says, ". . . reform is needed to prepare students for the twenty-first century" (33). He's talking about science in particular, but there is every reason to believe that his recommendation applies across the curriculum.

The overriding purpose of this book is to offer interdisciplinarity as a leading candidate for the school reform of the twenty-first century—not as a cure-all, but as the direction that we see to be most promising.

"Interdisciplinary" Learning and "Integration"

On the surface, defining our topic is relatively easy. "Inter-" is the prefix meaning union: "between, within / reciprocal / occurring, played, carried on, etc., between / involving two or more." The word "discipline," as we've shown, is a bit more difficult to define rationally. We'd like to expunge "discipline" of its connotations of punishment; we'll adopt the principle that a discipline is simply "an organized body of knowledge and/or a systematic approach to learning." Thus, interdisciplinary.

William Mayville (1978) has made subtle distinctions between ways of yoking disciplines, including terms such as *multi*disciplinarity (juxtaposing any set of disciplines, whether or not they show any apparent connection, as in music and math); *pluri*disciplinarity (juxtaposing disciplines related in concept, as in math and physics); *cross*-disciplinarity (where one discipline is viewed from the methodology of another); and *trans*disciplinarity ("establishing a common system of axioms for a set of disciplines") (9–12). We needn't quibble about these subtleties, although they are useful to think about. We'll use the umbrella term of "interdisciplinary" to represent them all.

Gordon Vars (1991) has suggested that there are essentially two kinds of discipline-merging programs. Borrowing terms that were first used in the 1930s, he describes "correlated" studies, where teachers from two disciplines approach a common topic from within their disciplines, and "fused" studies, a fully interdisciplinary program where the central focus is a theme, topic, or problem that is approached from many different disciplines. A "correlated" (or, in Mayville's terminology, "multidisciplinary") project, for example, might be done on the topic of Native Americans, with history and English teachers correlating their efforts. The history teacher might cover the history textbook chapters, show some relevant videos, and have the students do research on various Native American tribes, arts, and crafts. The English/language arts teacher might cover novels about Native Americans set in historical times and also have students study Native American myths, legends, and folktales. The teachers might make the connections between the disciplines explicit or might be content simply to have the correlation rub off on the students.

Correlated teaching, by the way, does not necessarily require team teaching. In elementary school, for example, a single teacher might correlate several studies in this way, using language arts and social studies to link materials (a good solution to the curricular chaos implied by Figure 1–1, by the way).

"Fused" teaching (Mayville's interdisciplinary, transdisciplinary, cross-disciplinary, or multidisciplinary) breaks down the disciplinary barriers further. Instead of teaching subjects in parallel, a teaching team or an individual teacher chooses a topic or problem and approaches it from as many different directions as possible. Let's suppose one selected the topic of living organisms, based initially on a chapter in a science book. The teacher(s) might have the students create a terrarium or aquarium, linking biology, math, and nutrition as students figure out how to stock and maintain living creatures. There might be a classroom library on "life," with language arts readings that would include fiction, nonfiction, drama, and poetry. The teacher(s) would plan lessons using the fields of astronomy and evolution to discuss the origins of earth and life (and in some states of the union, by law, including "creationism," the Biblical view of the origins of life). Probing into the realm of physics and general science, the teacher(s) might launch a discussion of how ants can lift so much weight, or how bumblebees manage to fly. Through health and P.E. there might be study of anabolic steroids and what they do to human life. The teacher(s) might even probe the inevitable conclusion of life by looking at death from the perspectives of science, math, literature, art, music, myths and legends, and so forth. The "fused" or interdisciplinary unit would draw intelligently on disciplinary knowledge on a "need-to-know" basis.

To repeat, we'll use the term *interdisciplinary* to cover the full spectrum of possibilities, including multidisciplinary efforts that correlate studies as well as fully fused programs and projects. We'll use the term to describe the work of individual teachers who correlate *or* fuse their work, and to describe major curriculum reform efforts involving large teams of teachers.

Another term that we will use as an omnibus is *integration*. In fact, some educators now prefer to discuss an "integrated" curriculum simply because the term itself cuts the ties altogether with the historical concept of disciplinary learning. We'll stick with the *ID* word, however, because the schools have deep disciplinary roots and, shortcomings and all, the disciplines have been and will continue to be major engines in the creation of knowledge.

InterMusing

Think about a school where you have worked, studied, or visited. Given the existing curriculum, are there topics that would lend themselves to the approach of correlation? Could one achieve a degree of curricular integration simply by pairing up units and courses from one, two, or several disciplines? Moving further, can you imagine ways in which learning could be fused, if not through teamed approaches, at least through the relatively uncomplicated strategy of introducing a greater range of disciplinary perspectives into the self-contained unit? How could you "mathify" science? How could you "historicize" mathematics? How could you use literature with science and math, fused *or* correlated? How could you inject a healthy dose of science into a history or English/language arts program?

The Traits of Interdisciplinary Teaching

We've discovered something interesting in our interdisciplinary teaching and our reading of professional literature—a number of new(er) teaching techniques and approaches tend to be linked with interdisciplinary teaching. Figure 1–2 shows some of these characteristics.

For example, where discipline-centered teaching tends to approach its units through concepts found in the disciplines (e.g., electricity, long division, historical novels), interdisciplinary teaching often begins with themes, issues, or problems (e.g., "life and death," "Native Americans"). Interdisciplinary teaching tends to favor *constructed* knowledge (that which students learn for themselves) over that encapsulated in textbooks, emphasizing student inquiry over teacher-set topics. It looks for connections with the real world, and tends to test people through actual or situational experiences rather than exams.

We want to add that Figure 1–2 oversimplifies the equation. The traits listed on the left column are not inextricably linked with disciplinary teaching, any more than those on the right are exclusively the property of interdisciplinarians. It is quite possible, for example, to teach a single-discipline idea such as the nature of the atom from an inquiry approach, so that students construct knowledge rather than simply apply concepts gleaned from the textbook. And by the same token, one can have a fully interdisciplinary unit whose aims are the mastery of school-centered concepts and knowledge rather than community-centered or real-world applications.

However, we want to reemphasize our observation that the kinds of teaching approaches shown in the continua in Figure 1–2 tend to be linked with two distinct schools of thought: If you favor a strictly disciplinary approach, you also tend to favor the teaching methods on the left. If you're interdisciplinarily inclined, you'll find yourself gravitating to the right.

As advocates of inquiry learning, as teachers who think students can create knowledge for themselves rather than always taking it out of a text, as believers in testing through life experiences rather than multiple-choice exams, we find that interdisciplinary approaches offer us a way into these classroom methodologies that gives a degree of coherence and integration to our own teaching.

The final continuum on the chart deserves particular comment. Traditional disciplinary instruction has always valued the teacher as expert or specialist, for the teacher's main job was to explicate concepts to ensure student mastery of the discipline. Without diminishing the value of teacherly expertise, we see that the inter-

Discipline-Centered	Multidisciplinary (correlated study)	Interdisciplinary (fused or integrated)
Disciplinary concepts		Issues or problems
Curricular goals, objectives		Questions, inquiry
Canonical or standard knowledge		Constructed knowledge
Units centered on disciplinary concepts		Thematic, topical units
Lessons		Projects
Individual study		Small group and project work
Textbooks		Multiple resources
School-centered		Real world/community-centered
Knowledge for own sake		Knowledge in service of inquiry
Tests		Portfolios, authentic assessment
Teacher-as-specialist		Teacher-as-resource

FIG. 1–2 *Some Traits of Interdisciplinary Teaching*

disciplinary approach casts the teacher in a new role: that of resource. Rather than being simply the "knower," the teacher becomes one who knows how to help other people come to know and come to discover for themselves. This means that one does not have to be a master of *all* fields and disciplines in order to teach from an interdisciplinary perspective (whew), though it surely helps to have intellectual curiosity that extends beyond your college major and minor and draws on your training in the liberal arts—including those required courses like Art 101 and Math 101! The interdisciplinary teacher is one who can find materials, help kids find materials, understands something of how inquiry works in various fields, and can assist students in conducting genuine inquiry on their own. The interdisciplinary teacher, in fact, is one who can guide students as they invent or reinvent disciplines on their own. Instead of teaching the approved five steps of the scientific method, for example, the teacher will have science students conduct genuine experiments, coming to know what it is scientists do, how they think, how they solve problems. The teacher will have social studies students look at primary materials and make generalizations about what people thought and did in the past. The math teacher will move away from those endless artificial problems in the text and have kids apply math in real life situations. The language arts teacher will have students learn writing skills by writing about real purposes to real audiences, and will help students make connections with other kinds of composing: music, art, and dance.

The kinds of pedagogies associated with interdisciplinary teaching, in turn, give classrooms a new and different look. Marianne Everett (1992) explains, "Many adults today do not understand interdisciplinary curriculum with its child-centered approach to teaching and learning. This doesn't *look* like 'school' to them. They are unaware of 80 years of research, done in the twentieth century, on how children learn" (57).

Moving into interdisciplinary teaching, then, is difficult not only for teachers, but for parents as well. As we will emphasize throughout the book, one should begin cautiously, trying things out, testing them, and exploring new directions. In coming chapters, we will suggest many ways to do just that.

More Bold Claims for the Interdisciplinary Approach

Before moving on to give some specific examples of this obviously large beast we call interdisciplinary learning, we'd like to let it feed on and engulf several other major and allied approaches. Exciting and important curriculum work has been going on in the names of:

Holistic Education

Rather than beginning with knowledge—disciplinary or interdisciplinary—holistic education focuses on the whole child or learner. It emphasizes the linking of values and knowledge, and it focuses on creating classrooms where students take up their learning as wholes, without fragmentation of learning skills or knowledge. Holistic educators recognize that from their earliest moments, children are seeking comprehension and synthesis of their universe, trying to make the pieces fit, trying to make meaning and understanding within it. In that quest, the holists point out, youngsters don't create meaning one fact or formula at a time, and they certainly don't make distinctions between academic fields. Thus many of the projects that one finds described in holistic education literature are distinctly interdisciplinary in nature.

Global and Multicultural Education

Marshall McLuhan was one of the first to recognize that our world has become a "global village" as a result of mass communication, satellite transmissions, and instant electronic access. While a few educators still cling to an approach that emphasizes western traditions, many have called for a broadening of the curriculum to take up global concerns through teaching materials drawn from a rich variety of cultures. William Reeves, for example, answers his own challenging question, "Who Wants a Color-Coordinated Cross-Cultural Core Curriculum?" (1993) by calling for "horizontal integration" of curricula. Noting that there is little sentiment in favor of dropping the DWEM (Dead White European Males) *completely* from the curriculum, he adds that the "principle of horizontal integration can be used to produce a cross-cultural curriculum" (56). He proposes as an example an interdisciplinary unit that might begin with *The Blue Hotel* (Stephen Crane's novel of a Swede who visits the west, becomes involved in gambling, and is eventually killed), which could be horizontally taught with Amy Tan's *The Joy Luck Club* (four Chinese women try to become part of American culture while keeping their identities), V.S. Naipaul's *The Enigma of Arrival* (an Indian born in the West Indies experiences racial conflict while trying to become integrated into the social fabric of England), and Nadine Gordimer's "A Chip of Ruby" (an Indian couple encounters the difficulties of living in South Africa). Global education lends itself to interdisciplinary teaching, too, because worldwide issues—global warming, homelessness, peace in our time, hunger, aging, commerce, the quality of life—cut across the sciences and the humanities and require interdisciplinary knowledge for solution.

Multimedia Education

Perhaps less a philosophy of education than a dedication to using the best that modern technology has to offer, multimedia education breaks down classroom barriers electronically. Although the classroom is still the proverbial independent castle, any classroom with a computer, a modem, and a phone line is now a part of the global village, giving youngsters opportunities to seek answers to their questions from kids in other countries, from specialists here and abroad, through elaborate electronic webs. Media educators are bringing in such naturally interdisciplinary materials as interactive videodiscs, and they are helping students learn how to use the full range of electronic retrieval devices that are becoming standard fare in even the smallest libraries. Although there is still a great deal of debate over the role of television in children's lives, many multimedia educators argue, "Bring the best of it into the classroom." Some would argue, in fact, that if we merely plopped kids in front of the television set and had them watch Cable News Network, the Discovery Channel, Arts & Entertainment, and public broadcasting (and maybe a little MTV at recess), they would be at least as well and probably better educated than they are presently with the use of textbooks. (Of course, we need to carefully recall that in their day, textbooks were the new multimedia adventure of their time, opening up new horizons for readers.) Multimedia educators also want students to be able to use media for communications, so it becomes important for students to learn the how-to skills that enable them to alter computer programs and to use them for their own ends, to use photography and video creatively, and even to write for media production.

These movements toward interdisciplinary/integrated/holistic/global/multimedia curricula are gaining a very substantial foothold in the schools. In the elementary grades, for example, whole language and integrated teaching approaches are beginning to break the mold of subject-by-subject instruction; middle schools have been curricular leaders in modeling interdisciplinary instruction sponsored by teams of teachers; many high schools are exploring interdisciplinary approaches within and across disciplines; and colleges and universities are showing not only a willingness, but an unusual eagerness and vigor, in breaching the traditional fortresses between disciplines.

There is not uniformity of agreement on these matters, of course. We think it's fair to point out that there are trends in contemporary education that are headed in directions other than those we have identified as interdisciplinary. These include the push toward common learning at all grade levels (Hirsch 1993), establishment of national content standards discipline by discipline, and the effort to establish a national testing program that could easily re-entrench old disciplinary models. We should note, too, that there are some who feel that the best route to a coherent or integrated curriculum is *not* to interdisciplinize, but to realign the structures within existing disciplines and thus teach them more coherently. The Bradley Commission on history, for example, has come out in favor of a hierarchical knowledge model that links the knowledge of college professors and doctoral students with the aims of history all the way down to the lower grades (Gagnon n.d.).

Jerre Brophy and Jan Alleman (1991) also warn that curriculum integration can go too far. They observe that "just because an activity crosses subject-matter lines does not make it worthwhile; it must also help accomplish important educational goals." They object to interdisciplinary activities that are forced, unnatural, or silly (e.g., drawing a hungry face as an arbitrary linking of art and social studies in a well-intentioned "hunger" unit). They feel that activities should be defensible "even if they did not include the integration feature" and should "foster, rather than disrupt or nullify, accomplishment of major goals in each subject area" (66).

Perhaps not surprisingly, we share the concern of several of these writers. We've indicated our respect for the traditions of the disciplines, and we think it is clear that there is widespread agreement that students *should*, after all, master the knowledge and skills of the Big Four and myriad other school disciplines. Further, the last thing we want for interdisciplinary teaching is to become a procrustean model or a mere gimmick: one more new fad to squeeze into the curriculum in formulaic ways.

There is more to be said, but we will close this section by briefly recapping the ties we see between interdisciplinary education and numerous exciting, evolving directions in education.

If you want to know precisely where we stand, we favor:

- integrated thematic education

- holistic instruction

- constructivist learning

- whole language teaching

- math, science, history, and everything else across the curriculum

- hands-on or active learning

- multicultural education

- multimedia education

- student-centered teaching

- education for critical thinking and problem solving

- global education

- community-directed or "real-world" education

An Interdisciplinary Sampler

Enough large talk about aims, goals, advantages, and disadvantages of interdisciplinary, integrated learning. It's time for some specifics, some examples of the range of teaching activities that fall under the umbrella of interdisciplinary learning and teaching:

- Giving new meaning to the phrase "hands-on learning," Lawrence Biemiller (1993) reports on "A Maze to End All Mazes." Students and faculty at Lebanon

Valley College in Pennsylvania spent over a month cutting paths in a corn field to create a 560-foot maze (with a stegosaurus outlined in the middle!). The idea came from Don Frantz, an alumnus interested in mazes, who had made contact with specialists in England, where the creation of mazes in hedges has long been popular. Employing math, geography, and cartography, the creators of this "maize maze" generated maps, then blocked out a grid in the cornfield and cut away. As a college/community project, the maze was then opened to the public for entertainment, raising money for the Red Cross. The project also led to study of Greek mythology and the story of the original maze dweller, the Minotaur. This is not your typical classroom interdisciplinary project, but it does help to expand the mind and encourage one to think of the potential of interdisciplinary learning to dramatically change the shape of education.

- Working as a teacher aide in Lynn Butler's fourth grade class at Caughlin Ranch Elementary School, in Reno, Stephen Tchudi gave the youngsters lessons in Esperanto, the international artificial language developed by Ludovic Zamenhof in the late nineteenth century. These lessons were presented as an adjunct to the language arts writing workshop and followed similar "language experience" methodology. The students learned Esperanto through creating fiction and nonfiction stories about themselves and their imaginations. Under the auspices of "Infanoj Cirkau la Mondo" (Children Around the World), an international Esperanto children's program, pen pals in other lands were found. Writing and reading in Esperanto put the youngsters from each country on an even footing, since everyone was writing in a second language. The Reno youngsters published two issues of an Esperanto newsletter that was mailed to their pen pals (Figure 1–3). They received over fifty letters, with art, postcards, stories, and good wishes. These were posted on a bulletin board and on a map of the world, helping to change the teacher's social studies unit on "international understandings" from a textbook chapter to a real-world learning experience.

- Andrea Foster, a sixth-grade science teacher at Sal Ross Middle School in San Antonio, describes an in-class simulation experience that involves math, science, careers, social studies, art, and language arts (1991). While studying the Leaning Tower of Pisa in a social studies unit on Italy, her students constructed a tower, topped by a Ping-Pong ball, from uncooked spaghetti and marshmallows (the latter left out overnight, she reports, in order to achieve a bit of stiffness). The children paid in simulated dollars for their "raw materials" and built the tallest tower they could. Towers were judged on the basis of height, use of raw materials, and construction techniques. This sort of activity shows one way that interdisciplinarity can be brought into the classroom without requiring expensive field trips.

- "Chocolate Chip Cookie Mining" has become a part of teacher lore. Kids are given chocolate chip cookies and toothpicks. The object in this simulation on environmental issues is to "mine" as many "nuggets" from the cookie as possible. Afterward, the students try to restore the "environment" by putting their cookie back together (a project of Humpty Dumptyesque difficulty).

- Shayne Konar (1991) from Grand Forks, British Columbia, draws on his students' interests in baseball cards as an interdisciplinary starting point. Using data on the cards, students keep statistics involving estimating, calculation, and record keeping. They work in geography by locating team locations on a map and calculating traveling distances; they employ art by creating their own baseball cards featuring kids in the class; they write baseball history; they delve into a language arts library featuring baseball fiction and nonfiction.

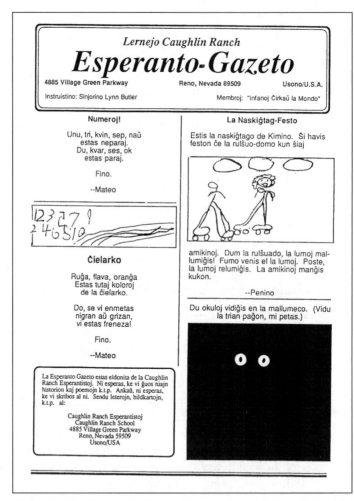

FIG. 1–3 *The "Esperanto Gazeto." Esperanto newsletter published by the fourth graders at Caughlin Ranch Elementary School in Reno. Lynn Butler, teacher.*

- Betty Carvellas, Brad Blanchett, and Lauren Parren, science, social studies, and language arts teachers from Colchester High School in Vermont (1993), describe a course in "Science and Society." Arguing that students need to see the connections between scientific/technical problems and moral/ethical decision making, they have students pick real-world issues—the use of Styrofoam at fast food restaurants, acid rain, toxic waste—investigate them thoroughly in a multimedia approach, and prepare proposals for solutions that are presented in town meetings and other public presentations. Their students have met with community leaders and even had visits from their U.S. senator as they struggle with and make genuine contributions toward solving community problems. Along the way, they obviously develop and polish their disciplinary knowledge and skills in English, social studies, and science.

This sampler is only the tip of the proverbial iceberg of interdisciplinary projects that are going on in classrooms around the globe. (The teaching units in Part 2 of the book provide many more examples, and you might pause in your reading to skim those right now.) In the next several chapters, we'll explore the ways in which you can begin developing imaginative projects of your own.

References

BEANE, J. 1991. "The Middle School: Natural Home of Integrated Curriculum." *Educational Leadership* 49 (2): 9–12.

BIEMILLER, L. 1993. "In Corn as High as a Dinosaur's Eye, a Maze to End All Mazes." *Chronicle of Higher Education* 40 (3): A47.

BROPHY, J. AND J. ALLEMAN. 1991. "A Caveat: Curriculum Integration Isn't Always a Good Idea." *Educational Leadership* 49 (2): 66.

CARVELLAS, B., B. BLANCHETT, AND L. PARREN. 1993. "Science and Society: Escape to the Real World." In *The Astonishing Curriculum: Language in Science and Humanities,* ed. S. Tchudi, 85–91. Urbana, IL: National Council of Teachers of English.

CAYNE, B. S., ed. 1987. *New Lexicon Webster's Dictionary of the English Language.* Danbury, CT: Lexicon.

CORDES, C. 1993. "As Chairman of Key House Committee Restates His Vision, Scientists Worry." *Chronicle of Higher Education* 40 (September 8): A26–A28.

EVERETT, M. 1992. "Developmental Interdisciplinary Schools for the 21st Century." *Education Digest* 57 (2): 57–60. Originally appeared in *Excellence in Teaching* 8 (Winter/Spring/Summer 1991).

FOSTER, A. 1991. "Towers of Spaghetti." *The Instructor* 101 (2): 24–25.

GAFF, J. G. 1989. "Interdisciplinary Studies in Higher Education." *Education Digest* 55 (2): 57–61. Originally appeared in *National Forum,* LXIX (Spring 1989): 4–5.

GAGNON, P. n.d. "Seamless Subjects, Seamless Reform: Learning and Teaching Together, from Pre-School to Ph.D." Washington, DC: National Council for History Education.

GAUR, A. 1984. *A History of Writing.* London: The British Museum.

HIRSCH, E.D. 1993. "The Core Knowledge Curriculum." *Educational Leadership* 51 (1): 23–27.

HURD, P.D. 1991. "Why We Must Transform Science Education." *Educational Leadership* 49 (2): 33–35.

KONAR, S. 1991. "Play Ball." *The Instructor.* 101 (2): 25–26.

MAYVILLE, W. 1978. *Interdisciplinarity: The Mutable Paradigm.* Washington, DC: American Association for Higher Education.

MILLER, M.A., AND A.M. McCARTAN. 1990. "Making the Case for New Interdisciplinary Programs." *Change* 22 (3): 28–36.

REEVES, W.J. 1993. "Who Wants a Color-Coordinated Cross-Cultural Core Curriculum?" *USA Today Magazine.* 121 (March): 56–7.

VARS, G. 1991. "Integrated Curriculum in Historical Perspective." *Educational Leadership* 49 (2): 14–15.

VIADERO, D. 1993. "Students Fall Short on 'Extended' Math Questions, Analysis Finds." *Education Week.* 15 (7): 16.

2

New Life for Old Disciplines
Finding Links and Likenesses

In the introduction to *Deschooling Society* Ivan Illich (1970) makes the following statement:

> The current search for new educational *funnels* must be reversed into a search for their institutional inverse: educational *webs* which heighten the opportunity for each one to transform each moment of his living into one of learning, sharing, and caring. (ix)

The movement Illich rejects has been called the *empty vessel* approach, teachers pouring the wisdom of society into the empty vessel that is the student. Illich advocates for an approach that places students in an active role as learners and recognizes them as participants in the creation of knowledge, worthy of sharing their discoveries with others, ultimately for the betterment of all. This approach is a powerful one, a vision that we think can be made to materialize through the interdisciplinary approach this book describes. The "web" is a fine metaphor for those situations encountered in life that present human beings with a need to think and learn. People are snared by situations, sometimes as mundane and commonplace as the dripping of a faucet, and compelled by the problems the situations present to use their intellectual and physical abilities to cope. In the interdisciplinary classroom we propose that teachers and students spin the webs, creating for one another the need to seek and apply knowledge and skill, to share with one another in order to solve the problems they face.

A Vignette

A group of fifth graders is huddled around a computer screen. Students excitedly call out computer commands to the girl sitting at the keyboard. Their goal is to move a car made of Lego building materials to a line marked on the classroom rug with a piece of masking tape. When it reaches the line, the car is to stop. The electric motor in the car is controlled by a computer through an interface device that is a part of the Lego TC Logo system, an instructional tool designed to help students learn basic science and engineering concepts. The students are using the Logo programming language to get the car to do what they wish it to do. The girl at the keyboard, taking a suggestion from one of the group's members, types in the command "on 5." The Lego car moves about halfway to the line. The students bring the car back to the starting point and several suggest that "on 10" is the correct command. But "on 10" causes the car to move over a foot beyond the line. The logic seems right, but the result is wrong. The students are puzzled, truly perplexed by the car's actions. They are snared in the web! (Lafer and Markert 1994).

The car that the students are trying to stop on the taped line has no brakes. The computer can only turn the motor on or off. At the end of the period of time signified by "on 10," the computer shuts down the motor. But the car has built momentum that causes it to continue moving forward without the motor's help. "On 5" moves the car halfway, but doubling not only increases the amount of time the motor remains on, it also increases the amount of momentum the car can build.

The students are not defeated. Their chatter gets louder, the sentences longer, the excitement more evident. They scratch their heads, tilt their chins toward the ceiling with fists beneath for support. They think and they talk, sometimes to themselves, sometimes to others. "If we try seven . . ." "How about . . ." "Dang it." "All right, look, the car just keeps going after the motor stops. How far? We've gotta stop it short of the line. Then it will coast. But how far short of the line?"

Harder but More Fun

The problem before them is a difficult one, made even more complex when the students are asked to move their car from the carpeted floor into the linoleum-covered hallway—different surfaces, different numbers. Frustrating! But when students are asked to share their feelings about the activity, one blurts out that "it sure beats doing school." Indeed, the students are not doing school in the manner to which they are accustomed. The purpose of their work is not simply to learn. Rather, they are learning in order to make something they care about work. Lost in the complexities of the task, most of the students are not even aware that they are learning.

And indeed, an observer may, with reason, ask if anything is being learned. Our answer to this question would be an emphatic *yes*. Despite the fact that there is no systematic discipline-specific teaching taking place, students are learning and, in a powerful way, learning how to learn. Motivated by the perplexity they share, they call upon one another for the knowledge each may possess. They have a need for information and a need for concepts that can take them to their goal, a need to understand and learn. So they work together because they need one another in order to solve a problem. Cooperation is learned in a meaningful way. And, when necessary, when the information at hand will not produce the desired results, they create information through experimentation, or they turn to other resources: teachers, books, students from outside the group, parents, and, if encouraged to do so, to experts outside the school.

InterMusing

Consider the Lego-Logo activity just described. Make as comprehensive a list as possible of the things you see students learning through their participation. Look for those that are directly related to specific disciplines, such as the concept of momentum; those that have value for multiple disciplines, such as problem-solving skills; and those that transcend the disciplines, such as cooperation and attitudes toward learning. Consider what use you could make of an activity like the Lego-Logo car project in your own teaching situation. For example, what English, math, science, social studies, or art value might there be in having students design the tallest possible free-standing tower from ten plastic straws, twenty paper clips, and thirty wooden toothpicks?

What of disciplinary content? Look first at the list you just compiled. The list of concepts and skills one could build is considerable. The students are obviously practicing thinking and language skills. The circumstances of the situation push them to develop new intellectual muscle. For instance, the web fashioned for this activity allows each group only four trial runs to get the car up to and stopped at the line. So students must think and talk through the possibilities before they run a test (the *twenty-one questions* dynamic). And the results of each trial must be carefully evaluated. Students have a need to know why the car acts as it does in response to the conditions of the situation and the conditions they set through their programming choices. The need to know leads to application of arithmetic knowledge and mathematical reasoning. The first trial leads the group to reason that if "on 5" takes the car halfway to the line, two times "on 5" should take it the rest of the distance. This is the proper equation.

But the situation, not the text, dictates the appropriateness of the response. The effect of momentum intrudes and what is mathematically correct is not situationally appropriate. At this point the concept of momentum has not been taught directly, has not been made explicit or labeled. But *momentum* does figure into the students' thought processes—something causes the car to continue moving after the motor has shut down—and this force is something with which they must contend. This is an opportune time for a lesson on momentum. Their experience will help them make sense of both concept and label. Velocity and its relation to momentum could also be taught in a most productive way at this time.

Friction too figures into the problem, and its relationship to velocity and momentum is now a concern of the students. A meaningful lesson can easily be related to this concern. Even complex engineering concepts can be fruitfully discussed given the context the activity provides. For instance, in light of the texture of the surfaces on which the car is to run, students can be asked to consider whether smooth, treaded, knobby, or studded tires should be used. This could easily lead into profitable discussions of traction, road and floor building materials, the effects of climatic conditions on these surfaces, tire and shoe design, fashion, merchandising, ethics, and advertising.

InterMusing

Okay, we said it. But we will leave it up to you to consider how the different topics mentioned in the last sentences above could be tied to the Lego-Logo experience. Think about the activity you came up with for the last InterMusing. What would be the value of tying together the topics you've found and relating them to the activity you devised? What disciplinary concepts could be taught in conjunction with each of the topics listed? What would linking the disciplinary concepts to these topics contribute to the quality of learning?

There is, of course, more math here, and much more than math. The problem students face has algebraic trappings. There are the givens, the facts at hand, and the unknowns for which students are attempting to solve. There is opportunity and incentive to review previously discovered formulas and to *create* new ones for finding the needed information. If the car goes two feet forward on "on 5," and five feet forward on "on 10," how many "on" units are needed to move the car four feet? One type of unit is being converted into another, feet and inches into the "on" units, and there is reason to expect play with ratios, the amount of momentum created by each unit of movement.

The list goes on as one unpacks each of the project elements. Students build the car from a set of instructions, so reading and following directions are practiced (perhaps one day they will join the ranks of those who actually do know how to program a VCR!). Students also read diagrams and charts identifying the form and function of the various Lego TC Logo components. They are allowed to modify the car, so there is discussion of possible design changes related to the looks of the machine and possibly of its aerodynamics. They work with the computer hardware and the Logo programming language. Another sweep at the activity would show many more learning events taking place, a tangled web indeed, and a very rich learning opportunity.

A Good Use of Time?

Rich, yes. But certainly a time-consuming approach, and one that we can guarantee will not be met with immediate approval from all. There are those who will argue that disciplinary knowledge and skill can be taught more efficiently, that things be done the way they have always been done. There is the hefty and expensive textbook the district has spent its good money on and the concomitant demand to cover the material contained within, not to mention those tradition-sustaining tests that keep teachers and schools accountable. Then too there are the students who have become comfortable in those traditions—students who will resist when the game they have for so long (and at so great a cost) agreed to play is supplanted by something different, something more interesting, perhaps, but something that demands more of them than simply figuring out the rules and following them.

Is the interdisciplinary approach worth the effort and time it takes to implement, defend, and use? Our answer is obviously yes, or we wouldn't have written this book. But let us resume our argument for the interdisciplinary approach by asking another question, the broader question, *What it is that students need from education?* We believe that for too long curriculum decisions have taken place without much concern for this question, made evident in the proliferation of assessments of educational achievement that work only to determine whether students learn what is being taught. Rarely have they been concerned with whether what is being taught actually helps students to achieve something of value and what of value students are able to do as a result of having *succeeded* in their studies in English, science, math, or history.

In recent years these questions about the *value of learning* have been applied to various disciplines and this has set in motion what we believe to be a rather productive reexamination of instructional processes. The most conspicuous of the disciplinary self-examinations have occurred in mathematics through the development of the *Curriculum and Evaluation Standards* (National Council of Teachers of Mathematics 1989), and in science through *Project 2061* (American Association for the Advancement of Science 1989, 1992) and the National Research Council's work on national science education standards (1993, 1994). Similar projects are presently underway in English and, as we write, a document outlining new standards for the social sciences is being released.

The results of these inquiries into the value of the learning taking place in the disciplines have been used as criteria for evaluating the efficacy of instructional practices and assessment methods and as the basis for recognition of the need for substantial changes in the way students are taught. New definitions of instructional effectiveness have begun to emerge. Ruth Parker (1991), speaking of changes proposed for mathematics curricula, writes that

> A long history of traditions has grown up around what is meant by a good mathematics teacher and a good mathematics student. As many educators recognize, however, those traditions have little in common with mathematics in the 1990s. (442)

Instruction based on the traditional view of mathematics, she says, "has resulted in a large number of students unable to use mathematics skills to solve even simple problems" (443). The focus on the *usefulness* of learning is also evident in the introduction to the *National Science Education Standards* document. "The standards," the authors state,

> will project a vision of science in which teachers create learning environments that enable students to acquire a body of knowledge while developing the intellectual skills that will equip them to use and increase their understanding of science throughout their lives. (12)

We expect similar statements to appear in the other standards documents.

The Need for a Change in Perspective: English as an Example

Since both authors are attached to the discipline called English, we will use it as an example of how an inquiring approach to the relevance of curriculum can change teaching in a discipline and lead to the valuing of interdisciplinary approaches. English educators have been asking, for some time now, what it is that the discipline is about. Those whom we believe to be the most perceptive have come to understand that the value of English is not to be found in the study of language itself or in students becoming familiar with certain texts considered by some to be "great." Rather, English, as a subject to be taught and learned, is *useful* when it (1) helps students acquire abilities that will allow them, through language, to come to understandings about their world, their fellow beings, and themselves, and (2) helps students to develop abilities that make it possible for them to share their understandings with others (Moffett and Wagner 1992; Tchudi and Mitchell 1989).

Such a view does not abandon study of great literary works, nor does it suggest excluding language mechanics as an area of concern within the discipline. It does, however, argue for changes in the way these elements are conceptualized for instructional purposes. Great books become resources that aid in the quest for knowledge and understanding, and knowledge of language mechanics is understood to be necessary insofar as it helps one to become adept as a communicator.

Texts read outside school, be they "great" or otherwise, are usually not read to be *learned* in and of themselves, but rather, they are read for purposes beyond themselves, some for pleasure, certainly, but also to answer questions that arise in the minds of students as they interact with their world. Literary study aimed at helping students to become better able to *make sense* of text is automatically interdisciplinary since it helps them to formulate the questions these texts serve to answer— questions that are rarely about literature itself. *The Pearl* is not about literature, nor is *Beowulf.* Both are about life. So too *The Magic School Bus* books that children love to read. The interdisciplinary approach allows literary study to become purposeful for students because it allows literary study to reveal itself as being responsive to real needs. It provides tools for solving problems, tools that help students more effectively answer important and meaningful questions. The power of a *responsive* interdisciplinary approach is that it situates works of literature in the contexts that give them their greatness, reattaching literature to the important questions it tries to answer. Students need not be *told* of its value since, so situated, the value of texts is *experienced*. Students introduced to literature in this way are more likely to become life-long readers and good judges of the worth of what they read.

Language mechanics too must be situated in meaningful contexts if students are to understand their usefulness and use them appropriately. What students need is the knowledge and understanding that will allow them to make language choices that are appropriate for the situations they encounter—whether the situation be writing a personal letter, designing a poster, or scripting a play. The goodness of language choices is largely determined by situation. Consider the fate of the aspiring country and western singer whose songs adhere strictly to the rules of the school sanctioned standard dialect: He ain't bound to visit Opry Land soon.

Better than Disciplinary: Situated Curriculum

InterMusing

While acknowledging the importance of both "generalized learning" in schools and the teaching of "general, widely usable skills and theoretical principles," Lauren Resnick in her Presidential Address to the American Educational Research Association (1987) points out that there is "discontinuity between learning in school and the nature of cognitive activity outside the school." One major difference, says Resnick, is that "school cultivates symbolic thinking whereas mental activity outside the school engages directly with objects and situations." Use your own experiences in considering this statement and list the ways in which school learning and learning outside the school have differed for you. Is there a difference in the processes of learning that took place? In the quality of learning that resulted?

We have used English as an example of the importance of situation as a factor in the instructional process. All disciplines suffer when instruction causes them to become disconnected from the contexts to which they apply, from the situations that make their content and procedures meaningful, exciting, brilliant, great. As Boyer (1983), Sizer (1984), and Goodlad (1984) have pointed out, and as teachers and students continue to tell us, large numbers of those attending American schools are much too disengaged, much too passive in their studies. They fail to delight in the magnificence of the formulations of the sciences and the humanities. They are not "turned-on" by the genius of great minds and great ideas. This, we argue, is because instruction by discipline artificially obscures the naturally interdisciplinary situational contexts that give disciplinary knowledge and procedure its meaning and value. In other words, the isolation of the disciplines in traditional school programs drains the disciplines of their relevance by removing them from the complex and interdisciplinary problems for which they exist.

The interdisciplinary programs we advocate work to *situate* disciplinary instruction in problem-evoking contexts. In their search for solutions to these problems, students find the purposefulness of concepts and procedures. The questions that disciplinary concepts and procedures answer are the questions the situations are causing students to ask. This is the key to involvement; because situation creates a *need*, learning is *sought*, not *assigned*. Our own experience with the concept of *acre-feet* serves to illustrate this point.

Both of us over the years had heard of acre-feet but never really understood its meaning or significance until we were reintroduced to it during the Truckee River Project, a summer institute we run to introduce teachers to the thematic interdisciplinary learning. The Project's theme was "Water in the West" and focused, in part, on the effects of a six-year drought on the Truckee River, our region's primary water source. The term *acre-feet*, "the volume of water, 43,560 cubic feet, that will cover an area of one acre to a depth of one foot" (*American Heritage Talking Dictionary, Third Edition*), was first mentioned on a bus trip we took to view the upper reaches of the river system. Our guide, a spokesperson for the utility company that controls water in the area, showed us an almost empty reservoir and told us of its capacity, in acre-feet. She also translated acre-feet into the number of families a certain amount of water provides for over a year's time.

Several months later, during what seemed to be a drought-breaking winter, we took another trip, this time to the snow fields that melt to feed the Truckee system each spring. Our colleague David Fenimore, a member of the mountain search and rescue team, showed us how to use measuring rods to determine the depth of the snow pack. The rods indicated that we were standing on more than fifteen feet of snow. The question that our summer's training had taught us to ask was how much water this snowpack would yield once it melted. We talked about the water content of various kinds of snow, dug a hole so that we could see the strata that showed the layers provided by different storms, tested samples for water content, and then played with a formula David gave us for translating feet of snow into acre-feet of water. With little difficulty we could then make rough determinations as to how many families' water supply was contained in the area we could see from where we stood. Acre-feet had taken on significant meaning. The concept had become a part of the way we think and speak about our world because we had learned about it in the context of a meaningful situation to which it could be applied.

Our point is that teachers can greatly increase the power of learning by allowing students to become involved in situations that invite them to learn. A rather simple example of a unit of instruction designed to provide such an invitation is one created by students in one of Lafer's courses. The unit calls upon middle school students to build and operate a snack cart. The *situation* the cart builders find themselves in requires understanding and application of mathematical concepts such as gross and net revenue, board feet (they need lumber to build the cart), and cost per board foot. The situation provides incentive for accurate calculation and the use of those calculations to determine if the enterprise can be made profitable. Once presented with the fact that a certain percentage of the gross must be used to pay for materials, product, and other "overhead" expenses, and the notion that "mark-up" must reflect these factors, the mathematical formulas that allow for the calculation of percentages can be explained in a meaningful way, their elegance revealed in their power to provide means for coping with the contingencies of the situation the cart-building project creates.

Harder but More Fun

Situations that are authentic tend to be interdisciplinary simply because most of the problems people face cannot be explained or solved through application of a single discipline. Such interdisciplinary learning leads to what we believe to be a qualitatively superior kind of learning. We tried to show this through our description of our encounters with acre-feet. Gilbert Ryle (in Gage, 1984) distinguishes between "knowing what" and "knowing how." Prior to our trips to the reservoir and the snow field, we knew the "what" of an acre-foot. We understood it to be a unit of measurement representing a large amount of water. What we didn't know, and what our experiences taught us, is "how" the concept applies to real-world issues and concerns. Once the "how" was discovered, our understanding of acre-feet became useful.

InterMusing

Using Ryle's distinction between "knowing what" and "knowing how," how might students' understanding of the mathematical concepts mentioned in the snack cart example differ from those of students learning the same concepts outside the context of a situation? Find a concept that you would teach in your discipline and consider it in relation to "knowing what" and "knowing how." What is the difference in understanding, and what might be the consequences of this difference? Would the teaching of this concept benefit from its placement in a situation? Think of other projects you might offer to students of a similar type, for instance, redesigning the school cafeteria lines, creating a Japanese garden in front of the school, or even building a better mousetrap!

The Criterion of Usefulness

The *criterion of usefulness* asks whether the learning that takes place allows students to effectively act upon the world and with their fellow beings. In other words, can they use what they know to determine proper actions, and can they act upon these determinations? Stephen Willoughby (1990) in his book *Mathematics Education for A Changing World* claims that traditional mathematics instruction does not. "Most people who find themselves in a situation that requires mathematics," he writes,

> either don't recognize that good decisions depend on mathematical thought, or don't make the best decisions because they are unable or unwilling to think mathematically. (1)

The National Committee on Science Education Standards and Assessment (1993) contends that high school science instruction presently is "a deluge of disconnected facts" that fail to prepare students to develop informed answers to such basic questions as to whether it is best to ask for paper or plastic bags at the supermarket. Among the goals stated in the *National Science Education Standards* are that students, as a result of their education in science, be able to incorporate "scientific inquiry skills" and "scientific fact . . . in [making] personal, civic, and political decisions." In a similar vein, Joseph Julian of the Maxwell School of Citizenship and Public Affairs at Syracuse University and Benjamin Barber, director of the Whitman Center for Culture and Politics at Rutgers University (in O'Neil 1991) argue that current practices in civics education lead students into passive civic lives by failing to attend to the development of intellectual skills that encourage and enable individuals to become active participants in the democratic process. Barber goes so far as to say that

> if students are to become actively engaged in public forms of thinking and participate thoughtfully in the whole spectrum of civic activities, then civic education and social studies programs require a strong element of civil experience— real participation and empowerment. (4)

So, in mathematics, science, and civics education, according to these educators, the bottom line is whether what is learned in school can be used by students to make the kind of decisions they will have to make as active participants in their society.

Robert Sternberg (1985) adds to the choir, leaping over disciplinary boundaries to argue that school programs generally fail to help students become critical thinkers, in part because the problems school programs ask students to wrestle with are relatively simple in comparison to those they will meet beyond school walls. For instance, school problems typically occupy a single disciplinary realm. A problem encountered in a math course automatically identifies itself as a problem requiring a math solution. Real-world problems do not so easily make apparent where solutions can be found.

Real-world problems, in fact, often fail to make their presence apparent. Consider how long it sometimes takes to realize that certain teaching methods are ineffective! In the Lego-Logo activity described earlier, the *problem* is exposed only after the "on 10" experiment produces problematic results. So, says Sternberg, the first step one must take in solving a problem is to recognize that a problem exists. Textbook problems usually end just about where the Lego-Logo problem begins: *If a car is moved five feet by the computer command of "on 5," what command must be given to move the car ten feet?*

The problems brought about by the Lego-Logo activity are also considerably more complex than are typical school text problems. The cause of the unwanted results is not revealed in the information the experiment produces, and cause must be discovered if a reasonable solution is to be found. Students must determine why the car goes beyond the taped line despite the correctness of their calculations, and this most definitely takes them outside of mathematics. The question of *where* to look for answers becomes a crucial one. According to Sternberg, the problems one finds in real-world situations are often "ill-structured . . . complicated, messy, and stubbornly persistent."

The students designing the snack cart problem discovered this. Build it and you can sell? No way! Selling requires business licenses, and the selling of some foods necessitates permits from the county health department. To sell food on school grounds one needs the permission of the school district, and in order to get such permission one must appear before the school board, and there are certain procedures one must follow in order to get on the agenda. Hot foods must be kept just so hot, and cold foods just so cold. And there are federal, state, and school district rules governing what kinds of foods can be sold to students attending public schools. Parents, too, are concerned with what their children eat, something the snack cart vendors need to consider. There are also the food service operators at the school. Some have contracts that give them exclusive rights to sell food on school campuses. Food services run by districts must sell a certain number of meals to be viable. The cart folk had better find out if their business will be welcomed. Other contingencies that could easily be overlooked: Non-toxic finishes for the wood; day-to-day storage of the food; finding vendors willing to sell in quantities reasonable for the volume of business the cart will do and at prices that will allow the cart business to be profitable; sanitary concerns such as food service gloves and nets for the hair; the packaging and handling of food. And it is inevitable that unforeseen contingencies will arise as the cart kids move into the enterprise.

A truth they will face is that the truth, outside the school, is rarely to be found on a given page in a given text. And they will find that the claim "But no one ever told us so" will excuse them from little. They will have to work to define their problem as well as they possibly can, ask as many of the right questions as they can, and find the resources that will allow them to answer those questions. And they will have to be ready to deal with the unforeseen, the quirky.

InterMusing

Make a list of problems that you have recently encountered while doing useful work around the house, at school, anywhere. Look at those problems and think about, or better yet, write down the steps taken to solve them. For example, have you put up a shelf or fixed a lock on a door? Or changed the format you use for recording grades? Give your students a similar task. Have students draw up a plan for rearranging seating in the classroom—or allow them to actually do it. Catalog the problems that arise as students attempt to carry out the task and the disciplinary and interdisciplinary knowledge and skill that must be applied to complete the task successfully.

The situation-based interdisciplinary instruction we advocate in this book prepares students to meet the challenge of complex real-world problems by (1) helping them acquire the wherewithal, the tenacity to press on despite the difficulty of the task and the frustrations of the moment and, this, in turn, (2) helps them to achieve the much-heralded goal of becoming competent lifelong learners. We want students to leave school prepared to deal with complexity and confusion, with contingencies seen and unforeseen, with the clear, the cloudy, and the quirky.

The students involved in the Lego-Logo project nicely demonstrate the quality of persistence. Despite the setbacks and confusion caused by the response of the car to their solutions, they continued their quest in a most enthusiastic way. Not only were they undaunted by the complexity of the task, they were *inspired* by it.

The Criterion of Meaning

James Moffett and Betty-Jane Wagner (1992), in *Student Centered Language Arts Curriculum*, have said that school should be harder and more fun. We think that there is a good possibility that the boredom students so often report as a dominant feature of their school lives is not caused by the difficulty of the tasks the school presents them, but rather by a lack of sufficient difficulty in those tasks to sustain interest. The tasks are too simple; they lack complexity and fail to create thought-provoking confusion. *Harder*, though, cannot be for the sake of harder. The difficulty must be inherent in the meaningfulness of problems students face. In part, this is the classroom Parker describes for mathematics instruction. "In this instructional environment," she writes, "persistence is valued over speed, thinking and reasoning over the quick right answer, and diversity of ideas over the notion of one right way to solve a problem" (442). This is not the classroom Sirotnik (1983) observed to be "implicitly teach[ing] dependence upon authority, linear thinking, social apathy, passive involvement, and hands-off learning" (29). "Our goal," says Parker, "is to develop students who are challenged by messy, ill-defined situations or complex problems; who are curious and have developed 'thoughtful habits of inquiry'" (243).

So What About Coverage?

Throughout the book we will present many examples from classrooms where students are moving in the direction Parker suggests. They are possible. They exist. We think the time is right for teachers to make the move because there is support for such change coming from many places. To cite the "standards" movements again, the *National Science Education Standards*, for instance, call for "learning in the questioning mode." "Inquiry in the classroom," its authors say,

> can and should engage students in inquiry as it is actually practiced—a series of creative, iterative, and systematic practices that lead to facts, concepts, principles, theories, and deeper understanding of natural phenomena." (p. 4)

The standards documents readily acknowledge that *coverage* in the disciplines will be affected by curricula that allow for discovery and provide time for students to persist in finding answers to the questions their discoveries raise.

In regard to this concern, the National Research Council says that "the quantity of factual science knowledge that students are expected to learn needs to be reduced so that students can develop a deeper understanding of science." "Subject matter," they continue, "is fundamental if it . . . motivates formulation of significant questions and is applicable to many contexts common to everyday experiences" (1993,1). Randy Moore (1993) in an editorial in *The American Biology Teacher* argues that the "fact-bound" curriculum represented in cover-to-cover classrooms communicates to students that "information is an end in itself." Much of the information that teachers feel compelled to "cover," he asserts, is "useless, "irrelevant," and meaningless in students' lives (260). Richard Paul (1994) goes so far as to point out that "the verb 'to cover' comes from a Latin root meaning 'to hide.'" "And," he continues, "in a way, it is not uncommon for 'coverage' to 'hide' what is really there." "Since everyone agrees that the purpose of instruction is the facilitation of valuable learning," he says,

> the key cannot be whether we in some way "include" something or "travel over" or "treat" it in some way in our course. The key is whether the manner of "dealing with" or "treating of" actually facilitates significant learning. (11)

So here is the justification for abandoning the cover-to-cover ethic.

As Moore argues, "we can't cover everything," and covering everything won't help students succeed in school, or in their careers. The information base is so dynamic and so large that it precludes the chance that any individual will encounter but a small portion of it. What students need, if they are going to be able to make reasonable decisions to be followed by reasonable actions, are:

1. the ability to recognize what information is needed;

2. the knowledge and skill necessary to discover the means by which this information can be acquired;

3. the ability to determine the relevance of their findings to the situation at hand;

4. the ability to make judgments concerning how acquired information is to be applied;

5. the ability to judge the value—the appropriateness and adequacy—of acquired information for answering the questions or solving the problems they face;

6. the ability to make decisions as to what to do if the answers or solutions they develop prove to be inadequate or inappropriate; and

7. the willingness to persist.

Playing with Interdisciplinarity

Assuming that we have convinced you of the efficacy of an interdisciplinary approach, we turn now to showing the ease with which interdisciplinarity can be implemented. We will also provide what we hope are comforting tips on how to find interdisciplinary "stuff," and use it to accomplish cherished curricular objectives.

Simply Interdisciplinary

Let's take a topic that is presently a more common part of curriculum, the teaching of a Shakespearian play, such as *Hamlet*. At first glance, *Hamlet* does not seem "useful" to students. Yet interdisciplinary possibilities abound when understanding of the play is tied, in significant ways, to what we know, or can know, about such things as ghosts (be they substantial, metaphysical, or metaphorical), duty, state, and love romantic and filial.

This knowledge may in part be derived from reading other literary works, but also from experiences with non-literary texts such as newspapers, textbooks from other disciplines, movies, songs, conversations, lectures, and non-textual sources such as direct personal encounters with the world, cogitation, and dreams. The complexity of this process is fascinating. Consider, for instance, the influence of scientific knowledge, be it broad or limited, in the undertaking we are describing here. Most contemporary readers are aware of a science that dispels the existence of substantive ghosts. This knowledge forces one to consider a range of possibilities related to a range of disciplines. Is the author asking for a willing suspension of disbelief and thus placing the ghost and the story in the realm of fantasy? To answer, the reader would obviously make reference to English studies. But psychology would also be a viable area of exploration for information regarding the process of suspending disbelief and the ramifications of doing so. The ghost might be a vestige of the belief system of the time and intended by the author to be understood as real. This *hypothesis* would lead the reader into historical and sociological explorations. Or the ghost could be understood to be the result of Hamlet's particular state of mind, leading again into questions that one turns to psychology to answer. In our classroom, then, the text of *Hamlet* would be supplemented with a book cart full of literature about ghosts and the supernatural. We might even invite students to watch *Friday Night Frights* on television and to explore their understanding of things that go bump in the night, and things that go bump in the head.

One's understanding of the disciplines mentioned all influence interpretation of the play. So, it could be argued, study in any of these areas enhances English studies and, thereby, is relevant material to be dealt with in an English course. The study of English, on the other hand, holds significance for other disciplines. *Hamlet* could easily serve as the subject for case study in many courses. If *Hamlet* is being read in an English course, for instance, a history teacher can use the play to discuss the relationship of the psychological temperament of individuals to the unfolding of historical events. A science teacher discussing brain physiology could easily take advantage of the fact that much of *Hamlet* is a study of the protagonist's mind.

Not only does literature reflect historical, psychological, and sociological realities, it also influences them. Thus, the reading lists of historically important personages are of great interest to scholars in many fields. Reading a book, or several books, known to have influenced a historically important individual is of value to both the history course and the English course, and, if the person influenced is a scientist, an artist, or a great teacher, there is a nice tie-in to courses in those areas.

So far we have addressed the interdisciplinarity in overlapping content. More important, perhaps, is the way interdisciplinarity plays itself out in the intellectual processes that overlap disciplinary boundaries. The processes in which one engages to *figure out* the meaning of books, short stories, and poems, for instance, are very much the same ones used to figure out how to stop the Lego-Logo car on the designated line. In both endeavors experience—worldly or textual—leads to hypotheses, their veracity confirmed or dispelled through the accumulation of further information through test (experiment) or through text. To use *Hamlet* again, evidence is presented throughout the play that argues for and against the ghost's substantive existence. The reader, and Hamlet, have to weigh the efficacy of each possible explanation against the evidence that the text presents. Our class might, then, include a debate on Hamlet's frame of mind or even a mock trial on whether he is guilty of the crime of "procrastination." At the same time the reader is made privy to Hamlet's thought processes. We watch his intellectual moves and make judgments concerning their correctness. Thus, the play, in multiple ways, serves as a lesson on reasoning, as does most, or perhaps all, *good fiction*.

Both the act of figuring out a text and the insight one gains by observing the characters deal with the contingencies of the situations in which they find themselves are lessons pertinent to a Lego-Logo project, the creation of a snack cart, or making decisions in business and marriage. Or to understanding the *reasoning behind* the Constitution, the discovery of the double helix, the *meaning* of the Pythagorean Theorem or understanding the genius of Beethoven or Van Gogh.

Themes Before Your Eyes

There are innumerable ways into focused interdisciplinary study, ways that might not occur to us because they are right before our eyes, or, as is the case with the example we are about to present, right there on our backs.

Our example concerns the purchase of a coat. As we will show, and as readers of *Consumer Reports* know, thoughtful consumption is no easy task. Consider too the relationship of the coat problem to the question we posed above concerning whether what is taught in school actually helps students achieve something that is of value. Should school prepare one to deal, in a thoughtful way, with problems so *ordinary* as the purchase of coat? If yes, need not the interdisciplinary complexities it represents (and we will show just how complex a well-reasoned decision about coats can be) be reflected in the work students are asked to do in the classroom? A coat purchase is, in the overall scheme of things, a relatively inconsequential undertaking. But consider the relationship of the problem-solving processes involved in a coat purchase to those in which one would engage to make informed and rational decisions regarding such questions as how to vote on a school bond issue or the viability of a national health care proposal.

Our example, because we like to toy with making the ordinary complex (see Lafer and Tchudi 1994), concerns an ordinary coat—a coat for recreation or dress. The problem can be given a more critical slant if, for instance, the garment is to be used for a polar expedition, a trip to the top of Mount Everest, or the moon. In using this more sophisticated type of coat problem, it might be interesting to obtain the specifications for clothing developed by organizations responsible for particular kinds of exploration such as the National Geographic Society, the Cousteau Society, and NASA. Students would see that the specifications are often very exacting and necessary for reasons of comfort and safety.

The polar, Everest, or moon coat can become the centerpiece of a most interesting interdisciplinary exploration. Students could, for instance, carry on research concerning the nature of the particular destination, then design a coat for explorers. They could also do this in response to their understanding of historical situations; they could create clothing to save the ill-fated Donner party. But back to our more ordinary coat. We still get an impressive list of questions the potential buyer might find worthy of having answered and an equally impressive list of disciplinary knowledge and skills that one could put to good use to find good answers.

As Sternberg notes, the first question that must be asked upon entering a situation is, "What is the problem?" That is, the problem must be properly defined, and here it is defined in relation to the purchaser's needs. Needs, in turn, are tied to the purpose or purposes for which the coat will be used. The list presented in Figure 2–1 shows purpose-related issues that may deserve consideration.

Destinations: Where will the coat be used?

- *Climatic conditions.* What temperatures can be expected with regard to season and time of day of activity? Are wind considerations a factor? Precipitation? Humidity? Levels of ultraviolet radiation?

- *Terrain.* What surfaces might the wearer be exposed to (ragged rock, water, sand)? What kind of flora will the user come into contact with (thistle, tree branches, poison ivy)? Does the wearer need to be protected from fauna (insects or reptiles)?

Activities: In what types of activities will the wearer be involved?

- *Physical requirements.* What kind of freedom of movement is required (arm movement, bending, etc.) What will be carried and what means will be used to carry equipment and/or materials (pack, pockets)?

- *Physiological consequences* of the activity. How much body heat and per-spiration will it produce?

- *Social requirements.* Is the coat's appearance appropriate for the occasions on which it will be worn? Is the wearer comfortable with the garment's appearance? Will it adequately impress those the wearer wishes to impress?

FIG. 2–1   *The Coat—Issues Related to Establishing Need*

InterMusing

Make a list of the criteria you would use in purchasing your next coat. How closely does your list match ours? Can you add?

Once the list of needs is established, one can begin to determine the features the coat must have if it is to serve the purposes of the buyer. While reading the list that appears in Figure 2–2, consider the information one must access and the thinking in which one must engage to make reasonable decisions. Sources of information must be located, and encyclopedias will be of very little help here. The opportunity is ripe for students to learn of research as a problem-solving activity.

Where might they begin to look for information that will answer the questions raised? It is much harder (and potentially more fun) to locate resources that will explain the thermal qualities of Gortex, polar fleece, and goose down than it is to find information on some of the more common topics students are asked to research. Student researchers might find it necessary to use the telephone books, telephones, and trade and consumer publications as research tools. They might speak directly to manufacturers, merchants, and even professional explorers. Or they might use the mails (of the "snail" and electronic varieties). And they are bound to discover the complexity of such searches, the dead-ends, the false leads, the bright sources that fail to produce, as well as the rich but hidden sources that a good search can uncover.

The questions posed by the coat problem most certainly necessitate an interdisciplinary search. Most are best answered at a point where several disciplines overlap or intersect. The climatological questions can only be answered through, at the very least, reference to *geography* and *meteorology*. But knowing the typical weather patterns of a particular geographical location may not be enough. The information one finds for a location does not ensure that conditions on a particular day will be like those that the typical patterns predict. In our region hikers have benefited from knowledge of the *history* of weather in the Sierra where Pacific storms can bring substantial snowfall in late June. Typically, the first snows usually come in mid- to late December; however, the fate of the Donner party was sealed by a tremendous storm that began on the third of November, 1846.

Geography, *geology, zoology,* and *entomology* would provide answers to questions of terrain, fauna, and flora. Questions regarding the physiological consequences of particular activities call for exploration in the realms of *biology* and *physiology.* The *physical education* course would be a good place to carry out experiments on the relationship of physical activity to the production of body heat and perspiration. *Mathematical* calculations would be necessary to translate units of activity into calories, and a physiological-mathematical formula would be needed to determine how much heat the body could be expected to release given the nature of an activity. One would also have to know how much heat must be retained by the coat to keep the body at a healthy and comfortable temperature, how much perspiration the body would produce for a given activity, and how perspiration would affect body heat—and heat inside the coat.

Then come the questions of which fabrics and which coat designs allow for the retention of the required amount of heat and the proper retention or expulsion of moisture. Questions of fabric lead into *physics* and *chemistry. Geometry*, coupled with physics and chemistry, would explain the heat and moisture retention qualities of particular weaves of particular materials. *Home economics* could play an important role in answering these questions. *Agriculture* and *botany* enter the picture to answer questions concerning the properties of natural fabrics such as wool, cotton, and goose and duck down—and questions regarding the ecological and economic advantages and disadvantages of using such materials.

InterMusing

Make a list of household goods that could be explored in a parallel fashion: kitchen appliances, televisions, furniture, an automobile . . .

Fabric

In regard to the conditions of use, the buyer might have to consider: the fabric's weight and durability; its capacity to resist moisture, dust, and sand; its capacity to resist puncture by sharp objects such as rocks, branches, and animal bites; its resistance to substances such as chemicals and minerals; its heat retention capacity; comfort factors including its response to body heat, perspiration, and outside temperature.

Design features

- *Body of the coat:*

    Fit. For comfort, agility, mobility. Accommodation for clothing to be worn beneath it and for what may be worn on top of it such as backpacks, overcoats, or ponchos.

    Appearance. (including color, which may be related to fashion considerations or safety concerns—certain colors attract insects and animals, some are good for camouflage, some are better if one wants to be sighted).

    Means for securing. Buttons, snaps, Velcro, zippers, ties.

    Places where secured. Neck, waist (or bottom), wrists.

- *Hood*. Fabric, insulation, fit, lining, securing devices, shape, detachability, means for detaching, stowability.

- *Pockets*. Size, number, placement and accessibility, means for securing, protection from elements (moisture, dust, etc.).

Quality issues

- *Hardware*. Buttons, zippers, snaps, Velcro, ties, etc. How will they respond to outdoor conditions (what are they made of, how does material respond to various elements wearer will encounter); are these components durable (how many times will the zipper zip?)

- *Fabric*. Is it durable and functional?

- *Manufacture*. Are components well made? Is stitching of good quality? Is the hardware properly attached?

- *Practicality of design*. Is the design one that will accommodate needs? Are pockets reasonably placed? Is pocket design adequate for the wearer's needs? Is the hood designed well in regard to needs? Is placement and design of securing devices sensible in regard to purpose?

Price

- *Affordability.*

- *Value*. Is the coat worth the price?

FIG. 2–2   *Coat Features to be Considered in Relation to Need*

Questions of coat design tap physics again in the form of *engineering*. If physiology confirms that most body heat is lost from the head, what kind of hood design is best for controlling this loss? The placement and type of securing devices, too, will determine the amount of air and moisture that can enter and leave the coat. Should the coat be fitted with grommets that allow air to escape, and where should they be placed?

Many of the questions posed above have ramifications for the nature of the coat's manufacture. For instance, are coat components sewn together or are they fused by heat or chemical processes? These are questions relevant to *technology*. What kinds of machines, for instance, are used to carry out this work? How were they designed and how do they operate? One might even become interested in the effects of the manufacturing process on workers, regions, and nations. Do the processes and materials used represent efficient use of resources? Do they produce ecologically harmful byproducts? Do they adversely effect those who work in the manufacturing process? And what are the *political, economic,* and *social* ramifications of purchasing certain coats? These questions could easily lead into the study of regulatory bodies and policies in *social science* courses, and the reading of literary works concerned with the effects of technology, technological change, and industrial and economic policy and practices on individuals and society. *The Jungle* and *Animal Farm* come to mind. There is also room to consider issues of attire and survival through fiction—Jack London's novels and stories would be appropriate, as would the journals of great explorers such as John Wesley Powell, Lewis and Clark, and Admiral Perry.

Into the Interdisciplinary Classroom

We conclude this chapter by offering some entry points for those who like the interdisciplinary landscape we have presented, but for one reason or another do not find it possible to buy it all. First, we know that many teachers work in schools where it is not possible to join with teachers in other disciplines to create an interdisciplinary program. As we demonstrated with our *Hamlet* example, a classroom becomes interdisciplinary simply by students going beyond disciplinary bounds to seek answers to questions that arise in the course of disciplinary studies. The science, sociology, and history of ghosts are legitimate areas of exploration to be undertaken as a part of English studies. As an entrée into interdepartmental interdisciplinary projects in the school, students can be encouraged to use teachers in other academic departments as resources. A history teacher, for instance, can send a student to a biology teacher to get information on a disease such as the plague.

If you pay attention to the questions that can and should arise as students study the meaningful content of your discipline, interdisciplinary connections will make themselves apparent. It does take time to answer or find answers to questions that pull teachers and students over disciplinary boundaries. But if those answers are understood to enrich disciplinary learning, then the time spent is easily justified. As we have argued throughout this chapter, interdisciplinary instruction arises naturally out of learning situations that are authentic. The questions that arise as a result of one's interaction with the world rarely, if ever, can be answered through reference to a single discipline, and these are the kind of questions that schools should be preparing students to answer.

Lastly, an interdisciplinary approach of any scale does not prevent students from achieving the legitimate objectives of specific discipline areas. Our local school district, for instance, lists among its grade eight science objectives the following:

- classify matter according to physical states

- identify chemical and physical properties of matter

- apply science to investigate a problem

- develop a working definition of energy

- explain how energy changes from one form to another

- explain respiration as the process of releasing stored energy

- explain how organisms convert stored food energy to heat energy

- explore the meaning of biosphere

- identify environmental issues

- investigate land, its use and misuse

- investigate air pollution in relation to the atmosphere and wind patterns

All of these, and several others contained in the district's guidelines, can easily be covered within the context of the coat purchase problem. Social studies objectives for the same grade include the following coat problem objectives:

- understand that satisfying people's wants for goods and services is the main purpose of economic activity, and that economic systems develop out of this activity

- name the major political entities and land forms in the United States

- understand the impact of geography on the history of the United States

- identify the pattern of migration of North American Indian tribes and their contribution to the United States culture

- articulate how the Constitution affects our lives

- understand how a bill becomes a law

- understand the complexities and consequences of one society encroaching upon another

- explain the reasons for the westward movement (e.g., Louisiana Purchase, Lewis and Clark expedition)

For the time being, we leave the reader with two short examples of addressing the objectives listed with the coat problem. Looking for answers to questions raised by the coat problem, issues related to the objectives can be discussed: the exploration of the polar regions had to wait until coats could be made that would adequately protect humans from the weather conditions they would face. Or, the coat theme can be infused into instruction directly related to the objectives. For example, aspects of the coat problem can be used to explain principles covered by the objectives: energy changing from one form to another could be discussed in relation to physical activity converting food to heat.

We will return to this process of making interdisciplinarity work in your situation, and making your situation work interdisciplinarily through the many examples we have to present. But we ask that you begin to think of the interdisciplinary options that are reasonable for your situation and that you use the exercise that follows to discover ways to satisfy the particular crocodiles you may be worrying about.

InterMusing

Just for kicks, list the curricular objectives in your discipline that your students could achieve while working on the coat problem, or any similar problem of your choosing. Could you cover a bit of U.S. history by having students explore the Gortex jacket or the microwave oven?

References

AMERICAN ASSOCIATION FOR THE ADVANCEMENT OF SCIENCE. 1989. *Science for All Americans.*

AMERICAN ASSOCIATION FOR THE ADVANCEMENT OF SCIENCE. 1992. *Update: Project 2061: Education for a Changing Future.* Washington, DC: American Association for the Advancement of Society.

AMERICAN HERITAGE TALKING DICTIONARY, 3D ED. 1992. Boston: Houghton Mifflin.

BOYER, E.L. 1983. *High School: A Report on Secondary Education in America.* New York: Harper & Row.

GAGE, J.T. 1981. "Toward an Epistimology of Composition." *Journal of Advanced Composition* 2: 1–9.

GOODLAD, J.I. 1984. *A Place Called School*. New York: McGraw-Hill.

ILLICH, I. 1970. *Deschooling Society*. NY: Harper and Row.

LAFER, S., AND A. MARKERT. 1994. "Authentic Learning and the Potential of Lego TC Logo." *Computers in the Schools* 11: 79–94.

LAFER, S., AND S. TCHUDI. 1994. "The Familiar Made Curious: The Case for Hometown Interdisciplinary Studies." *The English Journal* 83:14–20.

MOFFETT, J. AND B.J. WAGNER. 1992. *Student Centered Language Arts, K–12*. (3rd ed.). Portsmouth, NH: Boynton/Cook-Heinemann.

MOORE, R. 1993. "Editorial: Doing More Than Just 'Covering Information.' " *The American Biology Teacher* 55: 260–261.

NATIONAL COMMITTEE ON SCIENCE EDUCATION STANDARDS AND ASSESSMENT. 1993. *National Science Education Standards: July '93 Report*. Washington DC: National Research Council.

NATIONAL COUNCIL OF TEACHERS OF MATHEMATICS. 1989. *Curriculum and Evaluation Standards for School Mathematics*. Reston, VA: National Council of Teachers of Mathematics.

NATIONAL RESEARCH COUNCIL. 1993. *National Science Education Standards: July '93 Progress Report*. Washington, DC: National Research Council.

———. 1994. *National Science Education Standards*. Washington, DC: National Academy Press.

O'NEIL, J. 1991. January. "Civic Education: While Democracy Flourishes Abroad, U.S. Schools Try to Reinvigorate Teaching of Citizenship." *ASCD Curriculum Update*.

PARKER, R.E. 1991. "Implementing the Curriculum and Evaluation Standards." *Mathematics Teacher* 84: 442–449, 478.

PAUL, R. 1994. "Overcoming the Addiction to Coverage: Less is More." *Educational Vision* 2 (1): 11.

RESNICK, L.B. 1987. "Presidential Address: Learning In School and Out." *Educational Researcher* 16: 13-20.

SIROTNIK, K. 1983. "What You See Is What You Get—Consistency, Persistency, and Mediocrity in the Classroom." *Harvard Educational Review* 53: 16–29.

SIZER, T.R. 1984. *Horace's Compromise: The Dilemma of the American High School*. Boston: Houghton Mifflin.

STERNBERG, R.J. 1985. "Teaching Critical Thinking, Part 1: Are We Making Critical Mistakes?" *Phi Delta Kappan* 67: 194-198.

TCHUDI, S., AND S. LAFER. 1993. "How Dry Is the Desert: Nurturing Interdisciplinary Learning." *Educational Leadership* 51: 76–79.

TCHUDI, S., AND D. MITCHELL. 1989. *Explorations in the Teaching of English* (2nd ed.). NY: Harper and Row.

WILLOUGHBY, S.S. 1990. *Mathematics Education for a Changing World*. Alexandria, VA: Association for Supervision and Curriculum Development.

3

Intellectual Mileage from a Shoe
What Grows from Thematic Beginnings

T he shoe, that leather, canvas, or vinyl contraption we wear on our feet, is rarely afforded the stature of the "great idea." Nor, does it, at first glance, appear to have what it takes to act as a force to allow students, in their studies, to "really soar beyond the disciplines" (Ackerman, in Jacobs 1989, 29). In this chapter we will make a case for using the seemingly simple, common, and everyday elements of our environment as the basis for themes for interdisciplinary study. We will show that the shoe, or a rock, or as Whitman knew, a blade of grass, properly observed and considered, can reveal profound truths about the universe and the lives lived within it. Shoes, rocks, and blades of grass, as well as great dams, volcanoes, and geniuses do not exist independent of all else that is of nature and human creation. In fact, all that we have listed here inevitably interacts at some point in time and space, and if we wanted to, we could easily create a plausible life-scenario in which shoes, grass, dams, volcanoes, and geniuses all act and interact as essential components of a particular slice of the human drama.

We will refrain from doing so here, but invite you to consider how these randomly selected elements, at various points in time and space, touch upon one another, affect one another, influence one another. It is this interconnectedness of things that interdisciplinary teaching helps to illuminate and affirm. Interconnectedness also allows us to take the seemingly inconsequential as a starting point for exploration that leads to understandings of great consequence.

InterMusing

Take a moment to remember a time when a seemingly small act, observation, or common object led to "profound" thought, an image in the grain of the wood on a door, an ant moving across the sidewalk, a spider's web, the weave of a piece of fabric. Try to recall the sequence of thought, how the "minor" act or object served to trigger thought, how once the trigger was released the thoughts eventually flowed into that bay of profundity. Why do such things happen, and what is it about the way we see and think about our world that allows this to happen? How important is this manner of thinking?

And so we begin our exploration that takes us into the sole, and the *soul,* of the shoe. By doing so we will illustrate how the disciplines have converged to make the shoe, and how both the invention and the consequences of the shoe have been the theme for many a serious interdisciplinary study. We will use our interdisciplinary investigation of the shoe to get at the properties of good themes and the instructional dynamic they create. We will consider where themes are to be found, how they are selected, and how they are exploited. We use the shoe because we think it serves as an extreme example, because it is something so common, so well known that it is difficult to conceive of it as something worthy of study. Here we will try to show the fascination that can be found in the shoe. In Chapter 5 we will consider how themes so seemingly mundane as the shoe can become the object of fascination for students and the motive for focused interdisciplinary and disciplinary study.

InterMusing

In this chapter, we will do our best to exploit a principle we discussed earlier, making the familiar curious. Take a few minutes to look at the shoe you are wearing and ask of it as many questions as you can. When, for example, did the tying of a bow become the accepted way to secure the ends of the laces? Any question is a legitimate question.

And Whence Came the Shoe?

The notion of the shoe as a theme for interdisciplinary study came to mind during early intermusings concerning this book. The interdisciplinary theme was coloring perception in an extraordinary way, every thought and experience a potential line, paragraph, or chapter. It was "Celebrate the River Day" in Reno, and there, in the middle of the river, just at the site where the celebrants were gathering to honor the Truckee, was a mass of refuse pushed against a rusting shopping cart that acted as a dam. Certainly the irony was not lost on us. Oren Lyon's words had appeared just days before on the Internet: "When we walk upon Mother Earth, we always plant our feet carefully because we know the faces of our future generations are looking up at us from beneath the ground. We never forget them." Certainly there was opportunity here for many an interdisciplinary unit. But irony and ecology gave way to questions of less grandeur like, "How did all this stuff get here? Where did it come from? And to whom had it belonged?" These questions were sparked by the presence amongst the junk of a worn boot, partially wrapped in the pieces of a disintegrating pink blanket, all covered with river muck, twigs, soggy bits of paper, glass fragments, and soda cans. Whose blanket? Whose boot? What stories do the owners have to tell? And, in the spirit of interdisciplinary exploration, where might one turn to find answers to these questions?

One could, we supposed, begin the quest with forensics experts, those people who solve mysteries by looking at leftovers such as these. What would such people be able to discover through examination of the boot? What clues would it reveal to them that it would not reveal to the untrained? What processes, techniques, and forensics knowledge would they apply? Could an examination of the soles or the inner lining explain where the shoe had been worn and for how long? This would probably involve an analysis of the material on the shoe's bottom, research into that material's properties, and consideration of the kinds of forces that could cause it to wear in the way it had. Information could be collected from sources that describe the properties of various materials, and these sources would make reference to chemistry to describe the material's composition, and to physics to explain how the chemicals are treated to give the material the qualities it possesses. Experiments could be run to test how the material interacts with various surfaces. Residues could be lifted from the boot to discover what it had walked upon, and this might lead to a probe into where the residue elements could be found—a probe dependent on understandings of geology and geography, and perhaps botany and zoology.

The forensics experts probably could tell how long the boot had been in the water, and this would necessitate information about the absorbency characteristics of different materials, leading to the study of their molecular structures and the properties of the water that flows down the Truckee. One might be able to learn something of the wearer by the patterns of wear that could be detected on the inside and outside of the boot, the manner in which the wearer walked, his or her gait. Does he or she overpronate or suffer from excess supination? (Starzinger 1993). Does the wearer have a high arch, a normal arch, or a flat arch? Is the wearer black, Asian, or white? These questions, hints Melvyn Cheskin (1987), can be answered by looking at how the shoe has been shaped by wear.

A recent PBS program on the creation of the Holocaust Museum in Washington, DC, discussed how shoes found at concentration camp sites have been used to reveal fascinating historical insights into World War II atrocities. Researchers can, for instance, gain insight into the thoughts of people boarding the death camp trains by noting that many of the shoes worn by the victims were dress shoes, some of the women's high heeled. It appears, the curator of the museum explained, that many of those bound for Dachau or Auschwitz had no idea where they were being taken or how long their stay would be. They dressed for an occasion quite different from the one they so tragically encountered. The shoes were not of the type one wears for comfort, to stand in for long periods of time, or to traverse long distances. They wore their dress shoes. A terrible insight.

Back in Reno, the mystery of the boot in the river gave way to other questions about footwear, some that were, we would imagine, like those you generated when you accepted our invitation to the last InterMusing. One of the authors once lived in Eugene, Oregon, and there the shoe is lore because Eugene is the home to the father of the modern running shoe, former University of Oregon track coach Bill Bowerman. Bowerman is also the founder of the Nike Corporation, and the man who, it is claimed, brought jogging to America from New Zealand (Leutzinger 1993). It is said that one of the major problems Bowerman faced in developing a light and properly cushioned shoe for runners was finding a way to glue rubber bottoms to the upper part of the shoe. In experimenting with various compounds, Bowerman eventually acquired a crippling nerve problem from inhaling the vapors.

Bowerman's quest for the perfect shoe for runners leads nicely into the interdisciplinary complexities of shoes in terms of the relationship of shoe use to shoe design, of foot physiology to the physics and physical consequences of body movements, of the interaction between various compounds and different types of surface, and of the relationship that exists between the comfort a shoe affords and the psychological state of its wearer. Shoes lead to stories of great achievement in sports, and into the economics of the shoe business, its advertising, and its ethics. Is it true that behind every modern-day world record there is a physiologist, a chemist, a physicist, a psychologist, and a business manager?

Not only have world records in sports been influenced by shoes, so too have wars, the economic histories of towns across America, and the psyches of those town's inhabitants and their sociological complexion. The link between war and shoes is represented nicely in a small volume titled, *The Soldier's Foot and the Military Shoe: A Handbook for Officers and Noncommissioned Officers on the Line.* Written by Edward Lyman Munson and published in 1917, the book was prompted by an investigation into the "causes affecting the shoeing of the United States soldier" by the Army Shoe Board. During the study, says Munson, "it became evident that in very many instances the faulty conditions found were due to a lack of information on this important subject." Shoes are something most of us rarely consider, but, writes Munson, "Napoleon is reported to have said that he made war not so much with arms as the legs of his soldiers." Many examples, he continues, "could be given where battles have been lost and won by marching capacity."

> Waterloo was lost and history changed because of delay in the arrival of the expected French reinforcements—while the march of Jackson's so called "foot cavalry" in the Manassas campaign of 1863 turned Pope's anticipated victory into the defeat of the Second Bull Run . . . War has become a business in which each unit has its part to play; and the soldier whose badly shod feet are unable to carry him into battle fails at the critical moment of the purpose for which he was trained, and instead of being an added strength he becomes an encumbrance. The effect of bad-fitting feet upon the psychology of war is great. (1–2)

This said, Munson goes on to develop guidelines for the construction of shoes fit for the work of a soldier.

The quest for a good working shoe for the foot soldier begins with an examination of the anatomy of the foot and a discussion of the consequences of commercial shoe makers' inattention or lack of concern for that anatomy. "Mobility of the toes is naturally greater than the fingers of the hand, with all the delicacy of use required of the latter, yet it is completely lost sight of by the average shoe manufacturer" (14). Thus, "the perfect undeformed foot is found practically only in children and among savage, non-shoe-wearing peoples." The last point is illustrated with photos depicting the perfect feet of a four-year-old American child, the foot of Hermes as sculpted by Praxiteles, and those of members of the Bontoc Iqorrotes tribe of Lubuagan.

American soldiers' feet examined by the Shoe Board, we learn, were far from being perfect. In fact, due to the effects of poorly designed commercial shoes, "in the great numbers of feet examined . . . not one was free of some appreciable deformity or blemish" (24).

In short space, this book touches upon and interrelates anatomy, physiology, history and military science, psychology (the relationship of happy feet to good soldiering attitude), sociology ("all but a few civilians are so influenced by the subtle suggestive influence of manufacturers' styles as largely to disregard matters of fit, shape, and comfort . . ." [35]), manufacturing technology, physics (as in marching, "As the left foot leaves the ground, the force of gravity, acting as a result of the loss of equilibrium in a forward direction, causes it to swing outward and brings it to a position under or slightly in front of the body without muscular exertion" [29]), economics ("the cost of the military shoe is a consideration quite secondary to the one of efficiency" [47]), and engineering.

"In many sports," says Melvyn Cheskin, "you have to walk before you can play. In fact, the cycle of the walking gait lies at the core of many sports. Thus an analysis of the walking cycle is essential to understanding much athletic movement" (265). From military marches and the proper soldier's boot to the athlete's walking gait and the proper sports shoe, notice how things normally taken for granted are being carefully observed to derive valuable, sometimes critical, information.

There, on the feet of most of the students in the classrooms we visit, are shoes that result from great intellectual effort, but the effort that has led to the creation of the Nike, Adidas, Reebok, and L.A. Gear shoes is hidden from our view. These shoes are something very familiar that with very little effort can be made to provoke immense curiosity. At a tutoring session in Sutcliff, Nevada, we asked students to hold up the bottoms of their shoes and to compare the waffle patterns. We looked at the differences. Some patterns seemed to be simply for show. Others could be explained for their function. We noticed details about the shape of the toe or the height of the heels, the lacing configurations, the height of the shoes' tops. We examined the materials used in different parts of the shoe and considered the usefulness of air pockets and the padding inside.

What most people who wear these shoes do not know, and would never stop to consider, is that they are the product of biomechanical design, the antithesis of the commercial shoes Munson describes. These shoes are the result of careful "study of the body in motion" (Cheskin, 173). Biomechanics, "applying principles from mechanics and engineering . . . can study the forces that act on the body and the effects these forces produce" (173).

Athletes, whether they know it or not, are affected by such things as the "historesis curve" and "compression deflection." The former is defined as "a graphic representation of the relationship between the stresses or forces required to deform an elastic material and the observed forces when the load is removed" (Cheskin, 197). If you step on a piece of foam rubber, you create a depression in the material. As soon as you lift your foot from it, the foam begins to reform itself. The shoe geniuses are concerned with how much of a dent our feet put in materials like foam rubber and how long that material takes to spring back. The "curve" is important for determining which materials should be used in certain parts of a shoe. Consider its importance in light of the fact that when a 180-pound basketball player jumps from an 18-inch platform, "he strikes the ground with a force of 700 pounds. A 250-pound player generates a force of one ton when he drops from a height of three feet" (Cheskin, 183).

Athletic shoes are designed, in part, to reduce the punishment the various parts of the leg and foot take during particular activities. The *historesis curve* is used to determine the cushioning effect of a material and its ability to regain its cushioning ability after a particular action. *Compression deflection* is defined as "the amount of deformation observed in a material after it has been subjected to a compressive or impact load" (Cheskin, 196). Nike, according to an article in *American Health* by Page Hill Starzinger, "injects pressurized gas into thin plastic cells under the heels or the forefeet (the balls of the feet) or along the entire length of the sneakers. Asics, Puma, Adidas, and Reebok use ambient air—a fancy name of the Earth's atmosphere—to soften the foot's impact" (56). So there is a good reason for the "air" shoes! The article goes on to report that "a less heralded—but equally important—form of cushioning is provided by the midsole, the material between the insole and the outer." Those participating in "high-impact" activities need "multi-density foam or rubber-based midsoles, because single-density foams lose resiliency quickly." There are, Starzinger tells us, a variety of foam and rubber types, ethyl vinyl acetate (EVA), polyurethane, and silicone phylon for the midsoles, each with its own elastic properties.

Elasticity has other ramifications for the athlete and the athletic shoe designer. *Newsweek* (1992) reports that "a running shoe has two functions."

> It must create friction with the ground; that keeps the runner from slipping, which wastes energy. It must also act as an extension of the Achilles tendon. After a runner pushes off with her back leg, the front foot lands with a force as much as triple her weight. The Achilles tendon compresses like a spring to store energy. As the runner rolls forward onto the ball of her foot, the tendon expands and pushes her ahead. The more energy the tendon stores, the greater the push. Good shoes increase energy storage by compressing and springing back into shape thanks to air pockets and foam wedges built into the sole. (58)

Thus, the reason for Saucony's Ground Reaction Inertia Device, the G.R.I.D., and L.A. Gear's carbon fiber Catapult Impulses (Starzinger, 57).

There is plenty of science, mathematics, and history too, if one wants to accept the history of the military boot or the evolution of athletic shoes as history. And we do think that one should accept such history. Look at Paul G. Faler's book on the history of shoe making in America, for instance. In *Mechanics and Manufacturing in the Early Industrial Revolution* (1981), Faler illuminates in a powerful way the ramifications of industrial change by focusing on the shoe industry as it affects the town of Lynn, Massachusetts, between 1780 and 1860. From this microperspective the reader is able to see the macro-implications of the machines science and engineering brought into being, their effect on industry, on towns, and on the people who lived in them.

The history of invention and mechanization in the shoe industry also lets us look at the problem-solving processes employed by those who created the machines. In his book *The Path to Mechanized Shoe Production in the United States,* Ross Thomson (1989) discusses the intellectual machinations involved in the invention of sewing machines used in the shoe industry.

InterMusing

Consider the following passage from Thomson's book in relation to what we said above about the intellectual processes put into play by students involved in the Lego-Logo project (Chapter 2). Then list disciplinary concepts and skills that come into play in this description of the problem of developing machines to sew shoes. How might the discipline(s) you teach use this passage?

"The operations and materials of shoe making preclude straightforward application of existing mechanical technology," writes Thomson.

> The simple hand operation of sewing posed a series of technical problems. On simpler materials such as cloth and light uppers, the sewer penetrated the material with a needle that had a thread-carrying eye at the end opposite the point, then altered the angle of the needle with one hand and the cloth with the other so that the needle repenetrated the material from the underside. Next, the sewer pushed the needle part way back through the cloth, grasped the point of the needle, let go of the eye, pulled the needle the rest of the way through the material, and finally extended his or her arm to take up the slack thread. The sewing machine hence had to solve an interlinked set of stitch-forming, material- or needle feeding, and tension regulating problems. (63)

This is an example of precise description derived from careful observation for a real purpose—the development of a machine to replicate the operations described. As we will consider below, this kind of observation and description, motivated by the desire to understand and create, has pertinence for and application in every discipline. The rigor involved in producing such a description is understood when it is actually demonstrated. We are still trying to create such a description for the purpose of inventing a machine that will tie the laces of our shoes.

Labor and Work

Okay. We've told you about what we learned about shoes as a way of illustrating where interdisciplinary thinking about a humble theme took us. Before turning to the classroom, there's one more connection we want to make, and it centers on the idea of labor.

Thomson's book is not so much a book about shoes as it is about the effects of industrial change—mechanization in particular—on human beings. The shoe and its manufacture provide a focus for the book that allows the author to accomplish his real purpose of examining broader, more abstract constructs that explain the sociological implications of invention. For instance, he deals with the consequences of the machine for the craftsperson. He contrasts "craft" and "mechanized technique," explaining that "in craft production, laborers hold a conception of the product and the method of its formation, which they then implement by the acquired, skillful use of tools." For the craftsperson, "labor is purposive and tools are means to achieve this purpose." In mechanized production, on the other hand, the machine is made to mimic the actions performed by the craftsperson and "labor simply allows the machine to function, and is therefore separated from the activity of conceiving and fabricating the product" (1).

Interestingly, Herbert Thelen in *The Classroom Society* (1981) characterizes the role of students in the typical instructional setting in much the same way Thomson portrays the laborer in a mechanized industry, in effect, as "separated from the activity of conceiving and fabricating the product." *Work,* says Thelen, is guided or directed by the nature of the situation with which one is trying to cope. One acts to affect the situation and sees the relationship between effort and the difference it makes. "We put the load close to the wheelbarrow's wheel," he says, "because that gives us the best leverage, not because that's the way Joe likes it or because that's the way we always do it." *Labor,* on the other hand, "is the application of a formula or technique over and over." The tasks are "cut and dried," involving little creativity and, thus, producing in the laborer little sense of a relationship between personal effort and outcome. Practice may perfect "technique," but the connection between improved technique and the results of one's effort is not for the laborer to understand. Thus, says Thelen, "the laborer is not psychologically involved enough to ask any questions about the task (only about the conditions of employment)." "Recall," he asks of us, "the disgruntled shoe makers in the factory: when they made the whole shoe, they were working, but when they shifted to assembly-line methods with each person just doing a small part of the work, they were laboring" (112–113). The relevance of our work here in relation to work and labor we hope will become evident.

Our present exploration touches only upon a little of what could be studied under the theme of "The Shoe." The questions you generated in response to the second InterMusing in the chapter, we would guess, would lead you into several other shoe issues we have not considered here. Why are men's shoes predominately brown and black? What are the physics of the pump and the wedgie, and what are the medical implications of the physics? Who and what determine what is fashionable? What is the psychology and the sociology of a particular style becoming popular? If you have an interest in finding answers to these questions, then the effort you would put forth to do so would be *work*. If you had no desire to know the answers but put forth effort to find them because you were told to do so, then you would be *laboring*.

Implications of the Simplistic: The Shoe as Theme

The point we are making with our shoe example is that thematic work can have rather humble beginnings. The things that are right before our eyes, if attended to, can lead to questions of the greatest importance and into study that touches in exciting ways upon the principles, processes, and concepts disciplinary instruction is intended to teach. We differ with those who believe that a theme necessarily has to be a "big idea" (Martinello and Cook 1994). We do not reject broader, and seemingly more academic themes such as "evidence," "tragedy," "humanity," "discovery," and "justice." At the same time, these more abstract notions can be examined, perhaps more effectively, by beginning with that which represents their concrete manifestations.

Thus, we find ourselves somewhat at odds with those who would reject themes such as the shoe by dismissing them as too trivial a subject for study. In *Interdisciplinary Curriculum: Design and Implementation* (Jacobs 1989), the theme of "transportation" is dismissed in favor of "argument and evidence" because "transportation does not give a very good view of math, literature, or physics, although it does not serve too badly in history" (Perkins, 70). It is also rejected because it does not "apply pervasively," while

> argument and evidence applies to all historical findings, to all literary claims, to all results in physics, and to all theorems in mathematics . . . the 'lens' of transportation applies to most subject matters only in segregated ways—such as time, rate, and distance problems in math. (70)

David Ackerman, in the same volume, rejects Gordon Var's (1987) suggestion of the kite as a legitimate theme for interdisciplinary study. Such a theme, argues Ackerman, cannot withstand critical scrutiny. The unit Var proposes, says Ackerman, would have "science students inquire into the history and social significance of kite flying, English students compose 'lofty' poetry, math students estimate altitude, and so on." Each discipline, he concedes, could "relate to the central theme," but, he says, the question that must be raised is, "Should each subject devote a portion of its instructional time to the interdisciplinary project?" Are the disciplinary topics generated by the theme valid within the disciplines, or are they going to cause teachers to give "short shrift to topics considered more important?" (27).

Ackerman offers four criteria, all related to the questions he poses regarding the kite theme, which he claims to be "intrinsic to the ideal of interdisciplinary education." For the most part, they serve as sound guidelines for determining the virtues of particular themes, or perhaps, as we will explain later, how particular themes are utilized. Thus, we feel it a worthy use of space to present the criteria and comment on them.

The first criterion is that the theme must allow teachers to cover "relevant concepts . . . significant to the school curriculum for a particular year or in general" (27). The theme, in other words, cannot dictate the concepts that will be taught. The history of kite flying, says Ackerman, "is not considered an important topic in the social studies curriculum," implying that the theme forces the social studies teacher to deal with this topic at the expense of more important ones.

We take a different approach, one that perhaps, wrests some control from the teacher as curriculum developer, but provides, we think, a better basis for disciplinary learning. Consider for a moment the purpose of the disciplines. They are indeed systems of knowledge and for each there is a content. But more importantly, the disciplines are systems, sets of procedures that allow those who use them to develop understandings of their surroundings, to answer questions that arise as human beings interact with the circumstances of the world in which they live. *From the questions* spring the disciplines. Without those questions, there would be no need for the disciplines. Yet the manner in which most of us are educated would suggest that it is otherwise. Thus, it is our belief that the concepts that are taught in the disciplines can best be taught *as a response to the questions students raise.* The role of the theme is to isolate a portion of the universe for study and study is the pursuit of answers to questions that the focus raises. The exercise below is intended to get you into the frame of mind for making the familiar curious.

InterMusing

Look around you. Let your eyes focus on something in the sky, at your feet, to the north, the south, the east or west. Think about that something for a moment. Think about what it is, about what it reveals when you look upon it, about what it does not reveal. Now formulate at least three interesting questions about it, questions that you really would be interested in having answered. Then think about how you would go about answering them.

Everywhere we look, there are things we know something about, but also do not know some things about. For instance, as Susan and Stephen Tchudi's new work in progress would have us do, consider the next manhole cover you find underfoot. What does it cover? There is a question that leads to study of the whole infrastructure of a city. What design and engineering principles went into its creation? Who made it, and where was it made? Of what is it made, and why was this material chosen? Is the pattern on its surface functional or simply decorative?

Consider the implications of each of these questions, not only in terms of the kinds of information they might reveal, but also in terms of sensitizing students to the complexities of the world. How many would know, for instance, of the deliberations that occurred at city hall, at the city engineer's office, in laboratories, and in factories before this cover could be made and placed over this particular hole? To get back to Ackerman's criteria, this questioning process, and the questioning attitude it supposes are neglected by school curricula. Yet both process and attitude are essential to the health of all disciplines and to the institutions that utilize the knowledge of the disciplines.

Turning back to the kite, does this theme violate the first criterion? Does it prevent the teaching of important disciplinary concepts? We think not. If the disciplines are what we think they are, tools for exploring and developing understanding of what has been discovered, then an exploration into the history of kites is a legitimate use of social studies time, because it is being used to develop students' understanding of how the social sciences are used to make sense of particular types of phenomena, how they work to answer certain kinds of questions. The kite and the shoe are the result of and the cause of significant events in the history of human beings. This is easy to see if we consider what *would not be* if either the kite or the shoe had not been invented.

Kites nicely illustrate important aspects of the process of invention, and they can be used to show how ideas and invention interrelate, and how they are built upon other ideas and inventions. The principles of flight learned from the kite provided knowledge essential to developing modern aircraft. The complex machines that so profoundly affect our lives today have origins in the seemingly simple inventions of the past. This is a basic and essential introduction to the concept of progress, and a path to understanding and appreciating the contributions of the past. Such an appreciation, it seems to us, is basic to the study of history. Study of the kite can be used, then, to teach students the meaning of modernity. The social significance of the kite thus becomes highly significant.

The third criterion Ackerman presents calls for the theme to represent something that is "valuable for students to think about and assimilate into their way of looking at the world." Interdisciplinary teaching, he says, derives power from "the interplay of disciplines in illuminating complex phenomenon" (29). We agree, and so too with the fourth and final criterion, that interdisciplinary approaches and their themes must contribute to "broader outcomes." We assert, however, that the theme need not be the complex phenomenon to be illuminated. Instead, the theme, as we have said before, is a *focal point* for exploration, exploration that works to reveal valuable, complex phenomena. Consider the examples we have offered so far. The shoe leads easily not only into the complexities of anatomy and physiology, but also into the complex principles of physics and engineering. And all of these complexities are made more valuable for students when they interact to provide answers to complex questions that arise as they examine that common and familiar entity, the shoe. Among the valuable and complex thoughts the shoe theme can be used to provoke are those that cause one to realize that all things have underlying complexity, that all that surrounds us can be toyed with, manipulated to reveal greater levels of complexity. We agree wholeheartedly with Ackerman when he says that "interdisciplinary teaching may help shape the learner's overall approach to knowledge" (30). We would add that the best interdisciplinary teaching will positively affect the learner's overall approach to making sense of the world in which he or she lives.

Themes

What is a theme? A theme is simply a clump of stuff for study, stuff bounded by certain parameters that allow for focus. One teacher whom we know of has her students throw a hula hoop onto the desert land that surrounds their school. What exists within the bounds of the hoop is the focus of their studies. Themes are jumpstarters for creating curiosity and need, a reason to seek and apply information and skill.

We offered the shoe as an example of the kind of thematic starting point that interests us. And, as we have said before, we do not reject the broader, seemingly more academic themes like those Ackerman proposes, "humanities," "science/technology, society," and "evidence," or those Perkins (1989) sees as providing "lenses worth looking through" such as "argument and evidence," "change," "dependence and independence." These are all good principles to explore and to think about. So too James Beane's (1990) themes for early adolescents: "transitions," "identities," "interdependence," "wellness," "social structures," "independence," "conflict resolution," "commercialism," "justice," "caring," and "institutions." But we do not think that such themes are necessarily the best starting points for exploration. Rather, they are themes that are discovered along the way. "Evidence," for example, is not so much a theme to be studied directly as it is a tool for discovering truths about such things as spiders, rusty nails, shoes, the industrial revolution, nuclear power production, and religion.

Christine Pappas, Barbara Kiefer, and Linda Levstic (1990) offer "wash and wear," "changes," "let's eat," "giants," and "digging up the past" as sample themes for kindergarten through sixth grade classes. Sherri Winnett (1993) suggests the study of amusement parks. An article in *Ties* magazine (Parkhill 1993) invites the study of roller coasters, and Marriott invites students to study physics in their Great America parks. Roberts (1993) focuses on dinosaurs. Janet Northrup (1989) has students explore "fast foods," and Ann Alejandro uses "cars" as a theme (1989). Elsie Nigohosian (Wepner 1992) uses endangered species to teach social studies, science, mathematics, language arts, music, and computer skills to elementary students. Dale Andrews, a teacher at Billinghurst Middle School in Reno has developed a thematic unit centered on the building of a bicycle trail that would follow the path of the old Emigrant Trail. Lee Hurren, Marley Carlin, Nancy Wells, and Sharon Soule, once students at the University of Nevada, Reno, created a unit on Cinco de Mayo. Another group of students, Gina Leonard, Milissa LiCon, Abigail Kirst, and Forrest Gorden wrote a unit that would have students establishing a colony on Mars. Within each of these themes, the important abstract concepts with which Perkins, Ackerman, and Beane concern themselves can be discussed.

The themes we prefer begin with something that is tangible, something that can be observed, smelled, tasted, or seen. We like these themes because we feel they lead students into and through important learning processes in a very natural way, from observation, to curiosity (questioning), to exploration, and to knowledge. This is the pattern of thoughtfulness we believe schools are obligated to help students understand, because it gives them a sense of how knowledge is made. It is, we think, the pattern that characterizes the thought processes of thinking people, of thoughtful people.

The Qualities of Good Themes

A theme is simply a focal point for study, an event, an object, an idea that evokes in students curiosity or a need to know. As such, it provokes investigation. We now present our list of the qualities of good themes. The list, we think, could also be called "qualities of good curricula," because good themes are only as good as the curricula they generate. We will say more about this later. For now, as you read through this list, consider the implications of the principles for instruction, interdisciplinary or otherwise.

1. Good themes cause students to generate interesting questions and to pose intriguing problems. They provoke curiosity. They confuse. As such, they provide reason for learning. Dale Andrews proposes to his students that they begin a project that will lead to the building of a bicycle path through Reno that will follow the route of the Emigrant Trail. Certainly the idea creates curiosity about the trail and the people who used it. Textbooks are helpful here. But in order to build a bike path that follows the original trail they need more specific information. History texts can tell them what the trail was and where it was, but in a general way. Dale knows that the trail ran through what is now Reno, but where exactly? The text will tell of events that occurred along the trail, but where will they get information telling them what took place along that portion of the trail that their bike path will cover? Once they find the route the trail took, how will they go about finding out who now owns the property? How will they obtain right-of-ways? According to Dale, students will discover that the trail's course runs directly through one of Reno's shopping malls. What will they do about it? These and a multitude of other questions will have to be answered, questions about materials and costs, amenities, maintenance, liability. If the path follows a historic route, how will that his-

tory be represented to those who use it? And who will use it? How does one go about finding out? Demographic studies?

2. The questions students raise in response to good themes provoke thought and, inevitably, thought about the thought processes, or *metacognition*. Good themes cause learners to think about things they have not thought of before, or to think about them in different ways. One of the reasons we like the idea of making the familiar curious is that it pushes students to understand the nature of their own understandings, to understand that in most instances, to varying degrees, they are partial and idiosyncratic. Thorough use of good themes causes students to consider how they know what they know, and this, in turn, leads to similar examination of perceived knowledge. A recent project at Billinghurst, a local middle school, asked students to explore the issue of water use along the Truckee River. Truckee water flows from Lake Tahoe in the Sierra Nevada mountains, through Reno, and out to Pyramid Lake and the desert farming community of Fallon, Nevada. It provides water for the cities, irrigates farmer's fields, and fills Pyramid. It is a limited resource even in the best years when there is good snowfall in the mountains. At the time the unit was used, the area was in the midst of prolonged drought. Public disputes over who should get the limited amounts of water available were hot and heavy.

At the onset of the unit, students were surveyed to find out who they believed most deserved to have Truckee water. They were then placed in teams, each of which studied the needs of a different Truckee user group. One team worked to discover all it could about the claims of the Paiutes who owned Pyramid Lake and needed water sufficient to allow the sacred Cui-ui fish to spawn. Another team studied the needs of the residents of Reno, and those of the tourists who stay at the hotel-casinos that provide the bulk of the town's revenues and most of the jobs. A third team examined the concerns of the Fallon farmers, and a fourth those of recreational users upstream whose spending sustains the economies of Sierra towns like Tahoe City and Truckee.

As the unit progressed, perceptions began to change and students were asked to monitor those changes. The views reflected in the initial surveys were affected by students' contact with the people whose lives were touched by the issues and the new information they were collecting through their research. The question of "how we knew then" as opposed to "how we know now" was discussed, not only in relation to the issue at hand, but also in regard to how this experience pertains to "knowing" at any time about any issue. Students had to concern themselves with their own taken-for-granted beliefs, with the issue of "common knowledge," and with the meaning of information as it relates to the act of making important decisions that affect the lives of real people. They knew by unit's end that the meaning of facts changes as the perceiver's attitude toward them changes. They learned the importance of knowing not only how *they* thought, but how other people think.

3. Good themes help students to discover *what they know* and *what they know*

how to do is pertinent to finding answers to questions and problems themes raise. At the same time, good themes allow students to discover that what they do not know or cannot do is also necessary for answering questions and finding solutions. This process of inventorying assets in the face of need is a prime motivator for learning. If you need something and you do not have it, you have to find a way to get it. An interesting facet of this is discovering what it is that you have to have. Ann Hoyle and her students at Easton Middle School discovered what they didn't know but needed to know to run a school bank when Douglas Porter, a local bank president, graciously invited two bank examiners to audit a banking operation run out of Hoyle's classroom. The examiners told teacher and students that the bank they were running was in violation of the laws of the Commonwealth of Massachusetts. They were operating a bank without a charter and "charging interest at a usurious rate," 418 percent a year, to be exact. The bank also did not have a license to collect loans and a cease and desist order was issued (Bumstead 1983).

The group of students at the University of Nevada who developed an interdisciplinary unit having middle schoolers build a concession stand ran into similar problems. Food storage became a problem, as did the need to find sources of initial capital. There was also the problem of finding wholesale vendors who would sell them the relatively small amounts of food items the cart would require.

4. The questions and problems posed by good themes lead to thought that eventually leads to *exploration*. Exploration or investigation become necessary when the memory and other readily accessible archives of information are found to be insufficient to provide answers and solutions to questions and problems learners face. Exploration is the process of approaching the unanswered or unsolved. Thus, a theme must have built into it enough complexity to force students to reach beyond what they already possess. Good teaching can bring out the complexities embedded in almost any theme. Good themes, and good use of themes, ensures that exploration will not be easy, that students will have to be resourceful if they are to acquire what they need. Texts and library materials can be useful, but good themes should take students into new resources beyond the school grounds, into the community, into the world, into resources that are not so nicely organized or readily available. The bank and food projects necessitated students tapping into resources they likely never knew to exist, into regulatory codes and product catalogues. The ability to reason one's way to and through resources is an extremely important life skill that is rarely practiced in schools. Familiarity with the process of finding resources is best taught, we think, in the context of finding answers to questions and problems with which one is truly concerned.

In 1991, a group of middle school students became aware of the existence of decoy ducks made by ancient Native American craftsmen of tule reed. The decoys were depicted on that year's state duck stamp. Upon seeing the stamp, a student asked his social studies teacher, Duncan Monroe, where the decoys were. Thus began the RADD, or Recover a Duck Decoy project. The students' initial research, involving contact with the duck stamp's painter, showed that the ducks had been excavated from a cave on the Humboldt River in the 1920s, and that approximately twenty of the original ducks survive. Most, they discovered, reside at the Hayes Museum in New York City and not a single duck, the oldest decoys ever found in the Americas, remained in Nevada. The RADD project's aim was to bring some ducks home.

The students, and their teachers, discovered that the Hayes Museum had recently become a part of the Smithsonian Institution, and this, they found, meant that the decoys were now owned by the United States government. They found administrators in the Smithsonian who dealt with Native American antiquities and discovered that the actions of these administrators were overseen by a Board of Regents that included the vice president of the United States, the chief justice of the Supreme Court, members appointed by the president of the Senate and the Speaker of the House of Representatives, and others appointed by joint resolution of Congress. The best way to approach the issue, they discovered, was to contact their congressional representative, which they did, earning some a summer meeting in Washington, D.C. with members of Nevada's delegation.

Through their explorations they discovered the hierarchies of bureaucracies and government, who did and who did not have authority, and who to contact in order to get things done. Phone calls and letters to one source led to new sources who referred students to more sources. New vistas, new layers of authority, new twists on who had to be contacted, how they had to be contacted, and when they could be contacted were discovered. The students spoke to local Native Americans who knew about antiquities and the antiquities laws. They spoke to lawyers who worked with the Native Americans. They engaged anthropologists, artists, conservation groups, hunters' clubs (Ducks Unlimited had unsuccessfully been trying to have a decoy returned to Nevada for several years). They spoke to scientists of all types, including those concerned with climate and atmospheric conditions—the Smithsonian has very strict regulations regarding the care of antiquities, and Carson City, Nevada, where the decoys were to be displayed, is about 4,000 feet higher in altitude than New York City. The difference in atmospheric pressure caused by the altitude change could seriously affect the well being of ancient tule reed ducks. The northern Nevada climate is also different from New York's, and transfer of the decoys from a humid climate to a dry one could cause damage. Thus, a display case had to be built to compensate for these geographic and climatic realities. Skilled craftspeople had to be found to build a case to the scientists' specifications.

5. Good themes create a need and a desire for disciplinary and interdisciplinary skill and knowledge. Certainly the examples we have given thus far require

students to possess or to acquire skills and knowledge commonly taught through the disciplines. The bank project necessitated that students know something of how interest is computed. A project calling for the creation of a new city park requires that students be able to compute area and possess an understanding of the attributes and requirements of different types of vegetation. A project to place a colony on Mars necessitates knowledge of science, mathematics, and the social sciences. We would wager that the formula for discovering the area of a triangle could be made important in the context of this unit. So could the workings of the human cardiovascular system, and principles of physics such as gravity, fusion, and fission. History, sociology, and psychology could tell something of how the colonists might react to the conditions they would face. English, in tandem with the social sciences, might offer novels, short stories, and poems to give the planners a sense of the nature of human beings, their needs, their desires, their manner of interacting with one another. Home economics and physical education could inform the planners of the nutritional and physical conditioning needs of the settlers, and art and music could be considered in regard to the effects they have on individuals and societies.

6. Good themes cause students to seek and apply disciplinary (and interdisciplinary) knowledge and skill. Need and desire lead to action. And, conversely, action leads to need and desire. Embedded in good themes are the questions and problems that make the disciplines purposeful, and their purposefulness comes to be understood as students use disciplinary knowledge and skill to find answers and solve the problems the themes raise. When purposefulness is discovered, students grasp the value of disciplinary teachings and this creates a desire, and sometimes a need, for students to learn more about them. Application, in other words, can prove *that it works*.

During the RADD project, students in Carla Sankovitch's English class worked on writing and speaking skills. They used these skills to gain access to those who could be of help, to convince those they accessed of the righteousness of their cause, and to obtain the money they needed to pay for the ducks' flight home and the case in which they would be displayed. Even before they knew that their efforts had succeeded, they had come to realize the power of the written and spoken word. Those words brought recognition from the press, from the community, from administrators in important agencies including the Bureau of Land Management, the Smithsonian Institution, and the Nevada State Museum, and from leaders in state and national governments. They spoke to civic organizations, made their pitch to the press, met with the governor, and consulted with the state's two United States senators.

In their writing and in their speeches they had to show that they knew their stuff. To do that they had to accurately discuss history, describe events, present the science that Matt Munley helped them to understand. The Illinois Rivers Project had the same force. Robert Williams, Cindy Bidlak, and David

Winnett (1993) report that the project, as of the fall of 1993, involved a network of teams at twenty-two midwest schools, which

> work to produce scientific data, to research social and cultural information, and to solve problems on its section of the [Mississippi] river. All teams are trained in project procedures, conducting water tests, using computers to transmit data on the Southern Illinois Educational Network (SOILED NET), and writing for *Meanderings* (the student-authored book). (80)

Students involved in the project have used what they have learned to, among other things, carry out a successful campaign to get the Jersey County (Illinois) health department to develop a new sewer system; help a country club discover the cause of a fish kill in a pond on its grounds and to determine the proper amounts of fertilizer to use on its greens; engage the Environmental Protection Agency, the Army Corps of Engineers, and a county conservation department to force a land owner to stop dumping waste near a stream bank; halt the dumping of raw sewage into the Illinois River through a broken sewer system by forcing the mayor and city council of Henry, Illinois, to complete in a few years clean up work that was a part of a ten-year plan. Again, as with the RADD students, the knowledge and skill learned through the disciplines was applied with inspiring results.

7. Good themes provide intellectual goals that cause learners to naturally encounter the *whys* of the disciplines. Such understanding of the purposefulness of the disciplines' contents and procedures leads to a pragmatically grounded understanding of the *hows* of the disciplines, an understanding of how their procedures work to accomplish their purposes. Further, good lessons embedded in good themes solve the problem of students simply memorizing information and algorithms. Understanding the relationship of a procedure to the problems it works to solve makes the operation or procedure *sensible*. We think it is critical that students not only learn the disciplines in the traditional sense, but that they make sense of the inner workings of the disciplines they study.

In the city park project, designed by a team of prospective teachers, Larry Marlow, the math person in the group, uses the unit as an opportunity for making the procedures for finding the area of various geometrical shapes sensible to students. There are, of course, formulas that allow one to calculate area, but students often do not understand the reasoning behind the formulas. If a park is to have lawn, the park planner must know how much sod or seed will be needed, and with a finite (and these days, a tight) budget for construction of parks, he or she must be able to determine what the cost of sod or seed will be. Marlow's plan is to take students out to a park, have them use various measuring tools to discover the area of those parts of the park covered with grass, determine the amount of sod needed to cover that area, call a turf company for an estimate, and come up with a price for a new lawn. In the unit, students also need to consider the amount of water different park designs would necessitate.

The science teacher would deal with methods for determining the porosity of various soil types, the moisture requirements of different plants, evaporation rates, and the possible watering techniques that could be used. Students would also consider the effect of climate on soils and plants, and evaporation rates, all to determine what the cost of water for the park might be. Aesthetics, in relation to expense and practicality, also need consideration.

8. Good themes naturally lead to interdisciplinary inquiry. It is difficult to imagine a real world question or problem that can be answered or solved through reference to a single discipline. Themes focus on problems rather than disciplines, thus pushing students into the realm of real-world issues. If students are seeking solutions to problems derived from interaction with the world around them, integration of disciplinary knowledge and procedure comes naturally. The shoe example shows how disciplinary procedure and content intermingle as one tries to answer questions raised by the theme. For example, in trying to understand the evolution of the athletic shoe, physiology and physics become intertwined in a most pragmatic fashion. Viewed from an economic/historical perspective, the science of machines (which includes physiological and kinesthetic observations as well as physics and engineering) intermingles with the sciences that focus on behavior, sociology and psychology. To glimpse this intertwining one can pick up a company prospectus for one of the athletic shoe manufacturers. Aspects of research and development of the product are described in terms of the impact they have on the minds of prospective buyers:

> Utilization of CAD/CAM technology should reduce the time it takes to introduce new products to market by shortening the design and development stages and should enable the Company to respond more quickly to changing consumer preferences. (L.A. Gear 1993, 6)

9. Good themes build strong communities of learners. Good themes, because of their real-world complexity, cause individuals to pose unique questions and unique responses to the questions. These questions and responses are often of great interest to the group, since all members are focused on the theme and have a stake in understanding it. In this way, good themes create a learning environment in which the product of individual thoughts contributes in a visible way to the good of the community.

The social interaction a good theme can generate is crucial to the development of higher-order thinking. Piagetian scholars have argued that it is contact with the thinking of others that leads to critical thinking abilities. To think critically is, to an extent, to consider possibilities, the validity of different and sometimes opposing views and perspectives. The ability to do so, to juggle in one's mind contending possibilities, is learned through interacting with others and, in a social and external fashion, grappling with the differences that arise.

The water project described above is set up in such a way that contending views are ensured. Each group examines the claims of a different Truckee River water user group, and by project's end, decisions have to be made as to who should actually get the water. Almost all of the thematic projects we have discussed force meaningful group deliberation coupled with a need to make decisions that ultimately have "real-world" consequences. Even projects that exist in the realm of simulation, like the trip to Mars project, have the potential to create situations in which competing minds are appreciated for pushing the group mind toward the best possible answers and solutions.

10. Good themes promote what Lafer and Markert (1994) have called "cooperation in the strong sense." Cooperation is not mandated, but rather, evolves as the group pushes forth to accomplish collective ends. The agreement to disagree is central to good cooperative ventures; the refusal to disagree prevents groups from finding and selecting best possible answers. Cooperation in the strongest sense is based on the will and desire to succeed rather than based on a set of dictated behaviors advocated for the sake of politeness.

Selecting Themes

Good themes, simply put, generate questions that students are interested in having answered. They lead into exploration that creates a need for the good things the disciplines have to offer. Much of what makes a theme good is what teachers do with them, or what they encourage students to do with them. The shoe, at first appearance, has no business posing as a theme. Neither does a rusty nail. But consider again what we found in the shoe, the kinds of questions that would lead into interesting interdisciplinary and disciplinary study. The rusty nail is Aalbert Heine's point of entry into far-ranging interdisciplinary inquiry. Says Heine, former director of the Corpus Christi Museum, "Just one object in the museum, a square nail, rusty and bent, is all that is needed to open up the world, to introduce the flow of knowledge" (Martinello and Cook 1994, 76). One can, starting with the nail, investigate the history of houses built in the part of the city in which the nail was found, consider the "forces that bent the nail, the kinetic force of the hammer, and the forces of friction that hold it in the lumber." The nail can lead to discussions of electromagnetics, chemistry (oxidation), geology, anthropology, astronomy ("to discuss meteoric iron and to speculate about the core of the earth"), economics, and art. For Heine, write Martinello and Cook, "the nail can be seen as the center of the universe" (76).

And so can the shoe, an old mason jar, a fossil, or an old TV set found at the dump. These are things that have, as all things do, composition, history, utility, origins, significance. And each of these aspects of their existence can be exploited for interesting study. That old mason jar, for instance, is made from silicon (the same substance that makes computer chips possible) found in sand, which has a geological history and geographical significance. Someone, at some time, has used the jar to preserve food. To do this, a procedure was used by which air was removed from the jar to create a vacuum. Cut off from air, the food was preserved. Someone invented this process, one invention in a long line of inventions related to food storage, a most significant factor in the development and history of human civilizations. Again, how many questions can one spin by focusing on this jar? And how many problem-rich inquiry activities could be generated?

InterMusing

Take the question we just asked and come up with your answer: How many questions can one spin off the mason jar? How many problem-rich activities? Or, if you do not want to play with the jar, how about something within your field of vision at this moment? A light bulb? A radio or television? A hairbrush? Just how complex is the simple? Take a look at the ballpoint pen in your hand!

Good Themes are Everywhere

Good themes surround us. They are there for the plucking. We, as teachers, and as students, simply need to be observant and ready. Before we offer a list of categories of stuff to pluck from, we can't resist throwing in this tasty excerpt from Robert Pirsig's *Zen and the Art of Motorcycle Maintenance* (1974), not only because one of the examples below concerns buildings as beginnings, but also because it so nicely illustrates other points we have been trying to make. He is relating his alter ego Phadrus' attempt to deal with students in his English class who claim that they are unable find things to write about. "One of them," he writes,

> a girl with strong-lensed glasses wanted to write a five-hundred-word essay about the United States. He was used to the sinking feeling that comes from statements like this, and suggested without disparagement that she narrow it down to just Bozeman.
>
> When the paper came due she didn't have it and was quite upset. She had tried and tried but she just couldn't think of anything to say.
>
> He had already discussed her with her previous instructors and they'd confirmed his impressions of her. She was serious, disciplined and hardworking, but extremely dull. Not a spark of creativity in her anywhere. Her eyes, behind the thick-lensed glasses, were the eyes of a drudge. She wasn't bluffing him, she really couldn't think of anything to say, and was upset by her inability to do as she was told.
>
> It just stumped him. Now *he* couldn't think of anything to say. A silence occurred, and then a peculiar answer: "Narrow it down to the *main street* of Bozeman." It was a stroke of insight.

She nodded dutifully and went out. But just before her next class she came back in *real* distress, tears this time, distress that had obviously been there for a long time. She still couldn't think of anything to say, and couldn't understand why, if she couldn't think of anything about *all* of Bozeman, she should be able to think of something about one street.

He was furious. "You're not looking!" he said. A memory came back of his own dismissal from the University for having *too much* to say. For every fact there is an infinity of hypotheses. The more you *look* the more you *see*. She really wasn't looking and yet somehow didn't understand this.

He told her angrily, "Narrow it down to the *front of one* building on the main street of Bozeman. The Opera House. Start with the upper left-hand brick."

Her eyes, behind the thick-lensed glasses, opened wide.

She came in the next class with a puzzled look and handed him a five-thousand-word essay on the front of the Opera House on the main street of Bozeman, Montana. "I sat in the hamburger stand across the street," she said, "and started writing about the first brick and the second brick, and then by the third brick it all started to come and I couldn't stop. They thought I was crazy, and they kept kidding me, but here it all is. I don't understand it."

Neither did he, but on long walks through the streets of town he thought about it and concluded she was evidently stopped with the same kind of block that had paralyzed him on his first day of teaching. She was blocked because she was trying to repeat, in her writing, things she had already heard, just as on the first day he had tried to repeat things he had already decided to say. She couldn't think of anything to say about Bozeman because she couldn't recall anything she had heard worth repeating. She was strangely unaware that she could look and see freshly for herself, as she wrote, without primary regard for what had been said before. The narrowing down to one brick destroyed the blockage because it was so obvious she *had* to do some original and direct seeing. (70–71)

Here are some of the places where the "bricks" of thematic units can be found.

- Buildings
- Machines
- Food
- Events
- Places

- People
- Ideas/Concepts
- Endeavors
- Phenomena
- Issues

FIG. 3-1   *Where to Go for Good Themes*

InterMusing

As we go through the categories we ask you to create lists of your own, of things within your reach, things local, that might be worthy of becoming themes for study by your students. You may even find some of the things on your list worthwhile to study yourself. Who knows! An exploration into one of these little things could lead to something big, like an article somewhere for those who never thought to look closely at the thing themselves!

Things

We have already mentioned mason jars, rusty nails, and shoes, each of which can trigger months of interdisciplinary study. *Buildings*, as we've seen, also have potential. And they do not have to be at all elegant or prominently recognized in city tour books. We once had a conversation with a person from our local humanities committee who told us that our state was devoid of culture. No place, we argued, is cultureless. A corrugated sheet metal Quonset hut by the side of a railroad track is a cultural artifact, and, to say what is not so obvious, an engineering wonder—if you want to do a little wondering. Corrugated sheet metal is the result of cultural forces that led to the creation of sophisticated processes that utilize sophisticated machines. Someone built the structure, for some reason, and something, many things over the years perhaps, have gone on inside it. Do we know what goes on inside the building today? And by the way, who invented the Quonset hut (note that *Quonset* is capitalized), when was it invented, for what reason, and what is a Quonset? Why the corrugated design? What function do those ripples serve? What kind of culture does the building represent and what does its aesthetic quality say about our culture? Our city? The area in which it is found?

A student of ours, Christine Bates, not too long ago took off on a wonderful exploration into a now-shuttered hotel building that sits on a prime piece of the riverfront at the heart of Reno's casino district. Beginning with current controversies over the building's future, she traced her way back to the original owners and the development of their grand design, and forward to the hotel's closing day. From her findings she wrote a play with characters the likes of Marilyn Monroe and Arthur Miller, who stayed in the hotel, and Sammy Davis, who played the "Skyroom" for years but couldn't stay at the hotel because it was outside Reno's "Negro" lodging area. She had to see *The Misfits*. She viewed blueprints and spoke with structural engineers. She consulted with lawyers, with the building's newest owners and with friends and family of the original owners. She spoke with those who were campaigning to tear down the Mapes and with those who wanted it saved. There are buildings everywhere worthy of study, be they the Pentagon or an abandoned shack on the corner of Fifth and Main.

Machines are another rich category of things from which to pull themes. Ann Alejandro of Southwest Texas Junior College designed a "Culturally Integrated 'I-Search' Module" using the automobile as a *vehicle* for exploring human behavior and American culture (1989, 41). Neil Wangsgard, Jack Barett, and Bernice Servillican, members of an interdisciplinary team at Billinghurst Middle School in Reno, also used the car as a focal point for a unit. Students were placed in groups, each of which adopted a particular era in American history and an automobile or group of automobiles from Harrah's Automobile Museum. By unit's end, students had created dioramas depicting their era for display in the museum.

An article in the local paper described an earth-moving machine's visit to a local elementary school. According to the article, students were absolutely fascinated by the huge yellow tractor. It isn't difficult to conceive of earthmover-inspired units that could include lessons touching on ecology, geology, physics, engineering, ethics, and more for students at any grade level. A visit to a manufacturing plant of almost any kind can produce the same kind of fascination and the same kind of opportunities for teaching numerous disciplinary concepts. And there are smaller machines, in businesses, in entertainment centers, and in schools. How does a video machine work and how are videotapes made—the technical and the theatrical aspects? Certainly there are computers to study and there are machines to invent for the colonists on Mars, for dealing with the water problems in the Truckee Meadows or in Iowa City, and for feeding and watering the gerbils automatically over summer break.

Civil engineering projects and infrastructure have great potential for generating themes. The theme of "dams" opens the floodgates for wonderful things to study and learn by, as can the systems that deliver useful commodities such as water, gas, and electricity to our homes. How does water get to the faucet, and what happens to it after it goes down the drain? Who maintains these systems, and what are the consequences of the way in which we treat the waste? What are the consequences of taking water from rivers and the ground? Consider where study of the power grid can take us. Some of us end up in coal mines considering the animals (and perhaps the humans) that died to produce this fossil fuel. Some of us have to look at the rivers and streams whose energy has been harnessed to turn the turbines. Others have to deal with the realities of nuclear power production.

Streets and highways offer a source of fascinating study. Consider what can be learned once one begins to ask questions of the roads that run through every city and town. Where do they go? What are the places they touch in terms of the people who live there, the geography, the climate, industries, events, history? What are the road surfaces made of and why? Are the same materials used along the entire route, or are different types of materials used in different places? Why? How were the highways built, who built them, and when? Who paid for them and how? Has the road changed over the years? How so? Why? Have changes in the road caused changes for the towns and cities along the route? And, of course, there are metaphorical roads and metaphorical dams, and all are tied into political systems and processes, human debate and deliberation, and universal principles that govern the physical world and its creatures.

Food is another tasty area for interdisciplinary exploration. Units on nutritional needs lead into studies of geography, history, human tragedy, invention, ecology, chemistry (the chemical make-up of foods as well as the chemical additives in foods, pesticides, weed killers, etc.), machines, irrigation systems (back to the rivers and streams), techniques of food preservation, food processing, and the marketing of food, the latter leading one into the supermarket and the worlds of merchandising and advertising. Dissect a Twinkie and consider all it represents, from production through its nutritional and sociological implications. All of this regards food for humans. Study food chains and the consequences of tampering with them. Different animals have different nutritional requirements and different digestive systems to accommodate their diets. Their diets have much to do with habitat, with the lives they live, and with the creatures who share their niches. Food can encompass the study of restaurants, food carts, and politics. Study the social service agencies that deal exclusively with food, food stamps and WIC. Study the stories and histories of gatherers, growers, hunters, and producers. *The Grapes of Wrath* has much to do with food production in the United States, and so does the classic television documentary *Harvest of Shame*.

On a summer's day in 1993 the people of Ely, Nevada, and surrounding towns gathered to witness the demolition of the Kendicott smokestack. The fall of the structure had symbolic meaning for those towns. It was another sign of a declining economy, the end, perhaps, of the era in which copper mining was the primary source of jobs in the area. On that day one great demolition feat would reduce the product of a great engineering feat to rubble. The tower, used for some aspect of the copper production process, would fall into itself rather than over. The explosives experts had some tricks at hand that would pretty much ensure that the stones and concrete would fall into a heap and spare the homes that would be crushed if the tower were to fall, in a piece or pieces, in their direction. So what was the purpose of the tower? What was the process that turned raw ore into pure copper? What is copper, and what is it for? What was, is, and will be the role of copper in the lives of the people of the area? Not too far from the site of the tower that was, abutting the tiny company town of Ruth, is one of the largest human-made pits in the world. From this pit was extracted the ore, some of which was treated by the process in which the stack was involved. There is talk of opening the pit again. Some are delighted by the prospect, perhaps most of the residents of the area. And there are some, including an environmental science professor from the University of Nevada, who warn that further digging is likely to affect the aquifer from which Ely residents draw their water supply. A political battle involving local, state, and federal officials as well as the mining company that wants to reopen the pit can tell much about how these entities intermingle, how environmental law is made and enforced, the rights of mining companies under the present mining law, the fight to change that law, the original rationale for that law, and the consequences of it remaining in place or being changed, for Ely, for the nation. By considering the who, what, when, where, why, and how of the Ely stack, every discipline is given access to a rich vein of study. Is the fall of the stack symbolic of the end or the beginning? And what might either mean for Ely and its environs?

Events like the grand demolition do not happen every day, but grand events, or events with less grandeur, do take place on a daily basis, and there is no reason to avoid taking on events of the past. There are holidays, fairs, elections and inaugurations, deaths and births, stock market crashes and resurrections, sports events.

(We have two interdisciplinary units in hand, one by a group of students at our university, the other by Susan Yeager [1988], that use the Olympic Games [now every two years] as an entry point of interdisciplinary study. Consider the disciplinary material that can be showcased under this theme! The students' unit includes a culminating project involving the development of an Olympics for the school and community.) There are concerts, space flights and plane crashes, celebrations and protests, battles won and battles lost, murders and trials, crimes and pursuits, the opening of films, the release of a new video, a television documentary, a scientific breakthrough, a scientific problem, a new business comes to town, an old business leaves, a road is opened, a flood hits town, an earthquake rumbles through Los Angeles, a hurricane ravages Florida.

Almost any event can be tapped for study. In the last two years or so Steven Spielberg has offered teachers from elementary school through college a feast of movie events rich for nourishing the interdisciplinary appetite. *Jurassic Park* put dinosaurs on everyone's mind, as well as chaos theory, gene splicing, and the negative as well as the positive potential of technology, especially computers. *Schindler's List* almost became a historical event unto itself, focusing most of the nation on the Holocaust. Spielberg made *Schindler's List* available to schools, and many took advantage of its great teaching potential. The showing of the film, or the showing of numerous other films, can be used as an event to spark interdisciplinary exploration. Books too can be made into events that lead into interdisciplinary explorations.

People, famous, infamous, and not so famous, make good starting points for interdisciplinary study. In one Nevada town a man who had been principal at the high school for thirty years was about to retire. At 70 years old and a 60-year resident of the town, a "this is your life" project could have put a truly human face on the world this man experienced and knew of, a study that could have consumed the content and processes of all of the disciplines.

Oral history projects such as Foxfire and Marian Mohr's Snake Bank to Spring Hill projects focus on the lives of residents of the communities in which the projects take place. Students learn the art of interview, familiarize themselves with the diversity of their communities and the riches diversity has to offer, come to know many adult citizens and appreciate the relationships of individual to community and community to individual. Within the context of an oral history project all disciplines can be touched upon by finding individuals whose vocations and avocations cause them to have knowledge of disciplinary concepts.

The famous and the infamous of local or more global notoriety can easily launch fascinating interdisciplinary study. In the Reno area we have several local "celebrities," some alive, some gone. There are the founders of the city's older casinos, their names made famous by the bright lights that still spell out their names on the businesses they founded, Harrah's and Harold's. There are those who made their fortunes by striking gold in the Virginia City mines, the inventors who developed the procedures for shoring the mine shafts and for extracting gold ore from the dirt, not to mention a Virginia City newspaper man by the name of Mark Twain. There are the people behind the names of our schools. One of the new schools in the area is named Sarah Winnemucca Elementary. Sarah Winnemucca was a nationally known leader of the Paiute people and persistent advocate of good education for Paiute children. And then, of course, there is Jessy Reno.

There are explorers to explore, artists, artisans, perpetrators and victims, survivors, scoundrels and saints, empire builders and managers, engineers and architects. Who designed the Hoover Dam? Who built it? There are business leaders and business regulators, chiefs of industry and those who work in industry. What does it mean to be the CEO of Harrah's or Harold's? What does it mean to be a manager or worker in those buildings?

Ideas, concepts, issues, and endeavors, big and small, can be used as themes. We have already alluded elsewhere to some of them. Knowledge itself can serve as a theme for interdisciplinary study. Tchudi and Lafer once taught a course titled "Knowing the Unknown" (1993) that explored how it is that we come to know what we say we know, and what it is that we *have* when we do know. "Science," or "history," can, in and of themselves, serve as themes to be explored. The question of what science is leads one to inquire about the history, processes, and imperfections of science; the nature of scientific reasoning; the people of science; treatment and use of science; the consequences and implications of science; the relationship of science to other areas of endeavor such as art and literature (science fiction, for example); and the future of science. Among the themes Tchudi and Mitchell list in *Explorations in the Teaching of English* (1989) are "loneliness and alienation," "maturity and mortality," violence in America," "new journalism," "our town," "innocence and experience," "surviving," "gods and goddesses," "ambiguities," "police stories," and "literature from prisons." These themes have great expansive potential.

Amusement parks qualify as *places*, as does the piece of ground encircled by the hula hoop thrown onto the desert. The Quonset hut, the city park, the boarded hotel, the river, the opera house that provided the brick for Persig's student's contemplation—all are potentially viable thematic material. All places have a history and a form that has much to do with natural forces and some with human endeavor. There are whole cities, individual neighborhoods, and neighborhood ponds. A school itself can be made the subject of study; it sits on a piece of land that was home to something other than a school at one time; someone decided to build it, name it, open it on a particular day on which there must have been some kind of celebration. The school and the community were the focus of a kindergarten through sixth grade interdisciplinary project used at Brown Elementary School in Reno. There are distant planets and colonies, utopias and distopias, places of geologic and geographical significance, homes, business buildings, hotels, parks, museums, caves, forests, lakes, tide pools, and even empty lots that might be of interest.

Last in our list is a category we will simply call *phenomena*. Some we have mentioned already, such as earthquakes and hurricanes. Weather in our area has much to do with how people here live their lives. There isn't much agriculture in our part of the world because the climate is so dry. The dryness is due to something called a "rain shadow." We have also been experiencing another phenomenon known as drought for about the last seven years. In past years we have heard of cases of the plague caused by fleas that travel on fur of rodents, and recently we have been warned about the deer mice that are carrying germs that cause something called a Hantavirus. There are varieties of the flu that visit us from year to year, historical plagues, famines, extinctions, meteors crashing into Jupiter, comets, climatic changes, the Big Bang.

Choosing from Among

We seem to have said that just about anything can become a theme. They're there for the plucking. But we do think some care needs to be taken in that plucking. Certainly different themes will appeal more to children of particular ages. Up to a point, that is. Most any theme can be made relevant and exciting for most children. The "evidence" theme suggested by Perkins (Jacobs 1989) at first glance is a theme for older students, students of middle or high school age. However, the concept of evidence embedded in a dinosaur theme could be made interesting and understandable for much younger children. Patricia Roberts (1993) in her book-length description of a dinosaur unit offers numerous dinosaur books for children in all grades and suggests activities that encourage students to "chart what is based on observations and what is based on conjecture" (42). These activities come close to being lessons about evidence.

We have already positioned ourselves as favoring themes that emerge from the readily observable and allowing the more abstract to arise from the study of the tangible. Themes most certainly can emanate from books, or films, or other second- or thirdhand sources. But we favor those that allow students firsthand access. Thus, we are advocates of teaching that begins with local themes, the study of the nearby. The Truckee River Project, which we mentioned before, takes its name from the river that runs through our town. The river is within walking distance of our classroom and we can, and have, during the course, travelled from one end of it to the other. We can dip our feet in the subject of our study. Our focus on *our* river does not stop us from discussing the Owens River and Mono Lake and the diversion of their waters to Los Angeles or the floods on the Mississippi and Ohio. Our local focus helped us to make better sense of the works of John Wesley Powell and the "hydraulic" society Mark Reisner discusses in his book *Cadillac Desert* (1986).

Learning the Territory: Advancework

Knowing what is *nearby* for students is a critical aspect of making themes work. When we speak of the local, understand that we are not restricting experience to that which is strictly of the locale. A unit on kites, such as the one described in Vars (1987, see above) is made local by the fact that students are familiar with kites, have flown kites, and can build and fly kites during the unit. So too with a unit based on the Lego-Logo project described in Chapter 2. At one point, as an extension of the original Lego-Logo project, Lafer worked with a fourth grade teacher to develop a unit that began with the building of Lego-Logo machines and moved to the study of simple machines and the physical principles upon which they operate. The unit then had students examine the nature of work, work as it relates to different geographical locations, the relationship of culture to work, and work to the topography of various regions of the world. During the unit students looked into family histories to see what countries they or their ancestors may have come from and to inquire into the work and the tools of labor their predecessors may have employed. They read maps, wrote letters, did interviews. The Lego-Logo experience led into and served as a reference point for a unit on the theme of work and culture.

The benefits of a theme having local roots can also be accrued if themes are attached to that which is timely. As this book was being written, both Richard Nixon and Jacqueline Onassis died. They were both figures of a past most of our students are too young to have experienced. But their deaths are in the present, and there are commemorations on the television, in newspapers, in magazines, and retrospectives through all media channels. Richard Nixon and Jacqueline Onassis have, in effect, *localized* portions of the past and caused questions to be raised anew about the consequences of the past on the present. Probes into the public and private lives of currently active politicians and celebrities are being discussed as they relate to press treatment of Richard Nixon and John Kennedy. Hillary Clinton's behavior as first lady is compared to that of Mrs. Onassis, as is the treatment of each by the press and the public. Today's news stories can be used to localize the past. The recent election of Nelson Mandela can easily be used to take students into the history of the Civil Rights movement in the United States, into the study of racism as it existed then so that it can better be understood as it exists now. The naming of Sarah Winnemucca Elementary School offered a good excuse to explore the history of indigenous peoples of our area and, for that matter, the history of indigenous peoples in the United States, Africa, India, and anywhere else that colonization has taken place.

ADVANCEWORK   Effective *localizing* depends upon one knowing those for whom they are localizing. To this end, we finish this chapter with a discussion of what we will call *advancework*, a term we have borrowed from Friedberg and Driscol (1992). Advancework calls upon teachers to engage in scouting missions to find out what is close by physically, in terms of relevance, in terms of timeliness. During this mission, one explores and records impressions of the terrain and comes to an understanding of the significant landmarks in the culture of the student. The shoe, for example, is for many students a significant cultural landmark. It is an item with attachments to status and group membership, heroes and dreams, the economics of childhood and adolescence. Discussion of shoes can tell us much about who students are, how they think, how they see themselves, and what influences their thinking.

For the sake of convenience, we divide the region to be explored during advancework into two territories, one the world of the mind—the inner terri-

- Consider the concepts you (and your colleagues, if you are a part of a team) wish to teach and/or are mandated to teach.

- Find local manifestations of the concepts, principles, ideas, content, etc., that you intend to teach.

- Consider the kinds of experiences students can have with these local manifestations that will allow them to become involved with or curious about the concepts the disciplines you are to teach. *Cause* the experiences to cause students to ask questions that the disciplinary teaching will answer.

- Engage students in these experiences, facilitate the question-asking, and provide the means or guidance necessary for them to find the answers they *need*.

FIG. 3–2 *Considerations in Making Thematic Decisions*

tory, the other the physical world—the outer territories. The inner region includes such aspects of students' lives as their emotions, feelings, thoughts, fears, and dreams, the psychological manifestations of their relationships, aspirations, and preferences, and their sense of self in relation to family, community, school, and the larger world. The outer category includes people, places, and things outside themselves.

Of the Inner Kind Advancework related to the inner world is centered on getting to know who students are. This may be accomplished through observation of students operating in *their world* with friends, in the hall, at the mall, at ballgames and dances, before or after class in the classroom, and through discussion with students about their feelings and attitudes toward that world and the other realms they visit and of which they are aware. Student writing is another avenue. An assignment to play Dear Abby to Juliet can reveal much about the student's sense of relationships and life on the emotional plane. Surveys and questionnaires are also helpful and information obtained need not pertain only to those being surveyed. Much can be learned about the way in which they respond to the world in the questions students design for peers and adults. Interview activities can be designed to capture perceptions and feelings, and again, as much can be learned by looking at the interviewer as by examining the responses of the interviewee. What one wants to know about others can tell much about who he or she is. Many teachers we know use beginning-of-the-year interview activities, not only to open a window on students' inner sanctum, but as a way of allowing students to get to know one another so that the foundation for a classroom community can be laid. We like the idea of having students work through the interview process to develop character sketches of their classmates. Students, working individually or in small groups, are asked to find questions that they feel can elicit useful information about their classmates. The questions are then discussed by the class in terms of their potential for getting at what needs to be known. Each student then takes from the pool of good questions those he or she wishes to ask of another and carries out an interview. The interview data is then used to create a character sketch for presentation to the class. This is not only a good way of getting to know each other, but a gentle way of introducing meaningful aspects of the exploration process, the development of good questions, interview, assessment of data, and presentation.

Surveys and questionnaires can also be used and students need not be at the receiving end of these instruments. The questions they find important to ask of others, as we've said before, tells us much about who they are, what they consider important, how they perceive themselves and others and the world in which they live. Questionnaires designed for use with students' friends, family, teachers, and other significant others can tell us much about who they know and who influences them. At Silver Lake Elementary School, a teacher, Lucy Boersma, and one of the authors developed an interdisciplinary unit on work and machines. The unit was concerned with the kinds of work people do in different parts of the world. One of the initial activities was to ask students to collect information about their family origins, to find where their ancestors had lived and the kind of work they did. To do this, students developed interviews for their parents and questionnaires to send to relatives who lived at a distance. In doing this, students learned as much about their families as we learned about them. We know too that parents and children learned more about one another through the interaction the exercise demanded. This information about the families of the students came to us as a residual of our attempt to have students look at the relationship of the geological, geographical, and meteorological features of a region to the kind of work people did in various places and the relationship of customs and traditions to place and work.

Beyond actual classroom encounters with the students who populate our classrooms, much can be learned about the lives of students of various ages through books written for and about them and by viewing the television programs produced for their edification. The advertisements aimed in their direction are also telling, as are the many newspaper and magazine articles written about children and kid culture. Scout, Atticus Finch's daughter in *To Kill A Mockingbird,* tells us much about how children see and respond to the world. *Catcher in the Rye* provides insight into the mind of the adolescent, as does the writing of such authors as Paul Zindel, Judy Blume, and S.E. Hinton; films like the *Karate Kid, Rebel Without a Cause, Romeo and Juliet* (and *West Side Story*), *Grease,* and *Wayne's World;* TV shows like *Roseanne, Beavis and Butthead, Ren and Stimpy*; and the writings of Piaget, Erikson, and Bruner.

The knowledge derived from advancework of the innerbeing can generate a host of themes such as "family," "friendship," and "acceptance and rejection." Or it can be used to help students recognize the human dimensions of more concrete themes. For example, our discussion of the shoe as a theme touched upon the effects of mechanization on communities. We have reason to believe, from our own encounters with the media, journals, and school teachers, that many students are concerned with the stability of their parents' employment, or are (or have been) affected in significant ways by changes in their parents' work lives. A look at mechanization and its consequences for Lynn, Massachusetts, in the years 1780–1860 can have great contemporary relevance if the link is made. It may provide answers to questions students have about their own feelings, and their own feelings may cause them to feel empathy for the people who lost jobs in Lynn or are losing jobs today in Reno or Newark. Ultimately, the link may provide an answer to the question of why we study history or read literature!

Of the Outer Kind   Advancework of the outer kind causes one to explore the physical, social, and economic trappings of the world in which students live. Once again, for news of the broader kind, there are newspapers, magazines, films, and televisions reports. But what we are asking you to do is to actually get out into the immediate neighborhood to see the things that make up your students' surroundings, the things with which they are familiar and the things nearby with which they are not familiar. Scoping out the local is a good excuse for a working vacation, an opportunity to scout out, drop in, ask a question or two about some of the places you pass by and never visit. Walk or drive the streets, read community newspapers and flyers. Read the signs in the store windows. In Quincy, California, almost every store displays a red ribbon symbol. Without too much prying, one finds that the ribbon indicates solidarity with those fighting to save the area's timber industry. This tells you much about what is important in that community.

Find the local utilities and discover what they have to offer. Our power company is also our water company and there are people in its employ who hold great amounts of information about the region. Scout the neighborhood for ponds and streams, well-worn trees and interesting homes. Notice the businesses and know what they do. Familiarize yourself with their services, and, if you are curious, ask for a tour. Use your credentials as a teacher to explain the nature of your mission and see if you can get permission to see the back rooms. Take a look at the people and chat. And don't forget to thumb through the yellow pages. Much can be learned from almost any section. If you find a long list of Lagomarsinos in the white pages, it might be worth your while to find out who they might be. In Flagstaff, Arizona, there are an awful lot of Babbitts, and many businesses bearing that name. Who are these people?

The yellow pages are a fascinating resource with an incredible amount of information for those willing to take the time. Scan the subject index and land on any category of business that catches your eye. *Disabled services* strikes us as one that might have value for classroom studies and projects. *Forgings* makes me curious, as does *bee keepers' supplies. Puppets, parachutes,* and *railroad companies* all hold promise. There is a listing for *historical places* for *architects, automation consultants,* and *labor organizations.* How about *patent searchers* or *sculptors*? When we "let our fingers do the walking" we noticed three businesses of particular interest to us. One was Savage and Sons Plumbing and Heating. The top of its advertisement reads "Serving the Reno Area Since 1893." We figured that Savage and Sons would know a lot about important aspects of Reno's infrastructure. We called to find out if anyone would be willing to talk to us about history and received a positive response. The same thing happened with Commercial Hardware, a 91-year-old family-owned business. A call to the store led to an open invitation to meet with family members who knew the history of the business as well as much of the history of the Reno area. Another business of interest in our area is a restaurant called Louis' Basque Corner, not only because of the Basque cuisine it serves, but because it is one of the many Basque eateries with boardinghouses above them. A read of Robert Laxalt's *Children of the Holy Ghost* (1992) tells us that these hostelries served the immigrant Basque shepherds who came to Nevada many years ago.

InterMusing

This is your invitation to hit the streets. For the sake of better teaching, go to a place or event that you have been curious about, could become curious about, want to know more about. Just go! Consider what you might want to know about the place or the event and be ready to ask questions. Remember, you are on a mission for the sake of better education. Take advantage of your credentials and go where others are not allowed to go, ask the questions no one else has the opportunity to ask. Suggestions: Walk along the highway, under a bridge, along a stream bank or the railroad tracks. Walk into a bar (a friend of ours has taken a job as a waitress in a bowling alley to learn more about the town in which she now teaches), onto a farm, a ranch, an ag-supply store, into a grain elevator, onto a giant road-building machine, into a quarry or mine, an equipment rental yard, a cement factory, a mushroom farm, a hospital. Scan the phone book or look in a business directory. Take notes and consider how you might use what you have found in your classroom.

References

ACKERMAN, D. 1989. "Intellectual and Practical Criteria for Successful Curriculum Integration." In *Interdisciplinary Curriculum: Design and Implementation*, ed. H.H. Jacobs. Alexandria, VA: Association for Supervision and Curriculum Development.

ALEJANDRO, A. 1989. "Cars: A Culturally Integrated 'I-Search' Module." *English Journal* 78(5): 41–44.

ANONYMOUS. 1992. "The Science in the Sports." *Newsweek*, July 27, 1992.

BEANE, J.A. 1990. *A Middle School Curriculum: From Rhetoric to Reality.* Columbus, OH. National Middle School Association.

BUMSTEAD, R.A. 1983. "The Bank that Failed." *Principal.* 62(1): 40–42.

CHESKIN, M.P. 1987. *The Complete Handbook of Athletic Footwear.* New York: Fairchild.

FALER, P.G. 1981. *Mechanics and Manufacturers in the Early Industrial Revolution: Lynn,*

Massachusetts, 1780–1860. Albany, NY: State University of New York Press.

FRIEDBERG, H.J., AND A. DRISCOL. 1992. *Universal Teaching Strategies.* Boston: Allyn and Bacon.

JACOBS, H.H., ed. 1989. *Interdisciplinary Curriculum: Design and Implementation.* Alexandria, VA: Association for Supervision and Curriculum Development.

JORDAN, T. 1993. *Riding the White Horse Home.* New York: Pantheon.

LAFER, S., AND A. MARKERT. 1994. "Authentic Learning Situations and the Potential of Lego TC Logo." *Computers in the Schools* 11: 79–94.

L.A. GEAR INCORPORATED. 1993. *L.A. Gear Annual Report.* Santa Monica, CA: L.A. Gear Incorporated.

LAXALT, R. 1992. *Child of the Holy Ghost.* Reno, NV: University of Nevada Press.

LEUTZINGER, R. 1993. "Jogging Into History." *Old Oregon* 72: 21–23.

MARTINELLO, M.L., AND G.E. COOK. 1994. *Interdisciplinary Inquiry in Teaching and Learning.* Boston: Houghton Mifflin.

MUNSON, E.L. 1917. *The Soldier's Foot and the Military Shoe: A Handbook for Officers and Noncommissioned Officers on the Line.* Menasha, WI: George Banta Publishing Company.

NORTHRUP, J. 1989. "Can Students Become Better Consumers by Writing About Fast Food Chains?" *English Journal* 78: 41–44.

PAPPAS, C.C., B.Z. KIEFER, AND L.S. LEVSTIK. 1990. *An Integrated Language Perspective in the Elementary School.* New York: Longman.

PARKHILL, S. 1993. "Roller Coaster: A Marriage of Psychology and Technology." *TIES* 6(2): 8–14.

PERKINS, D.N. 1989. "Selecting Fertile Themes for Integrated Learning." In *Interdisciplinary Curriculum: Design and Implementation*, ed. H.H. Jacobs. Alexandria, VA: Association for Supervision and Curriculum Development.

PIRSIG, R.N. 1974. *Zen and the Art of Motorcycle Maintenance: An Inquiry into Values.* New York: Morrow.

REISNER, M. 1986. *Cadillac Desert: The American West and Its Disappearing Water.* New York: Penguin.

ROBERTS, P.L. 1993. *A Green Dinosaur Day: A Guide for Developing Thematic Units in Literature Based Instruction, K–6.* Needham Heights, MA: Allyn and Bacon.

STARZINGER, P.H. 1993. "Sneaking Around: Just Because the Shoe Fits, Should You Wear It?" *American Health* 12(2): 56–60.

TCHUDI, S. AND S. LAFER. 1993. "Knowing What We Know: Exploring the Unknown Across the Curriculum." *Language Arts Journal of Michigan* 9(2): 3–8.

TCHUDI, S., AND D. MITCHELL. 1989. *Explorations in the Teaching of English.* New York: Harper and Row.

THELEN, H.A. 1981. *The Classroom Society: The Construction of Educational Experience.* New York: Wiley.

THOMSON, R. 1989. *The Path to Mechanized Shoe Production in the United States.* Chapel Hill, NC: University of North Carolina Press.

VARS, G.F. 1987. *Interdisciplinary Teaching in the Middle Grades.* Columbus, OH: National Middle School Association.

WEPNER, S.B. 1992. "Technology and Thematic Units: A Primary Example." *The Reading Teacher*, 46(3): 260–263.

WILLIAMS, R., C. BIDLACK, AND D. WINNETT. 1993. "At Water's Edge: Students Study Their Rivers." *Educational Leadership* 51(1): 80–83.

WINNETT, S.J. 1993. "Technology for Fun." *The Technology Teacher* 3: 13–15.

YEAGER, S. 1988. "Tuning in to the Olympics." *Journal of Physical Education, Recreation and Dance* 59: 59–62.

4

Who Leads and What Follows?
Planning for Interdisciplinary Study

Space, the final frontier. These are the voyages of the starship *Enterprise*. Its five-year mission: to explore strange new worlds, to seek out new life and new civilizations, to boldly go where no [one] has gone before.

The *Star Trek* epigraph, known by just about every TV-watching American, serves as an interesting metaphor for interdisciplinary inquiry. At best, schooling should center on exploring strange and unfamiliar worlds. Although few of our students will actually fly in outer space, in a good educational program they will constantly encounter "new life and new civilizations" (including, of course, ancient civilizations that are unfamiliar to the student). Each authentic discovery creates a bit of new knowledge for the student. Thus it's appropriate for us to imagine that each of our students is on a quest where "no one has gone before." They will remake and reinterpret the world to make it *their* world, *their* universe.

On the other hand, as regular *Star Trek* viewers, we occasionally find ourselves impatient with the somewhat random approach apparently taken by the starship commander. Week after week the show opens with the *Enterprise* crew in some sort of jam: They are down on the planet Gork poking around and some ethereal creature gets stirred up and threatens them. Or they are cruising around on the edge of Klingon airspace and the bad guys take offense and come out to get them. It sometimes seems as if the whole show is based on accidental encounters as the Trekkers zip here and there in space. Are these folks true inquirers, or are they simply lost in space, making discoveries only because they keep stumbling onto script-worthy problems?

There is a danger that interdisciplinary studies may go on an intellectual adventure cruise without much of a plan in mind. Such a random or accidental inquiry-centered education might still be superior to what happens presently in the discipline-centered, fragmented curriculum. For example, one could do worse than to take the unit topics we offer in Part II of this book, adjust the readings and other materials to the students' grade level, and teach the topics in the order they appear in the book. Or in the reverse order. Or choosing every other topic.

One could do worse than to have an "interdisciplinary topic of the month" gleaned from the front page of the newspaper: this month "the weather" (since there is a hurricane making news in the south); next month, international relations in Europe or whatever is the center of international attention at the moment.

As happens in *Star Trek,* where an overarching unity is supplied via the philosophy of Starfleet Command and the rock-solid values of the captain, one can easily imagine considerable unity emerging from apparently random episodes. Just as the crew of the *Enterprise* shows a consistent set of values and skills in solving whatever problem shows up on the view screen, the skills your students bring to interdisciplinary study, guided by a few common principles of inquiry-centered learning, could lead to considerable coherence. In this apparently random curriculum, sooner or later students would think about human values and scientific endeavor, about the nature of history and numbers, about the value of music, literature, and art. And maybe they would bump into an intellectual Klingon or two who would stir up and challenge their values. They would certainly go where no person has gone before.

But is the random curriculum enough? Predictably, we think there are more possibilities.

Frank Betts (1993a) points out that from the start, people seek to find unity in their galaxy:

> Learning begins as an integrated experience as a newborn child experiences the world in its totality. The struggle to survive is the struggle to organize experiences into an understandable, coherent whole. . . . *Thus,* all early learning is inherently integrated—it is authentic. (13.7)

Marion Brady (1993) would add that "reality is seamless." He believes that "the primary objective of general education is to help students clarify their models of reality" (1–2). That is: The universe "out there" is not *pre*organized for human ends. To an extent, we are all lost in space, cruisin' around the galaxy, pickin' an occasional fight, tryin' to figure out what's lurking around the next corner or behind that hunk of green cheese. What makes us human (and what links us to the outer space travelers featured in any science fiction piece) is our ability to interpret the unfamiliar, to find patterns in it, to structure it in ways that make sense and will allow us to proceed with our quest.[1]

---

1. The view that the universe is not organized along absolute lines is not, of course, shared by Platonists and members of some religious groups. But since the birth of contemporary empirical science in the Einstein/Heisenberg era, most thinkers agree that the Laws of the Universe are human creations to explain the unknown, rather than absolute truths lying around the galaxy waiting for human beings to find them. Too, modern science has shown us the value of taking multiple perspectives on unfamiliar phenomena: What you are looking for tends to be what you see; therefore if you want to get more comprehensive explanations (or "truths"), you'd better structure your research to reflect diverse vantage points and methodologies.

InterMusing

As an experiment in finding patterns, try this activity, first taught to us by Katarina Cerney at the Henry Ford Museum in Dearborn, Michigan. To help museum curators learn that there are diverse ways of categorizing and presenting an exhibit, she has become a bag lady: She collects every conceivable kind of bag—shopping bags (especially with printed ads), sandwich bags, bags from fast food restaurants, an odd "bag" or two like a purse or piece of luggage. She brings in her bag collection, dumps it on the table, and has people discuss various ways of preparing a museum exhibit on bags. In doing this activity with our students, we split the class into groups of five, divvy up the bags, and have each group prepare its own exhibit. Some groups will cluster bags by function: to hold sandwiches, clothing, groceries. Others will categorize by materials: plastic, paper, string, and cloth. Still others may focus on the printed exteriors of bags and how they send messages about the bagger and the baggee. (What does an L.L. Bean book bag say about its carrier?) Still others will take a narrative approach and write a story that somehow includes each of the group's bags. The point of the activity is to help students see that "reality" is in the eye and mind of the beholder.

Some preliminary organization to the search for knowledge helps. *Star Trek* is not *Sea Hunt*. That is, Kirk and his crew are cruising around the galaxy, not beneath the oceans, like Lloyd Bridges or Jean Jacques Cousteau. Any quest implies that someone has thought enough about a problem to decide that a journey or exploration will be fruitful. If someone didn't think outer space offered some interesting knowledge, nobody would build rocket ships or telescopes; if someone didn't think that the seas have something to teach us, nobody would build bathyscaphes or research submarines.

The bottom line is that we believe interdisciplinary teaching should be much more than a random series of exciting experiences. Behind Starfleet is Starfleet Command and its Prime Directive; behind bathyscaphes of Cousteau or the Woods Hole Marine Biological Center are science organizations and leaders who say: "Go do this. It matters." Behind every good interdisciplinary curriculum will be teachers who, without knowing absolutely where the quest will lead and what will be accomplished, are willing to save kids the trouble of cruising the intellectual universe at random—teachers who say, "Let's get started this way."

Unfortunately, there are many conflicting forces operating on the helmsperson of the classroom starship. There is a pull between process and product—should kids master facts or learn skills and processes? Should they memorize factoids or learn to solve problems? There is debate over the knowledge that matters—should students learn mostly about their own western traditions, or does multiculturalism matter? Should students learn for learning's sake or be trained in employable skills? Should we teach *to* the curriculum standards or *from* them? Are we more concerned with breadth than depth? What are the ties between general education and specific training? Between local planning versus state or national mandates?

Between deductive and inductive reasoning? Of course, there are always the great debates over disciplines: Which are central and which peripheral? Is one discipline more important than others? If we have writing across the curriculum, shouldn't we have math and history and art and everything across the curriculum, too? The result of these pulls—"Hard to the right, Mr. Sulu; no, make that left full rudder"—is enough to drive the curriculum engineer crazy. "Scotty to bridge! Scotty to bridge! She canna take nae mare! I'm givin' her all we ga', and the curriculum drive is about to blaw."

Kenneth Bradford and Helen Stiff (1993) write of this sort of confusion:

> Anyone who has spent much time in schools has either undergone or observed the ritual of curriculum revision. Mandates or guidelines come down from the state or district or principal, and the machinery clanks into place. A committee is formed, and a schedule is drawn up. Arguments ensue. Factions arise. Horse trading occurs. Objectives are sequenced. Content is divided among the grades. The document appears in teachers' mailboxes. The document disappears into desk drawers, and the textbook reappears on the desktop. Routine reigns. (35)

"In the fragmented curriculum," Frank Betts observes, "you tend to get exactly what you see, the tangible bits and pieces, testable knowledge and skills" (1993b, 2.9). This curricular space junk just may be remains of the classroom starship after it was overtaxed by conflicting demands and did, in fact, "blaw."

What is needed is well summarized by Gordon Vars (1993), who says that the skillful teacher "leads [students] to expand their awareness beyond their immediate concerns toward an increasingly widening view of the world and the universe" (5).

In this chapter, then, we'll be addressing ways of extending the universe of the classroom. As we have stated consistently throughout the book, we'll be writing for people who teach in a variety of settings. Some of you will be on small vessels—in the learning pod of your own classroom—essentially charting your own course. Others will be a part of well-groomed teams like the crew of the *Enterprise,* part of a large-scale, integrated effort. Because curriculum planning for the classroom is a microcosm of good planning for the grade level or the school or the school district, the steps and stages for interdisciplinary planning are similar. What we present, then, is intended to guide the classroom teacher and/or the planning team in charting their way through the universe of education.

Getting Our Bearings: Help from Starfleet Command

Whether one teaches alone or as part of a broader, synthesized curriculum team, there is always guidance available from the outside; the teacher's Starfleet Command is what Ken Styles and Gray Cavanagh (1978) call, somewhat omi-

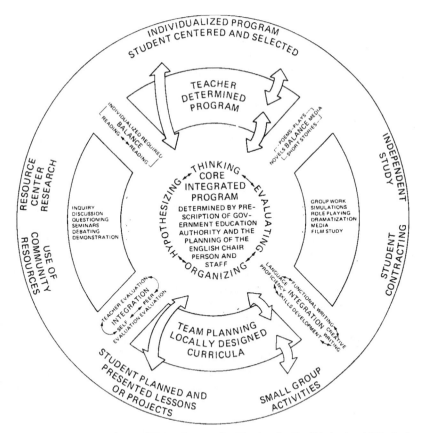

FIG. 4–1 *From Ken Styles and Gray Cavanagh. "Design for English in the 1980s," chart appearing in* The English Journal, *September 1978, p. 40. Copyright (c) 1978 by the National Council of Teachers of English. Reprinted by permission.*

nously, "The Governmental Education Authority." (See Figure 4–1.) Each teacher has some curriculum mandates of one sort or another, enforced more or less strictly. Sometimes this is the district-wide curriculum guide; sometimes it is a set of guidelines or benchmarks issued by a state or provincial education authority. Sometimes it is not a curriculum guide at all, but a set of examinations that students will have to take and that serve directly or indirectly as a measure of teacher competence.

InterMusings

Study the details of Figure 4–1. Styles and Cavanagh have done a remarkable job of portraying the complex relationships among curriculum, student learning style, and teaching strategy. Every time one starts an interdisciplinary project, it's useful to glance at that chart as a reminder of possibilities.

As Styles and Cavanagh show, there is an enormous amount of room, even in a mandated curriculum, for teacher and student choices. E.D. Hirsch (1993), one of the strongest advocates for a core curriculum, says that at best (or, we would say, "worst") content dictated from outside the classroom will never be more than 50 percent of the program (23). There will always be room for local curriculum or team planning sessions (for much more than 50 percent, we suspect and hope). There will certainly be room for enriched knowledge or skills that a teacher is free to explore, and there should be ample room for student input as well.

As we write this first edition of *The Interdisciplinary Teacher's Handbook*, there is a strong movement to create national standards for the school disciplines. Under the auspices of Goals 2000, a program launched by former President George Bush and sustained by President Bill Clinton, funding has been provided for each major disciplinary area to establish a broad national consensus on subject matter, and standards for students' learning outcomes: what should students be able to know and be able to do from their K–12 study of a given subject?

We are somewhat divided in our views of this national standards movement. Stephen Lafer is more positive, seeing the creation of standards as providing helpful guidelines for classroom reform. Stephen Tchudi is concerned about the implications of the standards movement for imposing a national curriculum and national testing programs. However, we agree that the discussions centering on national standards have led to significant innovative thinking in some of the disciplines and recognize that these innovations have strong implications for interdisciplinary teaching as well. We present, then, the cases of science, history, and mathematics.

InterMusing

Since these national standards are unfolding even as we write, we suggest that you take time to update yourself on any of those that apply to you. School districts, state departments of education, and national teacher organizations, as well as the United States Department of Education, can supply you with documents showing what's expected and required in your focal field. Analyze and evaluate these carefully. Are they sound? Do they mirror your own philosophy or contradict it? Can you see yourself comfortably teaching interdisciplinarily from the core of the mandated curriculum?

The Example of Science

Even before the federal push for national standards, the National Association for the Advancement of Science issued a blockbuster book titled *Science for All Americans* (1988, also discussed in Algren and Rutherford, 1993). Subtitled *Project 2061*, it acknowledged that much of school science instruction was failing—that the curriculum was fragmented, that principles of science were being taught in isolation, and that, above all, kids were not learning to apply scientific concepts in the real world.

People were particularly critical of what Bonnie Brunkhorst (1991) calls the "layer cake" approach, where, at the high school level, a year of biology has been stacked on top of the basic course in general science, with physics stacked on top of that and then with chemistry as the final layer. Brunkhorst and other educators influenced by the 2061 model are calling for "every science, every year." That is, they believe the sciences should be integrated throughout the school program and that science concepts and processes should be explored wherever they come up.

For example, suppose a group of fifth graders decide to establish a saltwater aquarium. In reading through the instructions supplied by the pet store, they would learn about the nitrite/nitrate cycle (chemistry); getting a good bacteria growth underway (biology); measuring the salinity of water through specific gravity (chemistry with supporting math); the amount of water to change each month (chemistry again, with more math); and the sorts of marine animals, vertebrate and invertebrate, that can live together comfortably in the tank (biology). Why should these youngsters have to wait until high school to learn the appropriate parts of these disciplines?

The genius of *Project 2061*, we think, was in moving beyond the fish tank level to discuss basic themes of science that can be treated at every level of schooling. These include "energy," "evolution," "patterns of change," "scale and structure," "systems," and "interactions." From these broad topics emerge thematic or unit topics such as "population growth," "personal health," "hazard control," "environmental health," "global change," and "risk assessment."

What intrigues us about these themes is that they could also be used as a structure for interdisciplinary learning. Taking the implications of *Project 2061* a step further, we would suggest the topics listed above can easily be treated from an historical point of view, from that of social studies, or literature and writing, or art, music, shop, and mechanics.

What we're suggesting, then, is that scientists and teachers involved in *Project 2061* may have provided a more expansive star chart than even they recognize. The themes they have hit upon may seem to have their origins in science, but they are actually categorizing topics that pull together a wide and interrelated set of human experiences. The themes of *Project 2061* are a view of reality and the human mind, not just of scientific states of affair.

As one thinks about the "government core" of the curriculum, then, one could do far worse than to take the unifying themes of science, integrate them in one's planning process, and develop teaching materials across the disciplines through them.

But there's more. Take . . .

The Example of History

People working on new standards for history/social studies have also discovered core themes for study. In its discussion of new standards for history, the National Council for History Education (1993) has found six "vital themes and narratives" that cut across human experience, "whether the subject be world history, the history of Western civilization, or the history of the United States." These include:

- *Civilization, cultural diffusion, and innovation,* which covers "the evolution of human skills and the means of exerting power over nature and people." (The graphic symbol for this theme is, interestingly enough, a quill pen and an ink bottle, suggesting immediately that this is a theme that can easily mesh with traditional English/language arts concerns for reading and writing.)

- *Human interaction with the environment,* presenting "the relationships among geography, technology, and culture, and their effects on economic, social, and political developments." Is this not science as well? And technology? Does history end with names and dates? Clearly not.

- *Values, beliefs, political ideas, and institutions,* focusing on "religions and ideologies" as well as "political and social institutions" including a consideration of "industrial and commercial development."

- *Conflict and cooperation,* illustrating "the many and various causes of war" and the "consequences of war and peace for societies and their cultures." This theme and the previous one, of course, have natural links across the curriculum, including both the humanities and sciences as well as technology and the applied arts.

- *Comparative history of major developments,* touching on the themes of revolution, reaction, and reform "across time and place," including imperialism, slavery, feudalism, "elites and aristocracies; and the role of the family; wealth, and merit."

- *Patterns of social and political interaction,* with emphasis on "the changing patterns of class, ethnic, racial, and gender structures and relations." These latter two themes serve to bridge a longstanding gap between teachers of history and teachers of social studies; thus the themes are an effort to integrate within the discipline itself.

Should those of us with roots in English/language arts be left out? Of course not—the themes cry out for the use of fiction, poetry, drama, and nonfiction. Nor would we want to ignore science and technology, which obviously have had major roles in revolution and reform, conflict and cooperation, and even the patterns of politics (witness the effect of the television set on the nature of U.S. politics).

The process of curriculum development advocated by the Bradley Commission on History next calls for division of the curriculum into subthemes as students approach issues in world, western, and U.S. history. The traditional high school course in U.S. history through chronology is replaced by one that focuses on subthemes: society, politics, economics/technology, ideas and images, and international relations.

Analyze the themes proposed by the history and science curriculum groups. What points of connection do you see among them? Is it conceivable that one could find enough common denominators to create a set of history/science megathemes? Could one factor in English/language arts? The fine arts? Vocational or community-oriented subjects? What would such themes tell us about the comprehensiveness of interdisciplinary teaching?

Also: Make a similar list of overarching themes or topics for your base discipline. If you are/were an art major, for example, what would be the core themes you would want to stress? Can you see connections between those and the history/science themes?

The Example of History: Part II

There is even more good work to be found in the architects of the new history curriculum. Intersecting with the overarching themes are "History's Habits of Mind," what the writers call "the perspectives and modes of thoughtful judgment" that are the "principal aim" of history, geography, and government. Among these habits of mind are for students to:

- understand the significance of the past to their own lives . . .

- distinguish between the important and the inconsequential . . .

- understand how things happen and how things change . . .

- prepare to live with uncertainties . . . realizing that not all problems have solutions . . .

- read widely and critically in order to recognize the difference between fact and conjecture, between evidence and assertion, and thereby to frame useful questions. (NHCE, 5–6)

These and other habits of mind (thirteen are listed) presumably get at what an historian does when thinking through problems. However, the reader will quickly see these are by no means limited to the discipline of history. We'd like students in shop and home economics and theater to be able to "frame useful questions" and separate "fact and conjecture" and develop other similar habits of mind.

Other disciplines are concerned with finding and describing similar or parallel thinking processes, so that once again, innovative work in one curriculum area leads us to thinking beyond individual disciplines and to consider practices and skills of knowing that are largely common to any field of inquiry. Which brings us to . . .

The Example of Mathematics

Over three decades ago, mathematics was one of the first curriculum areas to call for a radical departure from its traditions. The so-called "new math" helped students to understand principles and procedures rather than to rely on rote memory. Instead of stressing the times tables, for example, the new math taught about number systems other than base ten and showed how the idea of multiplication would work in *any* system, base three, base twelve, etc. Deemphasizing "the right answer," the new math emphasized habits of mind. Unfortunately, this approach was way ahead of its time. Widely misunderstood by parents, kids, and even many teachers, it was satirized as meaning that right answers no longer mattered, as long as you knew how you were messing up.

Three decades later, many of the constructive impulses have reappeared in the widely praised *Professional Standards for Teaching Mathematics* (National Council of Teachers of Mathematics 1991). As Stephanie Smith, Marvin Smith, and Thomas Romberg explain (1993), the new standards assert "that *knowing* mathematics is *doing* mathematics and *what* students learn depends to a great degree on *how* they learn it" (4). Rather than sketching out the details of what kids should know about, say, fractions or trigonometric functions, the math standards describe topics as diverse as "worthwhile mathematical tasks," "the teacher's role in discourse," "mathematics as problem solving," "learning environments," and "assessing students' understanding of mathematics."

Here, then, is a governmental or mandated core that is anything but restrictive for the teacher. The math standards are a jumping-off point for the teacher or, to return to our chapter's starry metaphor, a north star that can be used to take one's bearings and to plot trips in many directions.

Among the new directions being pursued by many mathematicians is interdisciplinarity. Recognizing that math has long been an isolated subject, even split off from science, Glenn Kleiman (1991) writes that "efforts to integrate mathematics with language arts, social studies, history, art, or music are rare indeed." He laments that "many people see mathematics as isolated from other areas of life, and devoid of creativity and aesthetics" (48). This is a dehumanized view, he suggests, and he proposes that people realize that math is a tool for humanity. He writes,

> To be human is to seek to understand . . .
> To be human is to explore . . .
> To be human is to participate in society . . .
> To be human is to build . . .
> To be human is to look to the future . . .
> To be human is to play . . .
> To be human is to think, to create, and to communicate. (48)

Each of those human elements, he explains, has a mathematical component, to which we add that his list of human traits seems to us a marvelous outline for a curriculum in any field! Couldn't we construct an art program by focusing on understanding, exploration, social participation, building, futurism, playfulness, thinkingness, creativity, and communication? Or a science program? Or a program in any other (inter)discipline?

InterMusing

Earlier we suggested that you compare the themes of history and society to look for common elements. Now we invite you to compare Kleiman's list of the characteristics of humanity with history's "habits of mind." Connections? Implications?

Where are we going with all this? First, we want to restate the point that the new "standards" in various disciplines are providing increasingly interesting and broad-minded views of disciplinary learning. The new directions we have described here are surely *not* those of the "good old days" of times tables, the periodic table, and the memorization of historical dates.

Second, by stressing overlap, we want to point out that even as the traditional disciplines search for new points of coherence, they are tending to go in a common direction: describing common broad themes and basic intellectual processes.

Third, the overlap points the way toward interdisciplinarity. For the teacher who is ready to bridge disciplines, the rationales and blueprints are already available.

The sad part about the national standards movement (in addition to its assault on local autonomy) is that it is woodenly discipline-centered in its approach. While each of the disciplines is working hard to come up with common aims that will satisfy the government's interest in standards, there has been no encouragement of interdisciplinarity, which, as we have argued, is the strongest trend in education generally. Goals 2000 will create an isolation in the curriculum that might more aptly be titled Goals 1850.

"The curriculum," writes Michael Apple, "is more than the facts and skills that we plan to teach. Beneath what we overtly teach in mathematics, social studies, language arts, science, and the other subjects in the planned curriculum lies a hidden curriculum . . . of tacit social and institutional values that we inculcate over many hours, days, and years." (1993, 2.2) Apple is particularly concerned about the social values that are impressed through the hidden curriculum of enculturation, especially children of lower socioeconomic status. But we feel it's important to point out that schooling has also had a hidden curriculum of pseudo–intellectuality based on conventional disciplines. A true curriculum for the twenty-first century will have to take the goals of the disciplines and push them to the next level.

Constructivism and Planning Models for Interdisciplinary Teaching

We have dwelt on the previous matters at some length for a reason: The "habits of mind" that we'd like to see cultivated in schools, along with the values that underlie the curriculum, and even the view of the universe that leads one to choose some themes or topics over others, are inextricably linked to the model for teaching one chooses.

If, for example, one is operating from a knowledge/skills model that assumes students learn the bits and pieces of a discipline and then apply them, one might rely heavily on one of the oldest models in education: teach/test/reteach (directly *teach* students basic ideas or facts; *test* to see if the students have mastered these; *reteach* the ones that haven't been learned). Old-style spelling and arithmetic are perhaps the clearest examples of that model at work.

By sharp contrast, in this book we are operating from the *constructivist* approach to learning. We see that students learn most successfully when they are engaged in *constructing* meanings for themselves or solutions to problems. Constructivism is *holistic* in its approach, meaning that it declines to break learning down into component elements, but recognizes that the elements are learned when they serve the function of solving a problem or creating a complete meaning. Above all, constructivism is linked inextricably to *authenticity* in learning—suggesting that for people to learn successfully, they must generally be engaged in tasks that they find useful, intrinsically interesting, or otherwise realistic. Much of what we know about constructivism is gained by watching people at work: scientists, historians, kids on the street, our own children, ourselves as learners.

Our constructivist model of how human beings approach learning also provides the basic model for interdisciplinary planning in the classroom. We admit to some oversimplification, but we see constructivist learners operating this way:

- *Learners sense dissonance between what they know or can do and what they want to know or do.* The doorbell is broken and they don't know how to fix it. They find themselves lacking an opinion when asked which political candidate they'll vote for. They think that skiing downhill looks like fun, but they're afraid they could never learn to do it. In other words, most learning is motivated by a kind of disequilibrium or dissatisfaction: The status quo simply won't do any more. (One of the worries teachers have about couch potato kids is that all too seldom does television create this sense of debit; couch taters could benignly watch sitcoms and talk shows until doomsday.)

- *Learners survey what they know.* One seldom starts on a learning quest out of total ignorance. Rather, people have background (what some call "prior knowledge") that gives them a head start on any learning project. A person may not know how to wire a doorbell, but she did repair that string of Christmas lights! He can't ski, but he used to be pretty good on ice skates. People may not know the views of the political candidates, but they know that if they read the paper, they'll learn pretty quickly.

- *Learners survey what they don't know.* Often this takes the form of questions: How am I going to fix this doorbell? Who knows about wiring and can help me? Does it matter whether I get to know the political candidates? Am I too old to learn to ski?

- *Learners set goals.* By george, on Saturday I'm going to get that doorbell working! By jean, I will get myself better informed about the election. By crackey, I'm going to learn to ski.

- *Learners gather information.* Out in the real world, people tend to gather information from any reasonable source: through conversations with friends, off the television set, by reading magazines, by asking questions of specialists. Schools tend to make learning more formal, using texts, library sources, and, of course, research. So in the doorbell quest, our learner might call up a neighbor who is good at fixing things for advice. Our people interested in politics might tune in more frequently to political programs on TV. Our skiing wannabe might buy a book or a video on downhill skiing.

- *Learners construct solutions; they hypothesize.* The constructivist learner is a maker of things: a tinkerer with doorbells and ski poles, a person willing to create ideological structures for himself or herself. The "habits of mind" we discussed earlier come into play here, for the best learner is one who is tentative, experimental, open minded, and a critical thinker. Most constructions are, in fact, "hypotheses," formal or informal: "Maybe if I put these two wires here, the dang thing will ring." "Perhaps if I decide to campaign for Candidate X, we can improve things in our town!" "Perhaps if I don't wax my skis quite so slick I can control myself better on the downhills."

- *Learners test and affirm or reject.* Much learning is trial and error. People hope that by thinking critically and through their education they will get better and better at making hypotheses that turn out to be correct for them.
    "Ding-dong."
    "You're welcome, Senator, I was happy to help."
    "Whooooooooooshski!"
    But the constructivist learning cycle is also recursive, meaning that we learn from mistakes and rejected hypotheses, going back to the beginning, to what we know and don't know, always starting from a higher level, even after a hypothesis fails.
    Finally,

- *Learners share and seek confirmation of what they know.* Most human beings have an irresistible and humanistic impulse to go public with their knowledge. This is more than mere show-offery. As scholars have long known, ideas gain validity when they are accepted by a community. Our novice electrician asks our neighbor over to inspect our doorbell (and to offer praise). Our political interest group becomes politically active now that its candidate is in office. Our skier basks in the glow of the admiring crowd at the ski lounge after dramatically skidding to a halt in a shower of snow.

We hasten to add that this is an approximation of the human learning process. We invite modifications and amplifications to reflect various approaches to learning and knowing. A feminist critique, for example, might say that we have offered a typical male paradigm, presenting the impression that all of life can be reduced to a neat set of procedures to be followed. A poet might object that our view of human learning allows too little room for the poetic/intuitive approach to things, which is to muse and mull over observations, to have insights and creative moments, for the poet is less interested in *solutions* to problems than in expressing the dimensions of them. A developmentalist might observe that the learning cycle practiced by a baby in the cradle is far different from that of a mature physicist contemplating a mathematical problem.

So we encourage people—you, the reader—to develop a view of the learning process that reflects such modifications. Our quest—your quest, we believe—is to develop the broadest, most comprehensive view of learning possible.

InterMusing

The outline above is our hypothesis about the learning process based on our reading, research, and observations of learners, which we continually test in our own teaching. We invite you to affirm, reject, or qualify our hypothesis. That is, look at our list and see if it fits with your view of learning. Some explorations:

- Review something you have recently learned, anything from a practical skill to a lesson of life to an abstract concept. Did your intellectual inquiry roughly follow the stages we outlined?

- Qualify our assertions by finding examples that don't fit; then figure out an explanation.

- Compare our stages of inquiry in a discipline you know: the historical method, the philosophical method, the scientific method. How close are the paradigms? How do they differ from discipline to discipline and from discipline to real life?

The S^2 Interdisciplinary Planning Model

Our approach to planning the interdisciplinary teaching unit, based on the constructivist learning model, is outlined in Figure 4–2. "S-Squared" model represents two traditionally opposed elements of learning: *structure* (to organize study and get it going in nonchaotic ways), and *spontaneity* (giving free reign to children's interests and imaginations within that initial structure). Squaring these, we believe, leads to a "multiplier effect" in this model. That is, when "multiplied" by each other, the planning elements increase student learning geometrically (just as 5 x 5 leads to a much greater total than 5 + 5).[2]

---

2. Figure 4–2 is really just a cover sheet, the first page, the tip of the iceberg in planning an interdisciplinary unit. Each of the squares in the S^2 model is supplemented with multiple pages in your teacher notebook: a page or several spelling-out goals, many pages of resources, even more pages of classroom activities.

TOPIC:			
	Math/Science	Humanities/Arts	Community/Vocational
Central Concepts 1. Mandated 2. Teacher 3. Student selected			
Resources 1. Class text 2. Library 3. Media 4. Networks 5. Research 6. Community: people/places			
Classroom Activities Whole class Small group Individual projects			
Assessment/ Performance Displays Performances Community action			

FIG. 4–2 *The S² Planning Model: Structure x Spontaneity*

SELECTING TOPICS   We've already had a good deal to say about selecting topics in Chapter 3. To review, it may well be that the national standards groups or other governmental agencies will provide topics ready-made. More often, we think, teachers will prefer to come up with their own topics and, as the school year progresses, more and more often the students themselves may propose topics for investigation. Just in case you need a few more ideas, we offer yet another list of solid interdisciplinary themes in Figure 4–3.

DESCRIBING GOALS, OBJECTIVES, AIMS   We use the phrase "central concepts" as catch-all phrase to describe what the teacher sees the unit as setting out to cover—its goals and aims. These are the basic ideas central to your unit (and, once again, the bit of white space provided on Figure 4-2 is too small to accommodate a detailed list—use extra pages as necessary).

The central concepts can be described as:

- major principles from the (inter)discipline that will be learned: *the scientific method, the nature of electrical circuits, the literary themes of good and evil, the historical causes of World War II*

- skills or processes, what the kids will do: wire a doorbell, write an essay, prepare an historical time line

- knowledges or understandings, what the students will cognitively understand at the close of the unit

- questions to be answered, what the students and teacher want to learn from the unit. We're especially partial to beginning units with *questions* rather than with goals or concept statements. A question has its own built-in assessment tool—"Did we answer it?"—and opens up the unit to a wide range of concepts, rather than a few identified at the beginning of the unit.

InterMusing

Describing concepts, goals, and questions to be answered is no easy task. For a unit or topic of your choosing, write down some essential concepts or goals or questions. Experiment with ways of writing these aims: What form permits you to most clearly express the central ideas you expect your unit to cover?

LEARNING ACROSS THE DISCIPLINES   We've divided the concepts on the S^2 chart into three basic areas representing math/science, the humanities, and practical or community subjects. Usually, you'll start planning with your own base discipline and move outward. That is, if you're a science teacher by trade, you might start your unit on electronic gizmos with some basic concepts about electricity and electronics, the history of the silicon chip, the techniques of miniaturization, and an overview of electronic devices that are available to the consumer. Then you would move out to discuss connections with humanities/arts and community (examining the impact of electronic devices on the home, talking to local experts, looking for applications of electronics observable around town). You can, of course, divide, subdivide and recombine the concept areas to fit your situation. If you're a science person working with a mathematician, for example, you might choose

The death of Communism	Prison reform
Young voters	The weather
Television programming	Divorce
College frats and sororities	Plastic surgery
Water supplies	Drunk driving
Marathons	English as a second language
The 1950s	Compact disc technology and beyond
Mass transit	Lawyers
Babysitting	Urban myths
Names	Any sport
Future automobiles	Future trains
Middle age	Charity
Endangered species	Painting
Sewers	Labor Day
Credit	Child-proofing
Scandals	Desktop publishing
False alarms	Electronic gizmos
Nerves	Awards
Business security	Pyramids
Savings	The glass ceiling
Gambling	Housework
Noise	Silence
Latchkey children	Drug legalization
Nobel prize winners	Soap operas
Self starters	Rumors
Race relations	Future planes
Toxic spills	Smoking
Taxes	Weight loss
Forest fires	School fashion
Wetlands	Earrings
Homelessness	Privacy
Peace	Puzzles

FIG. 4–3 *Still More Interdisciplinary Themes and Topics*

to limit your focus to those areas. If you're part of a well-integrated middle school teaching team, you might want to ignore the disciplinary divisions altogether and simply write down core concepts or goals regardless of disciplinary origin.

THE "REQUIRED" CURRICULUM   Most teachers will deal with some "governmental" mandates for their home discipline, and it is appropriate to list up front the material that "must" be covered. Too, we think it is important for teachers to include some of their own "must cover" concepts up front. Although we strongly favor including kids in the planning process, teachers shouldn't sell short their own expertise.

ENGAGING STUDENTS IN THE PLANNING PROCESS   In the 1960s, the early days of the present educational reform efforts, there was a good deal of talk about the "open classroom." Influenced by educators like Jonathan Kozol (1967) and Herbert Kohl (1967), many teachers realized that kids needed to be able to make choices in the curriculum, to enter their own opinions on the topic of "what we want to know." Some of the early efforts at engaging students in planning were pretty crude, leading to stereotypes of the open classroom as a place where everybody stood around wondering what to do next. It became clear that without the background to make choices, kids would have little to say, analogous to what would happen to most of us if we took our car to the mechanic only to have him/her say, "So what do you want me to do? It's your car!"

InterMusing

Despite the obvious drawbacks of simply opening the classroom to free choice, the totally open question, "What would *you* like to learn?" provides some fascinating answers and may be worth asking your students. *Don't* ask the stereotypical question, "What do you want to do today, kids?" *Do* try asking students how they would structure and restructure schools or a particular field of study if they were in charge. What would they do about class periods, bells, and buzzers? How would they teach science? Math? Language arts? When we've asked these questions, we've often been pleased with imaginative replies.

There is a growing body of evidence that students can be successfully involved in the learning process without the teacher losing control over the classroom or having it disintegrate into irrelevancies or a curriculum of MTV. We're excited by the interdisciplinary work at Sandy Union High School in Oregon (n.d.), where faculty teaming of science and vocational education programs led kids to create a multi-use trail system in an ecological preserve, to redesign a pond and watershed system, to improve the stream habitat, and to establish a migratory fish run. In Asheville, North Carolina, students decided to take action about pollution in the Pigeon River and made and implemented recommendations for changes that were regarded as highly controversial in their community (Williams and Reynolds 1993). In a California high school kids decided to tackle serious problems such as the greenhouse effect, pollution, gun control, homelessness, and the death penalty (Burke 1993), and sixth graders in Illinois had the vision to identify global issues such as world hunger as worthy of study and attention (Doane 1993).

How to go about it?

At a conference, we heard about a Denver teacher who took some of his high school math students to McDonald's for lunch, asked them to identify some major themes for study, and wound up buying them lunch and dinner as they talked about global issues such as aging, war and peace, the world economic structure, the greenhouse effect, and the safety of the world for themselves and future generations. Now, not every teacher can take the kids out for lunch, but the principle here is clear: *Ask* the students and *listen carefully* to their replies.

Some strategies for engaging students in the planning process:

- *Have lunch with students,* younger or older. Once a week dine in your classroom rather than the teachers' dining room and invite kids to stop by to tell you what they have been thinking, what they want to know.

- *Use the newspaper* as a source of ideas. Regularly take time to flip through a few of the lead stories and ask students what they think. In particular, ask them to tell you how they see the news relating to what you're studying, whether it is math, history, language, or an interdiscipline.

- *Discuss the government-mandated goals* for your class, the material you must teach; then open up the classroom and ask students to offer ideas on how best to go about learning the stuff.

- *Invite students to propose real-world applications* that can grow from your core teaching concepts. How could we apply levers to tasks around the school or home? How can we apply what we know about World War I to understanding the latest war, wherever it is?

- *Use brainstorming* to elicit student ideas. You write your topic in the center of the chalkboard or a sheet of chart paper (or, as we like to do it, on wall-sized sheets of butcher paper) and invite students to free associate for questions, to link questions, to follow a line of questioning as far as it can be pursued. Stephen Tchudi once demonstrated this technique for teachers on a topic picked more or less at random—locks. He found the brainstorming so interesting that he wound up writing a book for young adults on the topic: *Lock & Key: The Secrets of Locking Things Up, In, and Out* (1993). In brainstorming, no idea, angle, or possibility is ruled out as implausible or ridiculous.

InterMusing

Practice the brainstorming technique for yourself on the topic of interdisciplinary teaching. Stretch your questioning as widely as you can. Use this as an agenda for your own exploration of teaching ideas beyond the covers of this book.

- *Discuss what makes a good question.* Wiggins (see Betts 1993a) has argued that good questions are those that have no obvious or easy "right" answer, push toward abstract thinking, and at the same time, reflect students' personal interests.

- *Discuss the value of questions that cannot be answered easily.* Check your local or school library for books on unexplained mysteries (or have students discuss television programs of that ilk). Help students understand the limits of question-asking and have them mull questions that remain to be definitively unanswered—like the origins of the universe—and why it's important to keep asking them.

- *Explain your favorite questions,* giving students a sense of what you wonder about and why.

- *Set up a question box* at the back of the class, a place where students can deposit questions they would like to have answered. You can decide whether it is more fruitful to limit questions to (inter)disciplinary matters or to allow any question that the kids want to raise, including social matters.

- *Use contract or extra-credit learning activities.* Teach the core knowledge that you think is essential in your unit, but always provide opportunities for students to propose related work and ideas for recognition or credit. Prime the pump by giving students a few ideas about acceptable projects, then suggest that they design their own along similar lines.

- *Stock the classroom with books related to your topic and encourage browsing.* Whether or not you use a textbook, this supply of related material will trigger ideas from students.

- *Gradually increase the amount of student planning over time.* It would be naive, we believe, to call for heavy duty student planning in September; it's downright possible to suppose that by the end of the semester or the school year students can be taking the lead in proposing activities related to your field(s).

KNOWING HOW WE KNOW: THE ROLE OF METACOGNITION   For a planning system to involve students successfully, it is important to go beyond merely talking about student questions to discuss the concept of *metacognition*, or consciousness of the learning process. As students participate in planning, they become more aware of "learning about learning." But what does it mean to "know how one knows"? Learning is such a complex act that it sometimes seems naive to suppose that students could truly come to understand their own learning (just as most adults have just a glimmer of what goes on in their own brain).

To us, taking a "metacognitive approach" does not mean turning students into psychologists or brain surgeons, but it does mean helping students become aware of two things:

1. How does what we call "knowledge" come into being?

2. What are my own learning strategies and how can I best use them in school and life?

David Perkins (1991) has lamented that in the present curriculum, students seldom show significant insight into such subjects as math, physics, English, or history. That is, they may master the nuts and bolts knowledge of the field, but they don't wind up having any real idea about how the field works. Perkins looks particularly to students' writing for these insights and, too often, finds no evidence.

In our field, English, one clue is in the confidence students have in approaching a previously unseen literary work. We find that a surprising number of college English majors confess that when faced with a new piece of work (for scholarly reading, not necessarily reading for pleasure), they do not feel that they can successfully unlock the secrets. We place the blame for this phenomenon on the fact that too few English literature courses take a metacognitive approach; professors may lecture from or lead discussions drawing from particular critical approaches but fail to let students in on the approach, keeping its secrets to themselves.

Perkins recommends that to increase students' insights into (inter)disciplines teachers must first construct the curriculum out of "generative" topics (precisely the sort of approach we've been discussing here); second, teach for deep understanding of the field or discipline (essentially what we've labeled "metacognition"); and third, emphasize assessment in context (a topic we take up in Chapters 6 and 7).

To those ends, we recommend the following classroom activities for learning about how we learn:

- *Autobiography of a Value.* Have each student identify a value or belief that he or she holds as being very important, then write about how and why it became important. *Discuss:* Where do our values come from? To what extent are they based on knowledge? On teachings by others? On assessment of our own experience? How do our values shape how we look at the world?

- *Interdisciplinary Nontrivial Pursuit.* Have students write down questions about what they regard as important knowledge in the sciences, the humanities, the arts, the applied fields (e.g., "What is a classic?" "When was the Civil War?" "How do you calculate the hypotenuse of a right triangle?"). The student's idea of the correct answer is written on the reverse of the page, along with the student's estimate of the difficulty level of the question (1 = easy, 10 = extraordinarily difficult). As a cooperative game, the class tries to answer the questions, awarding the difficulty level in points to themselves for a right answer, to "demon ignorance" when they miss. *Discuss:* What knowledge do we value? Why?

- *The Pleasure of Proving Things Wrong.* The teacher writes down widely held but often unquestioned truths. Give groups of students five to ten minutes to prove these wrong: the world is round; the sun rises in the east and sets in the west; ghosts do not exist; water is wet; the sun will rise tomorrow; school makes people wiser. *Discuss:* How often do we operate on truisms that we don't bother to question?

**Professor Ferrington and his controversial theory
that dinosaurs were actually the discarded
"chicken" bones of giant, alien picnickers.**

FIG. 4–4 *FAR SIDE copyright 1993, 1994 FARWORKS, INC. Distributed by Universal Press
Syndicate. Reprinted with permission. All rights reserved.*

- *Proving the Improbable.* The flip side of the previous activity. Give small groups of students ideas that once held currency but have now been discredited and ask them to prove the obsolete idea is *true*: the world is flat; the earth is the center of the universe; you can walk on water or fire; telling the truth always pays off. *Discuss:* How often do we simply accept as a matter of belief that some ideas are "dumb" when we actually don't have a great deal of proof that is so?

- *Crackpot Theories.* Gary Larson's *The Far Side* (Figure 4–4) suggests the classroom idea of having students create a "crackpot" idea or theory: of life, of an ancient puzzle, of a sheer coincidence. *Discuss:* Why is it so easy to find sensible-sounding explanations for foolish ideas? Does this help to explain why some crackpot ideas die so slowly?

- *Brainmaps.* Borrowing and modifying an idea from Charles Hampton Turner's *Maps of the Mind* (1982), have students draw maps or sketches of how they visualize their minds. Are you a "gears and wheels" type thinker? A cluttered closet thinker? Is your mind a mathematical diagram? A musical score? A television tube? A video game? *Discuss*: How do you know how you think? How did you learn your particular way of thinking? How can you best use your own thinking style in school?

- *Mapping the Unknown.* Blindfold students and place them in an open room strewn with objects, from stuffed teddy bears to chairs and tables. Starting from a common point, the students then explore the room, taking notes on distances, directions, and objects encountered. Afterwards, they draw and compare maps of this "world." *Discuss*: How do different experiences create different versions or visions of the world? How many mapmakers does it take to get a truly accurate map? (This activity was freely adapted from *Project Ocean,* an interdisciplinary resource unit developed by the Farallones Society, San Francisco, 1987).

- *How to Lie with Statistics.* Find a statistics-laden article in the newspaper and bring it to class, say, data on unemployment, the gross national product, or the leading economic indicators. Then ask students to present those statistics in slanted ways to favor different causes or value systems (e.g., a union boss, a Democrat, a Republican, a banker, a person on welfare). *Discuss*: Are statistics "true" or not? How do we know when people are using statistics in a neutral or a slanted manner?

- *Writing Science Fiction.* The essential formula for sci fi is a "what if" that imagines something either contrary to popular knowledge and belief or an extension of a current phenomenon. Have students write short sci fi scenarios: "What if water ran uphill?" "What if the sun didn't rise?" "What if cable TV proliferates to 999 channels?" "What if schools run out of money?" *Discuss*: How do these "alternate universes" make sense? What do they tell us about our own views of "reality"?

- *Alternative Truths.* Help students see that knowledge is not cut-and-dried, that people are often in conflict about the truth. Our local paper recently carried an article carefully explaining why there cannot be a Loch Ness Monster, that the food supplies in that lake are simply too scant to support a critter of Nessie's size. The same week, a checkout counter scandal newsheet declared, "Loch Ness Monster Captured: There Are Many More Down There, Says Expert." Photographs of two Nessies about to attack a couple in a rowboat were shown. Find other areas where "experts" are in disagreement. *Discuss*: How do we resolve such differences?

S^2: Resources, Class Activities, Presentation, and Assessment

These aspects of the S^2 planning process will be discussed in subsequent chapters.

The sample units provided in Part II of this book were designed following the S^2 technique, so you might want to turn to that section now and review several of the units before proceeding. Of course, those units are merely outlines, and to be effective they have to be customized to fit particular classes, teachers, and students.

One way to test a planning model—S^2 or those that follow, is to use them to block out a single short lesson rather than a full unit. (Most will work either way, as a lesson format or a unit format.) For example, to test out S^2, choose a single concept such as the nature of health insurance or the nature of a black hole. Then work through the model and see where it carries you in terms of a lesson plan.

Other Planning Models for Interdisciplinary Study

THE BALANCED INSTRUCTIONAL DESIGN MODEL   Frank Betts (1993a) offers a planning model that has a great deal in common with our S^2 approach, and introduces some interesting and important elements. (See Figure 4–5.) This learning pattern begins with a "cue" event, "cue" as in a theatrical cue. Such an event, he writes, is "analogous to the musical score for an orchestra. It provides a common point of reference for all the players around which each can improvise while still retaining a connection to the work of the group" (13.23).

A cue for a unit would be linked to the central theme. It might be a book, a film, a video, a trip to a museum, or a guest speaker. The teacher follows it with "impressive acts," an input stage, where students read, listen, and observe, gathering data and information that extends their understanding. Eventually students move to "constructive" acts, where they start working out solutions to problems and applications of abstract ideas. Their applied learning is accompanied by "expressive acts," where students translate their understanding into writing, portfolios, or other kinds of explanation that serve to assess whether or not they have learned essential concepts beyond the ability to apply them constructively. "Reflective acts" chiefly involve self assessment, where students think about what they have learned and mastered in a unit. Betts also adds a phase of "celebration," which might be an exposition, fair, public performance, publication, or other way of going forth with student work so as to provide the public attention it richly deserves.

THE AUSTRALIAN PLANNING MODEL   Betts's approach also has much in common with an approach designed by Peter Forrestal (1986) of Australia, who describes five stages in planning:

- *Input*, where the teacher takes primary responsibility for locating core information, including textbook chapters, speakers, field trips, films, etc.

- *Exploration*, where the students, through whole class, small group, and individual activities, raise questions and find answers to problems, issues, and topics suggested by the "input" materials.

- *Reshaping*, a stage in which students work toward synthesis and application of

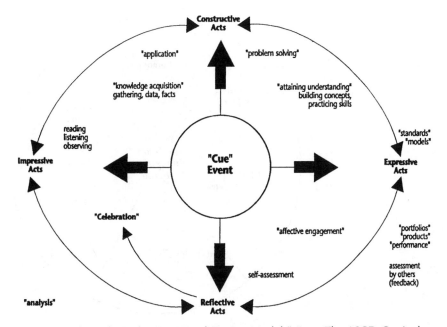

FIG. 4–5 *"The Balanced Instructional Design Model." From* The ASCD Curriculum Handbook. *Alexandria, VA: Association for Supervision and Curriculum Development, 1993, p. 139. Reprinted by permission.*

their learning, figuring out how to do something with the information they have gathered.

- *Presentation*, where new knowledge and ideas are presented to the class.

- *Reflection*, a time for students and teacher to evaluate the work that has been done.

Dividing the Pie

The two previous models could be used for discipline-centered or interdisciplinary concepts. The pie model forces one to think interdisciplinarily and can be used by the solo teacher, by several teachers working together, or by an entire school or department.

The procedure is relatively simple. (See Figure 4–6.) Write the central concept or theme to be explored at the center of a piece of paper. If it is directly linked to a particular discipline, write that in the center as well. Then, as slices of pie surrounding the main concept, show its interconnections with all concerned disciplines. What you'll get is a partitioning of content by particular disciplines. The pie can then be used for you to identify concepts or outcomes on a discipline-by-discipline basis. (At that point, one could use either S^2 or the Balanced Instructional Design to make the planning specific and concrete.)

FIG. 4–6   *The Pie Model*

We assume that this array of models gives the reader a pretty clear idea of what we have in mind. In the event you would like to see more ways of charting, planning, goal setting, and unit development, we refer you to Heidi Hayes Jacobs's book, *Interdisciplinary Curriculum* (1989) and Stephen Tchudi's *Travels Across the Curriculum: Models for Interdisciplinary Learning* (1991).

We hasten to remind the reader that the basic process of planning followed by *all* these models is essentially that of the constructivist view of learning. They can be summarized in simplest terms by an acronym for yet another planning model, this one used widely by people in the reading field: KWL.

What do I *know?*
What do I *want* to know?
What have I *learned?*

As Palmiasano and Barron (1993) have shown, a planning model is just the beginning of the teaching process. From the "organizing center" or curriculum "drivers" come all sorts of key decisions about what and how to teach. The basic plan will help one decide among instructional methods such as "guided discovery, problem-based learning, lecture, cooperative learning, didactic/direct instruction, Socratic method, individualized instruction, mastery learning, simulations, museum learnings" and others. It will help one take advantage of learning resources such as "electronic media," "computers, networking," and laboratories, and it will help one focus resources of time, money, materials and supplies, and "time/schedule" (7).

Finally, a *coda* on this whole discussion of planning: There's the story of the young high school assistant principal bucking for a higher job who printed lesson planning books and distributed them to the faculty. The books were to be filled one week in advance of teaching the lesson, both as an indication of instructional planning and as a sort of insurance that a substitute could continue instruction without missing a beat. There was much grumbling amongst the faculty. "How do I know what I am going to teach until I teach it?" The wily veteran teachers then hit on a strategy. They created a set of "dummy" lesson plans for the first week of school, then copied down what they were teaching the current week, day by day, in the appropriate blank for *next* week, creating the illusion of planning. The cynical veterans did have a point: In teaching, much *cannot* be planned. There are times when fortuitous discussions spring up, when just the right video becomes available. If our efforts in engaging students in planning succeed, there will be times when the kids take over the direction of planning altogether. Such occasions should be seen as celebrations, not as deviations from course.

At the same time, we'd hate to have our kids in a school where teachers didn't have much of an idea of what they would teaching week to week or month to month. A good plan, we think, will provide a framework or a blueprint with clearcut direction while allowing for and encouraging careful improvisational teaching when the time is right. That way, one's *structure* can lead to *spontaneity*. Come to think of it, that may be exactly what the *Star Trek* gang was up to all along!

References

ALGREN, A., AND F.J. RUTHERFORD. 1993. "Where is Project 2061 Today?" *Educational Leadership* 50(8): 19–22.

APPLE, M. 1993. "The Curriculum as Larger Environment." In *ASCD Curriculum Handbook*, Alexandria, 2.2–2.4. VA: Association for Supervision and Curriculum Development.

BETTS, F. 1993a. "Systems Thinking and the Integrated Curriculum." *ASCD Curriculum Handbook*, 13.1–13.33. Alexandria, VA: Association for Supervision and Curriculum Development

———. 1993b. "The Curriculum as System." *ASCD Curriculum Handbook*. Alexandria, VA: Association for Supervision and Curriculum Development. 2.9–2.11.

BRADFORD, K., AND H.R. STIFF. 1993. "Virginia's Common Core of Learning Takes Shape." *Educational Leadership* 50(8): 35–38.

BRADLEY COMMISSION ON HISTORY IN SCHOOLS. 1988. *Building a History Curriculum*. Washington, DC: Educational Excellence Network.

BRADY, MARION. 1993. "What's the Glue?" Unpublished working paper for the 1995 ASCD yearbook committee.

BRUNKHORST, B. 1991. "Every Science, Every Year." *Educational Leadership* 49(2): 36–38.

BURKE, J. 1993. "Tackling Society's Problems in English Class." *Educational Leadership* 50(7): 16–18.

DOANE, C. 1993. "Global issues in 6th grade? Yes!" *Educational Leadership*. 50(7): 19–22.

FORRESTAL, P. 1986. "An Australian Planning Model," In *English Teachers at Work: English Education in Five Countries,* ed. S. Tchudi, 242–245. Portsmouth, NH: Boynton/Cook.

HIRSH, E.D. 1993. "The Core Knowledge Curriculum: What's Behind Its Success?" *Educational Leadership* 50(8): 23–30.

JACOBS, H.H., ed. 1989. *Interdisciplinary Curriculum: Design and Implementation.* Alexandria, VA: Association for Supervision and Curriculum Development.

KLEIMAN, G.M. 1991. "Mathematics Across the Curriculum." *Educational Leadership* 49(2): 48–51.

KOHL, H. 1967. *Thirty-Six Children.* New York: New American Library.

KOZOL, J. 1967. *Death at an Early Age.* Boston: Houghton Mifflin.

(NAAS) NATIONAL ASSOCIATION FOR THE ADVANCEMENT OF SCIENCE. 1988. *Science for All Americans: Project 2061.* Washington, D.C.

(NCHE) NATIONAL COUNCIL FOR HISTORY EDUCATION. 1993. "National Standards Project—U. S. History." *History Matters!* 5(6): 6.

(NCTM) NATIONAL COUNCIL OF TEACHERS OF MATHEMATICS. 1991. *Professional Standards for Teaching Mathematics.* Reston, VA.

PALMIASANO, M., AND M.A. BARRON. 1993. "System for Integrative Learning." Presentation to the ASCD 18th Annual Conference, Washington, DC, 29 March.

PERKINS, D.N. 1991. "Educating for Insight." *Educational Leadership* 49(2): 4–8.

SANDY UNION HIGH SCHOOL DISTRICT #2. n.d. "A Step-by-Step Guide to Integrating Science Concepts and Vocational Skills in the High School Classroom." Sandy, OR.

SMITH, S., M.E. SMITH AND T. ROMBERG. 1993. "What the NCTM Standards Look Like in One Classroom." *Educational Leadership* 50(8): 4–7.

STYLES, K., AND G. CAVANAGH. 1978. "Design for English in the 1980s." *The English Journal* (67)6: 40–44.

TCHUDI, S. 1991. *Travels Across the Curriculum: Models for Interdisciplinary Learning.* Toronto: Scholastic of Canada.

VARS, G. 1993. "Core Assumptions and Beliefs Evident in National Board Standards for Early Adolescent-Generalist Teachers." *The Core Teacher* (43)4: 4–6.

———. 1993. *Lock & Key: The Secrets of Locking Things Up, In, and Out.* New York: Charles Scribner's Sons.

TURNER, C.H. 1982. *Maps of the Mind.* New York: Collier.

WILLIAMS, J., AND T.D. REYNOLDS. 1993. "Courting Controversy: How to Build Interdisciplinary Units." *Educational Leadership* 50(7) 13–15.

5

The Learning Quest
The Mystery, Magic, and System of Learning

Exploration

> Probably, the most pronounced of all is the deep-lying and powerful exploratory tendency. This is constantly manifested by the watchfulness of children of everything that goes on about them, especially the actions of things and people. (Ellsworth Collings, 1923 in Willis et al. 1993, 174)

As we have done throughout the book, we continue in this section to use for the purpose of example interdisciplinary flights that we have taken off on, as much to please ourselves as to explain the concepts we are trying to relate. For this section we use old Highway 40, a remnant of our region's past. As we describe this road that we have taken, we invite you to consider features of a territory that is local for you that might work as well interdisciplinarily as this one does for us.

We found this theme because our eyes were wide open for themes to exploit in our course and in this book. On one of our "advancework" outings, as we pleasurably pedaled our bicycles through a very productive work day—we were exploring the Truckee for our summer project—we became aware of fragments of road that now lay unused far below the roadbed of Interstate 80, the present trans-Sierra highway between Reno and Sacramento. The most dramatic remnant of an old road was an old gasoline station, now a junk yard, that sat out of the view of drivers on the interstate. An old gas pump, tall and slender, glass globe still intact, remained. The sight triggered thoughts of what motoring must have been like in the days before the superhighways.

We didn't concern ourselves with the road for a long time after the bike trip, but it came into consciousness when one of the authors had a revelation; he realized that the motels on Fourth Street in Reno hadn't always been old and dilapidated, hadn't always been the domicile of poor folk, but rather had served as overnight havens for motorists travelling on the old highway. It was one of those *saw it again for the first time* experiences.

Highway 40 became a theme that we wanted to explore. Topics flew at us like snow during a Sierra blizzard. Questions bred other questions. What route did this old highway take through the rest of Reno? What did Reno look like when Fourth Street served as a spur of the main east-west highway? What did the road look like up in the mountains, and what were the towns that it passed through like? What happened to those towns when the interstate came and bypassed them? What effect did the interstate have on Reno? On its neighborhoods and its businesses? We knew something of the answer to the last question; we had been looking at motels. And once we got onto the theme of *one* highway, questions regarding *all* highways began to present themselves. How are highways built, and who builds them? The highway we were looking at ran through steep and rugged mountains. How were roads such as Highway 40 and Interstate 80 engineered? What geographical, geological, topographical, and ecological issues came into play during the decision-making process? What were the political and social considerations given to the building of each road? Who made the plans and who carried them out?

As with the other themes we have discussed, this one had trappings that could be used to teach concepts in every conceivable discipline. It should be obvious that we were convinced that the theme would be a good one to launch productive questing. It had magical qualities because suddenly before us, and our imagined students, was a part of our everyday reality that, with a little scrutiny, was producing a wealth of interesting questions we had no reason to ask before. And the questions it raised had potential for making the knowledge and the procedure of the disciplines magical too.

With a theme in hand, organizational decisions must be made. What we want to do here is look at some of the options for setting up the exploratory phase of the interdisciplinary quest. There is no reason why an entire class or an entire interdisciplinary team cannot explore the same topics. A math teacher might teach a string of road-related math lessons. Chapter 8 contains a lesson outline for teaching cubic measurement using road-related examples. The English teacher might create a literature unit that takes on roads in both their literal and metaphoric manifestations, or a research unit that leads somehow to interviews with those who possess information about the road. Social studies teachers can use the road as a framework in which to teach aspects of history, about political processes, about the sociological consequences of road building, automobile travel, or the introduction of superhighways. In other words, teachers can do much of the exploration themselves and then use their findings to create lessons that have continuity and relevance. Such lessons can also be used to inform students of the mechanics of the exploration process and to show how disciplinary concepts are useful in such exploration.

We bend, of course, toward interdisciplinary explorations that put students in the role of explorer, and have spent a good amount of space putting forth our rationale for this. In terms of organization, a number of options exist, only a few of which we will present here. The dividing of themes into topics (towns on old Highway 40, engineering, economics of Highway 40) certainly makes possible small group or individualized explorations. It may be possible, too, to have a whole class or a team investigate a single topic. In fact, this may be a viable approach if the topic is complex enough to give several students reason to pursue it from several angles. One project organized in this fashion was the Billinghurst water project. The theme was the Truckee River and the focus was on exploring the needs of different Truckee River water users. Since there were numerous groups laying claim to the river's water, different groups of students were sent out to collect information without straining the informational resources. We have also seen teachers working in teamed schools divide students into disciplinary interest groups so that a number of students are approaching a topic from a science perspective while others are taking a humanities tack. Disciplinary experts can share their findings with those with differing expertise through activities such as jigsaw groups. In jigsaw, each student holds membership in two groups, a heterogeneous "home" group and a "focused exploration" group. Expert groups pursue a particular type of understanding, a mathematical perspective on the highway, for example, and then share what they have learned with the home group. Mathematicians in the home group receive historical or sociological information from those attached to humanities-oriented expert groups (see Clark 1994; Aronson et al 1978; Kagan 1992).

This arrangement need not prevent math experts from studying the literary side of the issue or the literary experts from gaining mathematical understandings. Teachers can stress from the beginning that all students will be assessed in all areas. Student experts can play the role of disciplinary coaches, sharing their knowledge, skill, and their enthusiasm for a particular discipline with others who have different inclinations. Project-oriented jigsawing, where home groups are responsible for using the knowledge they have accumulated to develop a product, can lead to truly authentic kinds of cooperation and authentic lessons concerning the difficulties of collaboration. Experts have to communicate with non-experts; they often must convey their understandings to lay people for the sake of getting things done. This is often not an easy task. Project-oriented jigsaw in which experts of varying kinds work together to solve a problem reflects how truly functional communities work and the discourse problems such collaborative problem-solving situations create allow students to experience the real dynamics of participation in dialectic.

Another way to divide up thematic work, of course, is to have different students or groups of students pursuing different topics. As with the disciplinary groups, students in different topic groups will develop differing kinds of expertise that can be brought back to larger groups through jigsaw arrangements, presentations, or whole class or whole team projects. How students are placed in particular groups does present some problems, as does division of students into discipline groups. Certainly the option of having students choose their own groups is open. And it has its advantages in that students can choose groups according to their interests.

We do know, however, that students often make their decisions based on whom they will work with rather than what they will be working on. Sometimes the nature of the work can alleviate the problems of buddies choosing buddies. For example, in the Lego-Logo groups, students did choose their friends to work with. But friends, over a short period of time, became coworkers as interest in achieving task goals grew.

Teachers can choose which students go to which groups by some kind of random selection process or more methodically, basing selection on knowledge

Name(s)_____

Theme (title of proposed study) _____

1. Describe what it is that you will be studying:

2. Explain the reason for your interest in the theme you propose to study. Explain how you discovered the theme and how you came to see it as being worthy of study. What about the theme makes you curious enough to want to study it?

3. What questions do you want your studies to answer?

4. What do you expect to learn from your theme-related studies?

5. What skills or knowledge do you have now that will allow you to pursue answers to the questions the theme presents?

6. What additional skills and knowledge will you seek in order to answer the questions the theme raises, and where will you attain the skills and knowledge you need?

7. What resources, at this point, do you think you will utilize to find answers to the questions the theme raises?

8. How will you present your findings? What will you do with your findings?

FIG. 5-1   *Thematic Study Proposal Form*

obtained through advancework, considering aptitudes, attitudes, social skills, ineptitude—teachers do know of these things, or can devise means to find out. As we said earlier, surveys, writing assignments, classroom discussions, and observations are helpful in coming to understand who individual students are. One way to minimize protest is to inform students that they have been chosen for a particular group because the group needs their particular skills and abilities. Topic groups can, in fact, be set up so that advantage is taken of each student's strengths. Within groups, individuals can take on expert roles, pursing the topic from their expert perspective and sharing their expert understandings with the rest of the group, the individual contribution working for the good of the whole group.

Even informed group-making will not prevent some students from being less than appreciative about placement in a particular group. Sometimes this will be because they have been separated from friends. Our observations tell us that this problem dissipates as students become interested in the tasks at hand. The more interesting the topic, the sooner the pain of separation is forgotten. Collaboration with others who are not like oneself is, or should be, a goal of schools in a culturally rich and diverse society such as ours. Cooperative learning as a means to this end is the topic of numerous articles and books (see, for example, Sharan 1980; Cohen 1980; Miller and Brewer 1984; Slavin and Madden 1979; and Miller and Harrington 1994) that argue very persuasively that working students into groups with others they do not know or do not like can be highly beneficial for social development. Again, we have some firsthand evidence that the interest level a topic or task generates has much to do with how soon predispositions are overcome.

Which topic a particular group or individual is given is another problem to be faced if different groups are to be given different topics. Selection of members for groups, if based on knowledge of student interests, provides one avenue toward student receptivity.

Groups can also be asked to select their own topics through group deliberation. Their decisions can then be presented to the class and evaluated in terms of what others think exploration into the topic might turn up, or in terms of the contribution exploration into the topic might make to the goals of the class. Groups or individuals with the same or overlapping topics can discuss concerns in front of the whole class or in group-to-group conferences. All of these possibilities lend themselves to rich and meaningful interaction among students, to community building, and to growth in the ability to communicate.

Despite the effort made, individuals or groups might still be dissatisfied with the topic they are assigned. We have seen teachers guide students through periods of discouragement by nudging them toward seeing the value of the exploration in which they are involved. In the Billinghurst water project, for example, some students protested early on that the water user group they were assigned to investigate was one they did not support. But as the project moved on, the team of teachers pushed them gently into playing the "believing game" (Elbow 1973), causing them to collect information that eventually allowed them to discover all that was legitimate about their *client's* cause.

Many Directions at Once: Management

Management of classrooms in which students are organized into groups is covered nicely in texts dedicated to cooperative learning such as Elizabeth Cohen's *Designing Groupwork* (1986) and Spencer Kagan's *Cooperative Learning: Resources for the Classroom* (1992). We also recommend Yael and Shlomo Sharan's book *Expanding Cooperative Learning Through Group Investigation* (1990), and Richard and Patricia Schmuck's *Group Processes in the Classroom* (1992) as excellent resources for working with groups in the classroom. Certainly having different students working on different topics, or working on similar topics but in different ways, creates management and logistics problems different from those encountered when teaching from the podium. Instead of one lesson plan, it would seem, there would be a need for many, and in terms of supervision, the teacher would be monitoring a number of groups instead of one.

True, but our read is that many of the problems become non-problems if the dynamics of true investigation are allowed to come into play. In regard to the lesson plan, one outlining the broad goals of the learning process will suffice. For example, a goal such as "Students will discover resources to use for the purpose of exploration" can describe the work of all, even if all are not going in the same direction at the same time. As students work in their groups, time can be taken for whole class lessons, on techniques for finding resources, or on a concept that must be taught in one of the disciplines. Most classrooms in the interdisciplinary programs we have seen, in fact, more often than not function as traditional classrooms. The interdisciplinary investigative work takes place only on occasion, sometimes only once a week. Though we would like to see greater integration of disciplinary teaching into the investigative process, traditional teaching and interdisciplinary exploration can co-exist more than comfortably since exemplars for making disciplinary content relevant can often be drawn from students' exploratory experiences.

One can also develop plans to reflect the range of objectives that all students will be expected to achieve at some point, but not necessarily at the same point in the course of a unit. Such plans would reflect the teacher's intent to interject disciplinary content into group discussion when the moment was right. This could, of course, mean that a teacher would have to teach a single lesson several times. Or arrangements could be made so that at the right moment students could tap into resources made available to teach the concept. One could, for instance, have a teaching station in the room designed to teach the movement of a bill through a legislative body. Such a center could contain task sheets, books, video and audio recordings, and computerized hypertext materials that would teach the concept. Students could be introduced to group learning processes and then be asked to use these when the time was ripe for a concept to be learned. The teacher, if he or she wished for all students to learn a number of set concepts, would have to look carefully at the topics individual groups were involved with and make anticipatory judgments about how and when certain concepts fit into particular explorations. Rough plans could then be developed and a form of monitoring set up.

To demonstrate the different approaches we have just suggested, we will take the Highway 40 idea and break it into topics. Let's say that students are working in five different groups on the following topics:

Group 1: How the old road, Highway 40, came to be replaced by the new road, Interstate 80.
Group 2: The actual construction of Highway 40.
Group 3: The building of Interstate 80.
Group 4: The effects of rerouting on communities.
Group 5: The building of bridges.

Each group will, especially if the teacher *wills* them to, encounter legislative processes at some point in their explorations. Using the mass group approach, the teacher selects a single time for the whole class to become engaged in lessons on

Course: Social Studies
Unit: The legislative process
Interdisciplinary Thematic Unit: Highway 40

Monday
Group work. Groups will develop a list of rules, regulations, and laws that pertain to the topic they are exploring.

Tuesday
Share lists developed in groups. Ask students how they think rules and regulations came into being. Discuss levels of government.

Wednesday
Discuss decision making process as it operates in groups and the need for orderly decision making procedures within and among civic legislative bodies.

Thursday
Use issues related to the various group explorations to show the logic of systems of checks and balances. Follow bills related to group topics through the legislative process.

Friday
Group work. Students research the history of a piece of legis-lation related to their topic.

FIG. 5–2 *Weekly Lesson Plan*

the legislative process. Aware of what each group is exploring and where each group is in their explorations, the teacher considers the relevance of legislation to each of the topics as students in the groups understand it or will come to understand it. A lesson plan for such an approach for a single discipline course is presented in Figure 5–2 and looks much like a traditional lesson plan. The interdisciplinary explorations taking place, though, lend power to the teaching no matter what mode of instruction is being employed. Yes, even lecture benefits!

The plan presented in Figure 5–2 is, of course, unidisciplinary, but it need not be. Each of the topics has scientific relevance and reference to scientific concepts, scientific fact, and methods of science are bound to arise in literature students read concerning rules, regulations, and laws pertinent to their topics. Mathematics too, will most assuredly come into play—money always plays a role in legislative considerations no matter what they may pertain to. And when the disciplines come together to explain a single topic, the complexity of issues imbedded in the topic becomes apparent. The bridge-builders can design the safest and most elegant of bridges. They can build the bridge legislative bodies will pay for. Bring in issues of ecology and human displacement, and aesthetics, economics, and the reasons for the slowness of legislative processes can be understood.

For the sake of the disciplinary interaction we have just described, we heartily support teamed approaches. James Moffett, in an unpublished essay titled "Integrating Learning: The Rhythmic Curriculum" (ca.1991), calls for reconceptualization of the "the total curriculum," for the "smelting down [of] conventional subjects and methods and recasting the whole learning process as fundamentally and universally as possible" (1). In another essay, this one in his book titled *Harmonic Learning: Keynoting School Reform* (1992), he presents a rationale for "smelting."

> Though they differ in what they are about—in their information—government, economics, history, chemistry, and psychology share some common processes for making their information, for investigating. These are processes of observing and reasoning that characterize the human mind and determine how we make and store knowledge, although each field has its own concepts and frameworks that influence in turn how its practitioners observe and reason. (100)

The ability of disciplines to explain themselves and their concepts is increased when students are able to experience interdisciplinary fusion, when ideas and procedures from one discipline are linked up with those from others in students' minds.

In the lesson plan shown in Figure 5–2, the legislative process is the broad concept being taught in the social studies class. This teacher, we will imagine, is part of a team involved with the Highway 40 project. A mathematics teacher is a member of the interdisciplinary team and wants to teach ratios during the same period social studies is dealing with legislative processes. Mathematical ratios are easy to find in a unit that explores a highway, some basic ones being proportions of water to sand in concrete, or gravel to asphalt in a paving mix. And there are significantly more complex ones involving bridges and weight displacement, vehicles travelling sections of road per day and the effect of traffic volume on road wear as it relates to different surfacing compounds. All of these ratios have scientific implications— the chemistry of elements in cement, for instance, and the way in which they interact with water has much to do with the proper ratio of water to sand in concrete mixes used for particular purposes. Weight displacement and bridge structures to accommodate it are problems of physics. Ratios also apply to scales on maps, to representation in different legislative bodies, to measurements of vertical climb (height over distance ratios), and to issues of cost versus benefit: aesthetics, safety, ecology, human suffering versus capital outlay.

The concept of ratios, as a construct applicable in numerous ways to the contingencies of the real world, can be brought home through simultaneous mention in a number of connected courses, or the link can be made explicit through collaborative lessons that teachers from a variety of disciplines work to prepare. We are dealing with some powerful magic here. But the procedures are not so magical because the linking of concepts across disciplines derives from how disciplines are actually applied in real-world situations.

InterMusing

Take the concept of ratio and think of its applications in common activities in which you and your students participate:

food preparation	food purchases
dietary concerns	sports/exercise
daily schedules	travel
personal finance	reading
household projects	craft projects
care of pets	care of automobile
political decisions	philosophies

For each item that involves ratios, describe how those ratios are pertinent to different disciplinary realms: Food preparation includes recipes and involves ratios of measurement. Measurement of ingredients is related to taste and nutritional considerations, which are related to issues of physiology, chemistry, botany, culture, psychology, and even ethics (some do not eat meat!).

———

For part two, take a concept in your discipline and see how broadly you can spread it across other disciplines and realms of human experience. For instance, English teachers might try metaphor and analogy, history teachers conflict, math teachers volume, art teachers perspective . . . and consider how you can take advantage of their cross-disciplinary, cross-experience values to help students attain a better sense of their meaning.

The infusion of disciplinary content into thematic quests is not a problem, and we have offered two general ways in which it can be done, through whole class lessons that take advantage of the topics of student quests and through the use of stations that teachers develop for particular concepts to be taught to different students at different times. We also think it is possible for students to teach other students the concepts the curriculum prescribes, the disciplinary expert groups we mentioned above being one way for this to be done. In the schools we and others have dreamed of, disciplinary courses might be eliminated all together in favor of problem-based or situation-based instruction that would place teachers in the role of consultant in much the same way teachers in the Lego-Logo project instruct only in response to student questions arising from the activities. We go no further with this idea here, for we have yet to put our minds to a full blown exploration of its potential and potential problems.

On the other hand, as we have explained, we see instruction attached to interdisciplinary thematic quests making magic of the learning process as well as of the content and procedures of the disciplines. There is incredible potential in such methods to capture students' imaginations while informing them of the information and processes that are their intellectual heritage. That heritage is not something they should learn to sit on, but rather, it is something that they must put to use to build better tomorrows. "The next generation," says Moffett, "must have an education strong enough to survive its inheritance" (1992, 32).

The legislative process example and the one involving ratios are, we think, indicative of how interdisciplinary thematic teaching can help in developing students who are authentically knowledgeable and authentically able to participate in the task of making sense of the world and making the world work. The linking of disciplinary knowledge and procedure to the contingencies of the world—a polluted Mississippi, the creation of a business, the building of a highway, the preservation of an old hotel, or a purchase at the supermarket—imbues that knowledge and procedure with a work ethic. The disciplines exist for good reason and understanding them helps to get things done.

At the same time, the interlinking of disciplines to understand and solve real-world problems can, we think, can be used to bring about understanding of the interaction of values and disciplinary knowledge and procedure. The role of justice and concern for the well-being of others in the legislative process can be discussed as students examine decisions made in the building of the two highways. Is safety ever traded for reductions in cost? How do decision makers factor in the price of human displacement as homes are demolished to make way for a freeway? What is the cost of the destruction of habitat? How do we deal with problems that might pit human safety against the preservation of sensitive ecosystems? A shift in route to save homes or habitat may cost a great deal, or it may force the road up new and more dangerous gradients. Perhaps the safer and faster road will make travel from Sacramento to Reno easier, but what of the towns that will be forced off the map when they are bypassed? There is a different kind of mathematics at work here, a different science and a different kind of humanities that is tempered by the realities of numbers and physical and biological fact. Good decisions, we must teach, involve more than a set of calculations or a good heart.

Monitoring Progress

We said before that the system we would propose would be messy, and we think we have fulfilled our promise. However, we do want to tidy things up a bit before we move on. We have presented some rudimentary organizational formats that we think can be used in independent single subject classrooms and in teamed programs, or in multidisciplinary "self-contained" classrooms. Figure 5–2 shows a week's lessons for a class that is involved in highway exploration. The discussion of ratio across the curriculum implies at several points that interdisciplinary cooperation is involved. For both, students at different times are involved in group or independent work, exploring some aspect of the theme. Groups and individuals must in some way be monitored and managed. Students need guidance, and they need to work in a somewhat orderly and disciplined way.

Certainly, when students work in groups or individually, the teacher cannot observe all that they do, or do not do. We also want students to become self-managing and self-monitoring. The interest tasks generate, as we said before, constitutes a management tool. But interest in the task does not ensure that students will spend their time getting the work done. So we suggest that students be asked to monitor their own progress and to make public their records of that progress. Remember that the results of each group or individual's explorations eventually

Group _____

Topic _____

Response

1. Describe group's activities for the week. Specify what each group member contributed as you describe the activities.

2. Describe progress made toward answering questions stated in your exploration proposal.

3. What new questions have arisen, and how do you intend to pursue answers to them?

4. Are you having difficulty answering any of the questions you feel need to be answered? Describe what you understand to be the obstacles.

5. In your exploration, what use have you made of what you have learned in your courses? Is there information you need that you think these courses could offer you?

6. What resources have you used so far, and what resources do you need to locate?

7. Have you encountered any obstacles in finding resources? What is your plan for overcoming these obstacles?

FIG. 5–3   *Group Progress Reports*

contribute to the attainment of the goals of the larger group, the class or team. So public inspection of records of progress is authentically reasonable and instructive. Students must write the reports, and other students read them. Writers have an audience, and readers learn from the writing of fellow students.

The reports can take many forms and, if students submit proposals such as the one shown in Figure 5–1, they can be keyed to the questions on the proposal forms to show how far along the writers are in answering the questions they want their study to answer. Reports can contain information on changes in expectations, new questions that have arisen, knowledge gained and knowledge still needed, resources found and resources yet to be sought. For the report-makers, the document serves as a self-assessment tool marking progress and charting the course to be taken. For the teacher it is a monitoring tool that informs management. Groups or individuals not making sufficient progress need attention, and those that are progressing can be left alone. Students reading the reports can also help in management, offering advice to the reporting group based on what the report says about progress being made, obstacles being encountered, activities proposed.

One possible report format is illustrated in Figure 5–3. To facilitate response from students outside the reporting group, a response column is included. A better format for actual classroom use is to have response pages attached to the report. The first question tries to get at the issue of individual accountability, and there are advantages to a group report that includes information about the work done by individuals. The collective account may inform the teacher as to when he or she needs to intercede, but also provides insight into students' perceptions of group processes. If further individual accountability is desired, individual reports on personal contributions, problems, and needs can be required.

Progress reports, of course, do not need to be as formal as the one we have presented in Figure 5–3. Many teachers already use logs and journals, and student entries in these can be monitored to determine how explorations are progressing. Multiple-user journals and response logs can also be used. The multiple-user journals would contain responses to questions like those asked on the Figure 5–3 form, but group members would respond to them on their own. Such a journal might look like the one shown in Figure 5–4. The format would allow group members to gain an understanding of others' perceptions of the workings of the groups. Response logs are journals with space provided for the response of others. They differ from the format depicted in Figure 5–4 by not calling upon the log writer to answer specific questions.

Response to the reports, too, can come in different forms. We have suggested so far the possibility of written responses. Such response can come from individuals or as collective statements developed by other groups. Collective statements consume group time but the instructional potential is high as students discuss and develop suggestions for their classmates. Many kinds of arrangements can be made for promoting response. All students can be required to respond to all of the progress reports. The time constraints here are obvious. More manageable formats have groups with related topics reading each others' reports, random pairing of groups for response, or revolving schedules of response, groups 1 and 2 sharing reports, groups 1 and 3 and 2 and 4 the next.

Reports need not be written. Groups and individuals can be asked to develop presentations showing work-to-date on occasion in as elaborate a fashion as the curriculum will allow. Technology, both present and future, holds great potential for the quality of presentations, and reports serve as a good excuse for having students learn how to use presentational technologies. And while we like the idea of students presenting their reports for the inspection of other students, we also see value in students presenting their work-in-progress to teachers through formal and regularly scheduled conferences and through more informal monitoring and conversation. Teachers can develop check sheets or management logs that serve as a record of student learning and explorational progress. Such a sheet might contain a list of objectives to be achieved by students over the course of a semester or year. Evidence of progress toward achievement is noted and ready for presentation to students, parents, and administrators during conferences and at grading time.

```
┌─────────────────────────────────────────────────────────────────────┐
│  Group    _____                                    │
│  Topic    _____                                    │
│                                                                       │
│                            Group Members:                             │
│                       │ Bill  │ Jane │ Allan │ Sandra │               │
│  1. Describe group's activities                                       │
│  for the week. Specify what                                           │
│  each group member con-                                               │
│  tributed as you describe the                                         │
│  activities.                                                          │
│                                                                       │
│                                                                       │
│  2. Describe progress made                                            │
│  toward answering questions                                          │
│  stated in your exploration pro-                                      │
│  posal.                                                               │
│                                                                       │
│                                                                       │
│  3. What new questions have                                           │
│  arisen, and how do you intend                                        │
│  to pursue answers to them?                                           │
│                                                                       │
└─────────────────────────────────────────────────────────────────────┘
```

FIG. 5–4 *Multiple-User Journals*

The Look of Exploration

There is no single best regimen for leading students through exploration, and the role of teachers is somewhat ambiguous. At times they will lead, at others they will follow. As students pursue their quests and discover information, the nature of the information found will influence direction. Teachers take the lead by offering students knowledge of the tools available, through regular lessons offered in the classroom, through conferences with the explorers, and by putting students in touch with resources. They follow as they watch to monitor where new insights are taking students, giving guidance as necessary.

As we have suggested before, the rhythm of learning moves from observation to curiosity, or necessity to exploration, and it is curiosity or necessity that drives exploration. The teaching we are describing attempts as much as possible to emulate the rhythms that drive learning outside school. Something catches our attention, it puzzles or perplexes (Where are those ants coming from?), we sense a need to understand, then find the tools we need to bring about understanding. A student of ours, Larry Baden, noticed the braille inscriptions that are now found on most automatic teller machines (ATMs) and became curious as to why they were there. He questioned whether a blind person, after using the braille-coded keys, could read the screen messages that would follow. A blind acquaintance told Larry he too thought it impossible for a blind person to use the machines. Now they were both curious, and their curiosity led them to inquire at one of the banks with braille-inscribed machines. A bank official offered them a braille instruction manual for ATMs and told them that this copy was the first one his branch has ever given out, that no one had ever requested one before, showing how impractical some of the provisions of the Americans with Disabilities Act were. Upon hearing this, Larry Baden acquired a copy of the ADA and is now trying to discover whether the ADA is flawed or whether the bank's compliance officer is pitching the anti-ADA line. Baden and his friend also plan to test the instructions in the book to discover whether one who cannot see can actually make use of the machine.

Larry Baden's curiosity was the cause of his exploration, and the questions that marked that curiosity led him to tap resources that might help him to answer those questions. Those resources, his friend, the compliance officer, and the braille instruction manual, pushed him toward other questions that created a need for new resources, a copy of the ADA and, as he discovered, a lawyer to help him understand some of the fine points.

Resources

Resourcefulness is an essential attribute of those who are prepared to deal with the contingencies of a complex and changing world. Bound up in the notion of resourcefulness is the ability to find the resources one needs to accomplish the tasks one must or wants to accomplish. As with the content of the disciplines, we should be aware that we cannot begin to inform students of all the resources available, of all the resources they will ever use. Instead, *resource education*, if we can call it that, should give students a sense of the *boundlessness* of resources and cause them to think creatively about where to look for information. Students should have a good understanding of broad resource areas, knowledge of how to access resources, and the ability to utilize resources in the context of productive exploration.

Libraries

Larry Baden did not immediately turn to the library once he had become curious. Instead, he first turned to a friend, then to the bank, *then* to the library to discover what he could about the ADA. Our Highway 40 quest began when we spoke to longtime residents of Reno who remembered what Fourth Street used to be. With that information in hand, we too then turned to the library. No doubt, libraries are good places to consult in the quest for knowledge and understanding. Use them, but use them well because students often have little sense of what they contain beyond card catalogs, shelves of books, and encyclopedias. Nor do they understand their utility as a resource for exploration, since the utility of resources is directly related to its ability to satisfy needs or desires. We think that thematic interdisciplinary instruction allows the element of utility to become a part of student resource consciousness. When students learn resource savvy in the context of authentic explorations, they not only discover the magic of the resource, but acquire the ability to sustain the frustration that is often a part of research. Libraries *are* frustrating places *when they are properly used*. Note that we did not say "even when," for it is proper use that leads one into the labyrinth of catalogs and catalog cards, to indexes and files and new catalogs and even to new libraries or resources outside the library. What we are concerned with is *the attitude of quest* that we spoke of earlier, the desire to find, and the gumption necessary to keep pursuit alive in the face of obstacles.

Beyond sheer willingness sparked by need and desire is the fun and adventure of the quest, the magic of being bumped by things we've never known to exist, the magic of the realms of information that open up to us when we begin to *look*. Consider how a degree of freedom in the search allows futility to become utility. So often students are asked to do research on topics in which they have little interest, and a firm deadline for completing work on a narrow topic. We have seen the assignments that provide a topic, then call upon the student to find "at least one encyclopedia article, one book, and one magazine article" for the report. Even if they call for sources outside the library, an interview for instance, such assignments still convey the wrong message. It is the quest and the questions that propel the quest that should determine which and how many resources are to be used. So much school-sponsored "research" seems detached from the real desire to find. Students often experience futility in the research they are assigned, and that sense of futility is evident in the less than interesting reports they produce. If latitude is given so that some futility is allowed to become fun, then research becomes a quest. All consequences are not known before the pursuit begins.

We use ourselves as examples, admitting that we had a great deal of fun playing with the themes we have researched for this book. The shoe, for instance, *became* interesting because we gave ourselves the freedom to just look without any compulsion to come to a preordained-ordained end. Our freewheeling researches led us to a rich array of materials that increasingly made the subject more interesting and provided us with information we now feel we could use to write several *darn good* reports. We strongly suggest that on occasion students be allowed such freedom. Have students pick a topic as a starting point and ask them to discover as much about it as they can, with the proviso that they list all other topics of interest they encounter along the way. Let them have the freedom to take off on these other topics as they wish. The teacher's role is to continue throwing them into new resources that will lead possibly to new topics. As we will describe below, our own explorations took us from books to indexes to references to maps and outside the library through phone books to agencies and individuals, more documents, and sometimes back to the library again.

Students can be asked to track their course and create maps of their expeditions showing how they moved from one topic to another, from one resource to another. A map might be a simple narrative, similar to the one we provide below of our engagement with the highway theme, or it can take the form of a diagram or graphic. Maps can be used to discuss the features of various resources, those that allow users to find information in the resource (index, table of contents, keys) and those that point to resources beyond (citations, bibliographies). They can also be used to discuss the interconnectedness of topics, like that of Highway 40 to the Emigrant Trail and of the Emigrant Trail to the fateful expedition of the Donner party. The idea here is to give students a good taste of what it is like to be tossed around in a sea of resources without losing their bearings.

Getting lost is one thing. Finding one's way through is another, and unlike our experience with the shoe, the highway theme took us into the library with specific questions we wanted answered. Thus, we were more restrained in the side-trips we allowed ourselves. As we said before, our search began on Fourth Street with the question of why the motels were there. These questions led to queries, and the queries led us to the old highway and a set of questions about the highway that became our research agenda. We wanted to know what the old highway was like and how the interstate came to replace it. We wanted to know about the decisions involved and about the decision makers. We wanted to know if there was opposition to the new road or to its route, who designed the roads, and the details of the engineering of a highway through the rugged Sierra.

If we had been novice library users, this would have been an opportune time for lessons on how to proceed with an organized search, for someone to demonstrate for us how to track down specific kinds of information through card catalogs, indexes, and reference materials. Students who walk into libraries with research proposals that list the questions they wish to have answered have a need for the information library lessons can offer; the information they receive can be understood in a functional context so that even the fine print at the bottom of the catalog cards takes on relevance. Our hope is that students will come to understand that libraries are more than stacks of books—they are *systems* organized to facilitate the retrieval of information. Those organizational systems become wondrous when they satiate one's intellectual hunger. Tapping into the system, *really* tapping into the system, can indeed be a magical part of any learning quest.

Tapping into the system can also be a frustrating part of the quest, and we have witnessed students of all ages giving up searches without much fight. Tenacity is a quality with which educators should be concerned. Real learning is ultimately an encounter with the unknown, so a part of learning how to learn is figuring out how to cope with the surprises one is bound to encounter during any quest. Library work often leads to dead ends, to books that are not on the shelves, to references or magazines that our libraries do not stock, to books with great titles that have little to offer us in relation to our questions. In our quest for information on Highway 40, our plunge into our university's library landed us in very cold water. We typed "United States Highway 40" into the computerized catalog system and were told that there were 62,000 titles in the

```
AUTHOR      Vale, Thomas R., 1943-
TITLE  U.S. 40 today : thirty years of landscape change in America /
            Thomas R. Vale and Geraldine R. Vale.
PUBL INFO   Madison: University of Wisconsin Press, 1983.
DESCRIPT    xii, 198 p.: ill., maps; 26 cm.
NOTE          Includes bibliographical references and index.
LC SUBJECT Vale, Thomas R., 1943-
    Vale, Geraldine R.
    United States —Description and travel —1981-
    United States —Description and travel —1940-1960.
    United States Highway 40.
ADD AUTHOR    Vale, Geraldine R.
ALT TITLE    US forty today.
```

FIG. 5–5   *Catalog Card*

```
UNITED   is in 62962 titles.
STATES    is in 63065 titles.
HIGHWAY is in 405 titles.
40 is not in any titles. Therefore "40" is discarded.
Both "HIGHWAY" and "UNITED" are in 141 titles.............................
Adding "STATES" leaves 141 titles......................................

There are 141 entries with HIGHWAY, UNITED & STATES.
```

FIG. 5–6   *Library Computer Readout*

collection with the word "united" in them, 62,169 with the word "states," 404 with "highway," and none when "40" is added. Frustration, yes. But we were the survivors of many previous library excursions, so the frustration was somewhat sweet, more challenge than disappointment. We tried again, this time with the descriptor "highway forty," and up came a single title, *U.S. 40 Today: Thirty Years of Landscape Change in America* by Thomas and Geraldine Vale (1983). Cataloging systems, as ingenious as they may be, are quirky! Figure 5–5 shows what we saw on the computer screen. We recognized the clues on the card, the "note" show-ing that the book included bibliographical references, an index, and the three descriptors that could perhaps lead us to more materials. "United States Highway 40" caused a stir of excitement—it indicated that a whole category existed for our topic. But when we searched by subject using "United States Highway 40," we were given the screen depicted in Figure 5–6.

Quirky indeed! The descriptors were "LC Subject" descriptors, not necessarily descriptors being used in our library's system. Being more resource-rich than we expect many of our readers to be, our library provided us with computer access to the Library of Congress catalogs. Learning our way around that system was an adventure that tested even *our* mettle. Suffice it to say that we muddled through and after all our work possessed but a single title, the Vale book.

A single title in hand, we gave this book a very good looking-over. We read the authors' introduction on our way to the bibliography, and were told by the authors that what we would find within were photographs and commentary describing portions of Highway 40 as they existed in 1983. For every one of these photographs we would find another showing these same road sections as they existed thirty years earlier, in 1953. The 1953 pictures, the introduction said, were the work of George R. Stewart who had, in 1953, published a book titled *U.S. 40.* Why this book hadn't come up in our subject search we do not know, but when we called up the title itself, Stewart's book appeared.

The Stewart book offered us a good amount of information about the road, informing us that U.S. Highway 40 ran from Atlantic City to San Francisco; that it was the first transcontinental highway built in the U.S.; that it was conceived of by a group of private citizens known as the Lincoln Highway Association; that it was not built as a national highway project, but rather, "each section of the highway was necessarily local" (11); and that the road was neither straight nor marked with the signs we are used to today. Instead, marks painted on telephone poles designated the route.

InterMusing

Here we strongly suggest another type of advancework, a personal plunge into the pool of information contained in the libraries you have at your avail, however many, however large, however small and deficient. Follow a thread, any thread that is attached to questions that are of interest to you. Or take up a question at random, the name of a street in your town that may be meaningful or curious—and go to the library. Go as far as you can to find out as much as you can. As you are going, consider how you would direct students if they found themselves in your situation. Consider our meanderings, the way in which we found resources *through* the resources we'd already tapped. Consider the range of resources we can allow ourselves to be led to. What would students have to know about the library and about the materials they would encounter to follow such a path? As you play in the library, begin a list of research lessons that might be necessary, a list of problems that students might encounter, and solutions that might ease frustration. Do they know, for example, what the information on the catalog cards (or computer screens) means? Do they know how to use this information? Do they know about citations in text and in bibliographies? Do they know how to use this information to find clues that can lead to new paths? You will undoubtedly find limitations. But you will also find resources you hadn't known to exist, and resources contained in the resources. Your own search will give you a better sense of what they deserve to know.

As we moved through the Stewart and Vale books, we learned of many things, of towns old and new across America, of the industries that kept them alive, of their climates, and the plants and animals that lived nearby. Economies, we could see, were the creatures of regions defined by particular geographical and geological features. Geography affected climate, and climate and the geological features of the region gave rise to differing types of ecosystems, these producing the flora and fauna that allowed for the existence of particular kinds of industries. A wonderful web of interconnections and excuses for further exploration. So many questions, so many possibilities for learning.

Of course, we cannot afford to spend the time necessary for answering all of the questions such a search will raise. Exploration has to have some structure, and that is why we suggest that students create proposals such as the one in Figure 5–1. Those proposals, however, should not be adhered to ridgidly. Explorers must be given some latitude so that new discoveries and new questions can enter the quest. But the overall purpose of the exploration, the goal the proposal defines, must serve as a reference point for determining reasonable parameters within which such side trips are allowable.

Stewart's reference to the Lincoln Highway led us to look for titles related to that road, and we found several, including Effie Price Gladding's *Across the Continent by the Lincoln Highway* (1915), The Lincoln Highway Association's *The Complete Official Road Guide of the Lincoln Highway* (1984), and Drake Hokanson's *The Lincoln Highway: Main Street Across America*. The Vales' book, in updating the Stewart album, reluctantly pushed us off the old road onto the new, and once we moved off U.S. 40 onto Interstate 80 a new set of angles for exploration emerged. When we used "Interstate 80" as a descriptor we found Eleanor Huggins and John Olmstead's *Adventures On and Off Interstate 80* (1985). This book took us on a journey from San Francisco to the Great Basin, offering excellent descriptions of the natural, geologic, and human history of the country along the route. The excursion took us into the Gold Country of the Forty-niners, to Virginia City, and along the flumes that brought water to the Comstock mines and the miners.

Beyond Books and Back to Books: Maps and Newspapers

The books we have mentioned so far represent the start of our excursion into the library. Libraries are filled mostly with books, but not only with books. Some offer films, videotapes, slides, and now, multimedia materials. Our local public library checks out *puppets*. While we could not use puppets in our quest, we did find the map library at the university to be extremely useful. The newer books we'd found, *The Complete Official Road Guide of the Lincoln Highway*, Huggins and Olmstead, and the Vale book, all made mention of Interstate 80, but made no mention of dates for its construction. We wanted the dates so that we could search the newspaper collection for articles that might tell us about how people who were affected by its construction responded to the prospect of it being built.

The maps in the library were arranged by geographical location, and for each location, to our delight, several maps were arranged by date. We could flip through maps of the Reno area and the Sierra and find those maps that recorded the disappearance of U.S. 40 and the emergence of Interstate 80. A 1950s map showed U.S. 40 but no sign of Interstate 80. A 1955 map showed sections of the interstate in place, but not yet through Reno or the Sierra.

Beyond locating dates, we could use the maps to compare old and new routes and find the towns that existed on the maps *then* but did not now. On the old maps, for instance, we found the highway going through Polaris, Icehouse, and Gelatt, towns we had not previously known. Checking the newest maps, we found Polaris and Icehouse to still be worthy of a marker. Icehouse, we found, was originally a Southern Pacific Railroad station on Gray Creek. At one point, the creek was dammed and the pond that formed was allowed to freeze so that ice blocks could be cut from it to cool the Comstock mines and chill the California fruit that was being shipped east. Gellatt, a town shown on the 1940s maps to have been just west of the Donner Summit, may no longer exist.

When we did turn to the newspapers, we used 1955, the date of the first maps showing Interstate 80, as a starting point and scanned (no index exists for this newspaper) microfiche of the Reno newspaper until we found articles concerning the building of Interstate 80. The earliest mention we found was in the year 1958, and there we made one of our most interesting discoveries, Representative Walter S. Baring, the namesake of a well-known boulevard in the nearby town of Sparks. Baring first appeared to us in a boldly headlined article on the front page of the August 7, 1958 edition of the *Reno Evening Gazette*. The headline read "New Freeway Delay Threat Possible." The first line of the story states that "although investigations have proved all of his earlier charges to be false, Rep. Walter S. Baring may seek further delay of a Reno freeway route by a select committee of Congress, a local committee advocating for a Third Street Location has charged." Baring's complaint was that the manner in which the Third Street route had been selected was inappropriate and probably illegal, and that it would be more costly than a route he was advocating, one that would have placed the freeway on the northern rim of the city. Baring lost his fight, as today's Renoites know. The *Evening Gazette* of August 30, 1958, announces the "Expected Approval of Third Street Route."

The U.S. geological survey maps we had found helped us find dates for our newspaper search, which eventually led us to Baring. We think students should have a sense of how to make and follow research trails so they too can use libraries and the other resources we will talk about to make interesting discoveries of their own. As we said before, our foray into the literature of the highway began with a set of questions. We kept to those questions that led us to information that not only broadened our understanding of the area in which we live, but provided us with information that was of interest to others, to information that was not common knowledge.

We still wonder why Baring pressed so hard for the alternative route, and who his opponents on the committee were. The newspaper stories seem to cast him as an obstructionist, but at this point we have little sense of his real motives. We do know that the present location of the freeway does little to beautify the city and that a route at the northern rim would have had less of a neighborhood-splitting effect. Was Baring's call for a select committee probe a frivolous one? Or was he fighting the good fight for the people of Reno? We do not know. The topic is ripe for future exploration.

The newspaper articles gave us a sense of decision-making processes behind the development of the interstate highway system, sending us to books like Mark Rose's *Interstate: Express Highway Politics, 1939–1989* (1990), and Helen Leavitt's *Superhighway—Superhoax* (1970). The search took on a rhythm as it progressed, the same rhythm that we want students to move with as they explore. We think that time taken to teach them the steps, from question to resource, from resource to resource, and resource to answer, is time well spent. At the same time, it is necessary that students learn to improvise. So much of what we have done with our searches was driven by what we found. As with theme selection, we think it possible for teachers to gradually move students to independence by first demonstrating the process of resource selection, and then showing students how one copes with obstacles and dead ends. Teachers can discuss their own search frustrations and discuss the reasoning used to continue the search. This can be done on a regular basis in any class as teachers show how they have won *their* way to the understandings that form the content of a course, or through explorations with their students into the processes by which the knowledge-makers of the disciplines made the knowledge that is being studied. The stories of discovery are as important as the discoveries themselves and need to be told.

We also think it possible for teachers to run students through the process. Take the last InterMusing and move students through pertinent parts. Meander through a topic together. Such exercises can begin with discussions of current events. Look at the newspaper and land on a murder case, a civic controversy, or a political race. Have students highlight elements of the events that arouse curiosity, raise questions, or cause confusion. Then discuss the resources one might turn to for clarification. How, for instance, did the police determine who the prime suspects were? What are the ballistics tests that allow police to identify murder weapons? What of the legal and historical validity of local Native Americans' claims for land and water rights? Has the candidate for re-election really consistently lied about his voting record in the state legislature?

A Turn to Government Documents

Interstate highways, we had found, were and continue to be a controversial issue. Ben Kelly's *The Pavers and the Paved* (1971) was one of the books to which we turned to make sense of the process by which decisions about interstate highways are made. As with the other books we have mentioned, we scanned rather than read the books we found. We were looking for specific kinds of information and could not have possibly found the time to read through each and every book we discovered. How to look through books and documents is another lesson that should be included in the curriculum. We first turned to the table of contents, looked at the general introduction, then the introductions to the chapters that seemed to hold promise. After that, we read the chapters that seemed best suited to our needs. We thumbed through books, looking at charts, tables, pictures, indexes, and bibliographies to see what might be of use. From each book we took what we *needed*. Amongst the things we took from Kelly's book was this quotation from the introduction:

Unhappily, my good fortune as an author will be costly to much of the American public. Because of the new law, the business of building superhighways will continue to assert priority over urgently needed, less destructive kinds of transportation improvement for many, many months to come. Hundreds and possibly thousands of alarmingly expensive miles of additional Interstate and other expensive expressways will be in place through towns and cities that neither want or need them. Countless acres of settled neighborhoods, irreplaceable parks, and unpopulated (by man at least) open spaces will be seized and subjugated by pavement and cars. (vii)

How costly has the building of the highways been? And at what expense to other forms of transportation? How much private property had to be condemned for road building to take place? At whose urging?

Once an issue is in the hands of government, documentation is produced. Debate in the United States Congress is chronicled in the *Congressional Record* that is available in most public libraries. The *Congressional Quarterly* also catalogs the activities of the federal legislature. In looking for resources that might inform us on the issues Kelly raises, we found the *Federal Directory*, a comprehensive guide to all federal regulatory activities, and a number of government documents available in both the university and public libraries. We found one titled "financing Federal-Aid Highways," and another called "The Status of the Nation's Highways, Bridges, and Transit," and a series of yearly reports called "Revised Estimates of the Cost of Completing the System of Interstate and Defense Highways." The index of government documents we found on the university's computer system led us to articles like "Use of the Interstate Highway System Right-of-Way for Magnetic Levitation High Speed Transportation," which was concerned with the deliberations of a U.S. Senate committee working on this issue. Several of the documents

1. Congressional Gophers/

2. Congressional Directories/

3. Federal Legislation/

4. Miscellaneous Internet Resources on the U.S. Congress/

5. Guide to U.S. Government Legislative Documents at LC/

6. On-line Legislative Databases at the Library of Congress/

7. The Congressional Research Service (CRS)/

8. Other Library of Congress Services for Congressional offices/

9. Other Legislative Support Agencies/

FIG. 5–7 *MARVEL Services*

Choice			File
1	Congress, 1981–82	(97th)	CG97
2	Congress, 1983–84	(98th)	CG98
3	Congress, 1985–86	(99th)	CG99
4	Congress, 1987–88	(100th)	C100
5	Congress, 1989–90	(101st)	C101
6	Congress, 1991–92	(102nd)	C102
7	Current Congress, 1993–	(103rd)	C103

FIG. 5–8 *Listing from MARVEL*

were keyed to specific House or Senate bills that could easily be tracked down by using the index to the *Congressional Record*.

We know about the size of typical public school libraries, and we feel fortunate to have the access to documents our university faculty membership provides us. But the government documents we describe are not inaccessible to others. The on-line services of the Library of Congress provide indexes and documents. We took the "menu of services" shown in Figure 5–7 from the Library's MARVEL (Machine Assisted Realization of the Virtual Library) system that we accessed through the Internet. When number three is chosen, the menu shown in Figure 5–8 appears. The files track and describe legislation (bills and resolutions) introduced in the U.S. Congress from 1973 (Ninety-third Congress) to the current Congress (103d). Each file covers a separate Congress, as Figure 5–8 shows. Legislation can be retrieved by a member's name, a bill number, or a subject keyword. The Library of Congress service is available through commercial connections to the Internet such as America Online. Government documents are also available through Federal Depository Libraries, of which there is at least one in every state. A listing of these libraries is available on the Internet through the Library of Congress service.

Reference Works

Most students know where to find encyclopedias in the library, and in many small libraries such as those common to schools, encyclopedias *are* the reference section. But there are numerous other kinds of reference works that students should be made aware of and have the opportunity to use. In this section we describe some of the most interesting reference materials we encountered in our searches, realizing that we are privileged to have a research library on our campus. We will try to offer some hints as to how this material might be placed in the hands of students who go to school in places far removed from university and state libraries.

We were first drawn to the reference section because of our shoe expedition. We were looking for people we could interview or write to for information concerning the design, development, and manufacturing of shoes. We found the *Thomas Register of Manufacturers*, a set of books that lists by product all of the companies in the United States that produce a particular commodity. We looked under *shoes* and found not only the addresses and phone numbers for Nike, Reebok, L.A. Gear, Frye Boot, and Birkenstock, but also for those who produce the materials used in shoe manufacturing. We used several of the addresses listed in the *Thomas Register* to send out requests for information. Most of the companies listed toll-free phone numbers, and all could be reached by fax. One company sent us the book *The Art and Science of Footwear Manufacturing* (see Chapter 3); L.A. Gear sent us its annual report to shareholders and a packet of articles chronicling the company's history.

The *Thomas Register* was one of hundreds of references we passed on a trip we took down the reference aisles of our library. We got to know the neighborhood by strolling, rubbing an index finger over the bindings, and stopping to look when a particular volume caught our eye. The list we present here is by no means comprehensive, but it does get at the diversity of materials available and worthy of being known by students and teachers. Our estimate is that our fingers only touched about half of the references in the library and our selection rate was about one book for every five shelves.

The next InterMusing sends teachers into their school libraries or nearest research library for a trip down the aisles like the one we took. Such a trip, we think, would be a good one for students to make. A goal of what we are calling exploration is to familiarize students with the systems of information that are available to them. If there is little that is close, this is no reason to deny them information about what there is. In Chapter 9 we will distinguish between decision making that is cheap and that which is economical. If there is a *need* for students to have access to certain materials, then decisions that deny them such access are not economical, but cheap. If the materials cannot be purchased, then budgets should be written to accommodate occasional field trips. If for some reason it is not possible to take large groups of students to the nearest research library, then send delegations of students or adults whose job it is to gather materials for others. For the purpose of lessons on recovering information, teachers can use photocopied material so students can sample reference materials and learn about the systems of organization utilized in different works.

We are also aware of access problems beyond the problem of accessing the materials; some of these works are not for students of all ages. And some of what students find in sources such as the *Congressional Record* may be difficult for them to understand. All of what we list below may not be for you and the students you teach. Or you may want students to know that these resources exist without the expectation that they will use them immediately. There is, we think, value in such knowledge. Teachers can, as they do with other materials, help students interpret their meaning or pull from these documents those things that are meaningful and can be understood.

Do as we have done. Take a trip to the research library nearest you. Walk down the aisles in the reference section and look at the items that interest you. Thumb the pages to see what they contain and consider how you and your students might use them. Most reference works have introductions that explain their purpose and how they are to be used. You might want to photocopy introductory pages and some sample reference pages to make available to your students. Also, to appreciate the value of the resource, take a moment after you have completed your tour to note for yourself what you have learned. What kinds of things, besides new knowledge of the existence of these works, exist for you that hadn't before?

Indexes

Our searches led us to numerous indexes, several of which are available in computerized versions. Amongst the most familiar were the *Readers' Guide to Periodical Literature* and the *New York Times Index*. The latter goes all the way back to 1851, as does the microfilm collection of the *New York Times*. What might students learn from scanning the pages of the *Times* while, for instance, reading the play *Inherit the Wind?* The *Times* of London index catalogued an even longer period of time, taking us back to 1785!

We found indexes for almost every topic imaginable, a number of them dedicated to particular categories of biography. Most of these works were written in a style easily accessible to students in the later years of elementary school. We found the *Index to Authors* and an *Index to American Author Biographies*. There is an *Index to Scientific Biography,* and the *New York Times* publishes the *New York Times Personal Name Index* which leads to articles in the *Times* about particular people. They also offer an index of obituaries published in the newspaper.

There are a number of business indexes that guide one to books and articles published about work and commerce; there are also indexes in communications and journalism that lead to transcripts and recordings of broadcast news stories and speeches. There are indexes on criminal justice, theater, education, issues of ethnicity, film, Victorian periodicals, history, American customs, the American Revolution, and medieval studies. The *Oral History Index* and *Words on Cassettes* are interesting companion resources for teachers and for students involved in exploration. There are numerous indexes on music including the *Index to Children's Songs*, a *Music Psychology Index*, and a guide to the *Literature of Rock*. There is the *World Treaty Index*, an index on African affairs, one on *Goddesses and Wise Women*, a computer sciences index, a *General Science Index*, and several indexes on women's studies.

While students may not need to know of all these indexes, they should be made aware of their existence. We like best the idea of having students experience these materials within a context of need, the teacher pointing to various works when exploration would benefit from their use. It is also possible to introduce the range of materials available with "reference of the week" sessions in which teacher or students show and tell of reference materials they have found to be interesting and useful.

Reference Books

As with indexes, there are reference resources available for almost any topic one might need or desire to explore. Our interest in the nature of the polymers used in the construction of modern running shoes could have been answered by one of the scientists and engineers listed in *Who's Who in Technology Today* (Jones 1981), which provides biographical sketches of thousands of "individuals who are leaders in the most important areas of modern science and technology" (vii). Students interested in interviews may find this work and other "Who's Who" titles useful as they often provide corporate or institutional affiliations, phone numbers, and addresses. *Who's Who in Atoms* is much like *Who's Who in Technology Today*, providing biographical information, phone numbers and addresses for those involved in various nuclear technologies.

Weather of U.S. Cities (Ruffner and Blair 1987) is "a compilation of weather records of 281 key cities and weather observation points in the United States . . . to provide insight into their diverse climates and normal weather tendencies" (from title page). The descriptions are complemented by numerous charts showing "statistical cumulations to quantify normals, means, and extremes." We see many uses for this reference in math, science, geography, history, and economics. "How to Read These Reports" provides insight into the different aspects of weather that can be observed and described. A companion volume, *Climates of the States*, also has great potential for use by students. Lucy Boersma's Silver Lake elementary students could have used them well during their explorations into the relationship between work and weather. So too could students working on projects involving the design of "perfect" cities.

Our library hunt landed us a number of aviation references. *The Encyclopedia of Aviation* is an excellent work to use in studies in this area. It contains encyclopedia length explanations of all aspects of flying. *Jane's All the World's Aircraft* lists statistics for all of the planes in use today. *Who's Who in Aviation* provides the names and activities of those involved in all aspects of the aviation industry including engineers, airport managers, pilots, regulators, manufacturers, and flight instructors. Addresses and phone numbers are provided for most of those listed. *AeroSpace* provides facts and figures for "key technologies" related to aviation. *AOPA's Airports USA* is a yearly publication describing all airports in the United States. Intended for pilots of private aircraft, airports are described in terms of location, altitude, obstructions, lighting, runway facilities, fuel availability, and cost.

America, History and Life (Boehm 1965) offers "article abstracts and citations of reviews and dissertations covering the United States and Canada" (title page). This reference catalogs articles from numerous journals not only by subject, but by geographical region. The "List of Review Periodicals" describes a number of resources available for explorations into the history and the lives of people in every region of North America. We found a host of interesting journal titles in the list includ-

Modern English Biography
Dictionary of South African Biography
Rules and Governments of the World
Encyclopedia of Ethics
Encyclopedia of Religion
Dictionary of National Biography (British)
Biographical Directory of Governors of the United States
Biographical Directory of the United States Executive Branch 1774-1977
The Twentieth Century Dictionary of Notable Americans
National Cyclopedia of American Biography
Handbook of Middle American Indians
Encyclopedia of Architecture
International Directory of Company Histories
Million Dollar Directory: America's Leading Public and Private Companies
Corporate Technology Directory
Directory of Corporate and Foundation Givers
The Gallup Opinion Index
Constitutions of the Countries of the World
America Votes: A Handbook of American Election Statistics
Major Peace Treaties of Modern History
Constitutions of the United States: National and State
The New Grove Dictionary of Music and Musicians
American Music Index
Catalog of Political and Personal Satires

FIG. 5–9   *Other Interesting Reference Works*

ing *Western States Jewish History, Quaker History,* and *Labor History.* If we ever wanted to know more about Kansas there is *Kansas History,* and closer to home, the *Pacific Historical Review* and the *Nevada Historical Society Quarterly.* There is the *Journal of American Ethnic History* and a journal dedicated to American folklore.

Historic Documents (Dickerson 1973) is published by the *Congressional Quarterly* to provide "convenient access to documents of basic importance in the broad range of public affairs." Included are official statements by those involved in public affairs, Supreme Court decisions, studies, speeches, international agreements, papal pronouncements, and even "an Arctic explorer's field notes" (iii). The *Dictionary of American Military Biography* provides information about American warriors from the landing at Jamestown in 1607 to today. The sketches are of encyclopedia length and cover both the personal and professional lives of those listed. *Jane's Combat Support Equipment* is a trade publication that provides descriptions and many photographs of military equipment available in the world today. We found the advertisements such as those for Barracuda Camouflage and Fiat Production for Defense most interesting. We also like the chapter on portable bridges (great photographs) and the renderings of various types of mines and "minelaying" equipment. We can now better visualize what the "operations" we hear about in the newspaper are like and we can see students taking great interest in the information this work provides. We also have a better sense of how weaponry is promoted by its makers. Jane's publishes a number of other "catalogs," many for less lethal pursuits. *Jane's Ocean Technology* and *Jane's World's Railroads* attracted our attention. We can envision using all the Jane's works for the writing of quasi-accurate James Bond-type stories.

Peace has its publication too in the form of the *SIPRI Yearbook: World Armaments and Disarmament*, a publication of the Stockholm International Peace Research Institute that describes the numerous (and there are hundreds) agreements made worldwide that affect issues of war and peace. Many other references sit on the shelves of our library and those within your reach. Figure 5–9 is a list of some of the others we sampled. Be aware of their existence so you can point students in their direction when the time comes.

And Beyond the Library

We fully endorse libraries as excellent questing grounds. Libraries, however, are not the only repositories of documents, and documents are not the only repositories of valuable information. Some of us regularly tour the aisles of our local hardware stores, not to find items of particular need at a particular moment, but to see *what is possible*. The availability of a gadget sometimes leads to new and wonderful projects, sometimes to solutions for problems that have been put to bed because no known widget could at the time be found do the trick. Hardware store clerks have been known to be amongst the most helpful people in the world. We will more fully discuss people as resources later. First, we want to finish with the documents and access.

Electronics

Information and electronics are proving themselves to be extremely compatible. The libraries we used in collecting information for this book use computerized cataloging systems. CD-ROM indexes are available for numerous areas of inquiry; some are now "full text" services, meaning that one does not only find *references* to works needed, but the works themselves! We just discovered *English Poetry*, a CD-ROM package available in our university library that holds the poetry of 1,350 poets who lived between 600 and 1900. Numerous information packages on other topics are available for use at home and on classroom computers. A single page in a recent "multimedia" catalog lists *Multimedia Stravinsky: The Rite of Spring*, "an insightful exploration of this passionate and powerful piece," a program on dinosaurs, an encyclopedia, and a program that "includes street-level maps of the entire Continental United States" (Tiger Software Catalog).

And there are the "on-line" services that use phone lines to connect questors to unimaginable amounts of information. By the time this book is printed most everyone with a personal computer will have access to the Internet, through school networks or through the commercial network links such as Prodigy, CompuServe, and America Online. We will not even begin to make an attempt to explain all that is here. Instead we refer you to Harley Han and Rick Stout's two books on the subject, *The Internet Complete Reference* (1994) and *The Internet Yellow Pages* (1994). These books will introduce you to the realm of the "gopher server," "reader news," and "anonymous FTPs." Suffice it to say that every topic receives some attention on the "Net." Through the Internet one can tap NASA databases or find U.S. Geological Service seismology reports. *The Internet Yellow Pages* lists 49 categories of information available from or about the U.S. government. There is information from the Bureau of Justice Statistics. Documents regarding the Americans with Disabilities Act are available, as is the full text of the ADA. Census Bureau data is available, as are General Accounting Office reports. There is a bibliography of Senate hearings, a computerized file on congressional legislation that tracks bills and resolutions, daily summaries of White House press releases, a rundown of the President's daily schedule, and access to the Library of Congress (see above).

In looking for information relevant to our quests we found an "electronic newsletter" concerned with chemical engineering and several "mailing lists" dedicated to "computer-aided design." Scanning *The Internet Yellow Pages* index, we found nine categories of information on chemistry, fourteen listings under "consumer services," twenty-one under "economics," and nineteen under "environment." One environmental listserver informed us of the problem of mercury in the batteries used to light up one company's athletic shoes for children. Law, mathematics, music, philosophy, poetry, religion, technology, and telephones are all given listings that lead to vast stores of information on each topic.

The Internet also allows access into every field of interest. An explorer can use electronic bulletin board systems (BBS) to post messages of inquiry in various areas of interest. The "Usenet" system of "newsgroups" allows individuals to chat with one another, via the computer, about most topics. *The Internet Yellow Pages* contains 55 pages of newsgroup listings. The Internet also allows one to send messages via e-mail, and e-mail addresses for individuals with expertise in particular areas of interest may be found by using one of the many Internet e-mail directories. Most universities now have electronic directories for their faculty. These directories can often be accessed through the Internet and usually contain street and e-mail addresses, and phone and fax numbers.

Agencies and Organizations

There is information almost anywhere one chooses to go. Walk into the hotels and motels of almost any town and you will find brochures that contain information about the town, its businesses, and its attractions. Businesses often have printed materials describing products and services—we stopped by our local shoe stores to find out about the latest innovations in basketball shoes, touched the merchandise, and obtained booklets describing the benefits of various models. Bakers know about yeast, and florists, flowers. Louis knows Basque food and about the traditions of the Basque country. And the local mountaineering store has books and maps that provide information on the geography, topography, and geology of the mountains surrounding us. Businesses near and far can be excellent resources. The yellow pages and other business directories such as the *Thomas Register of Manufacturers* described above provide the addresses and phone numbers of people to contact for documents and interviews.

Government agencies, federal, state, local, and foreign, usually have great amounts of printed materials available for the asking or for small fees. Many federal government agencies are now making documents available through the Internet. An excellent resource for those wishing to acquire information by phone is the *AT&T Toll-Free 800 Directory,* which contains a subject heading index and listings by product or service offered. We found 59 listings under "shoe manufacturing" and more than double that under "shoes." We haven't yet taken the time to find the categories that would be relevant to our search for highway information, but we know we would find asphalt and cement manufacturers as well as associations related to engineering and construction trades.

We did find highway-relevant sources when we scanned the "State of Nevada" section in our local phone book. The Department of Transportation was an obvious choice. We also found the listings under "State Tourism Department" to look promising. Numerous other state agencies can be helpful in interdisciplinary explorations; we have listed in Figure 5-10 those in Nevada that are of interest to us. Look in your telephone directory under federal, state, and local governments and mark off those agencies within each that may be useful to you and your students. A simple scan will give you the awareness you need to be responsive to students when they do not know where to turn for information.

There are, of course, numerous local agencies with records and documents to offer. Our city has a community development department that deals with city planning, zoning, engineering, wastewater, and traffic lights. The finance department is responsible for issuing business licenses, collecting sewer fees, and dealing with risk management. These departments have documents available and people to speak with. The parks department has information on the construction and use of public parks. The county runs an Office of Emergency Management, a health department, the Justice Court, the coroner's office, a parks and recreation department, a regional transportation office, a road division, a Social Services office, and a voter registration division. Students can access material by telephone or by writing agencies for information. Visits by people from these agencies can be arranged, as can visits to the agencies.

InterMusing

Do a government agency search of your phone book and highlight all of the departments within each level of government that look interesting to you. Take at least five of those agencies and make a list of questions that agency might be able to answer. Take a few of the questions and pursue answers. Find out, for instance, who has knowledge of how traffic lights are programmed to allow for smooth traffic flow in your town or city. Or find out who has the map of storm drains that run below the streets. See if you can trace the history of ownership of

Buildings and Grounds (information on state buildings, historic sites, etc.)

Division for Aging Services

Attorney General

Business and Industry Department
- Consumer Affairs Division
- Nevada Office of Energy
- Building Standards
- Office of Industrial Development and Planning
- Mine Safety and Training
- Occupational Safety and Health Enforcement

Department of Conservation and Natural Resources
- Division of Environmental Protection
- Air Quality
- Mining Regulation and Reclamation
- Waste Management
- Water Quality Planning
- Wastewater Treatment Services
- Division of Forestry
- Natural Heritage Program

Equal Rights Commission

Gaming Commission (*Gaming* is a euphemism for *gambling*)

Gaming Control Board

Human Resources Department
- Aging Services Division
- Division of Children and Family Services
- Vital Statistics (birth and death records)
- Communicable Disease Control Program
- Tuberculosis Control Program and Clinic
- Environmental Health Specialist
- Engineers—Water Systems
- Engineers—Radiological Health Section
- Public Health Nurse—Family Planning Programs

Indian Commission

Department of Museums, Library, and Arts
- Nevada State Council on Arts
- State Department of Historic Preservation
- Nevada State Museum
- Archaeological Services

State Board of Pharmacy

State Demographer

Oriental Medicine Board

FIG. 5–10 *State Agencies*

an interesting house in your town. Test the ease with which people can be found who have information that may be of interest to you and your students and consider how the information these people hold may be of value in your teaching. Even if you are not yet involving students in exploration projects, consider how these human resources may be of value in showing students how disciplinary knowledge and skill is applied in real-world contexts.

Outside government and business, there are other resource-rich agencies and organizations to tap. Most states and regions have historical societies that serve as archives for documents and mementos of the past. There are museums, public and private, large and small. Automobile clubs provide maps and travel information, as well as consumer advice documents. Fraternal organizations such as the Elks, the American Legion, Scottish Rite Organizations (Masons and Shriners), Eagles, Moose, and the Veterans of Foreign Wars have documents and interesting people to share. There are business and trade associations such as the Better Business Bureau, the Chamber of Commerce, the Builders Association, the medical associations, and the Bar Association that are willing to share information and perspectives. Trade unions are another resource. So too are colleges and universities, extension agencies, hotel and convention bureaus, local and regional humanities committees, and organizations such as the National Rifle Association, the Sierra Club, ranch and farm bureaus and organizations, the American Civil Liberties Union, and hunters organizations such as Ducks Unlimited. Clubs, recreational organizations, and churches can be informative, as can political organizations such as the League of Women Voters, the offices of the political parties and the offices of those holding political office.

These resources need not be reserved for older students. Certainly some of the records and documents these agencies and organizations have to offer are beyond the comprehension of youngsters. But knowledge of their existence and the bureaus and agencies that hold and distribute them can be made palatable. To know, for instance, that someone, some organization is responsible for thinking through the problems of traffic lights and sewers adds a dimension of civic understanding that many adults fail to attain. Knowing of and meeting with the people who work in these agencies and organizations helps students to begin to understand the complex web of entities and individuals that make up a community and allow it to function.

People

Using people as resources has so many seemingly obvious benefits that we recommend phones and fax machines as standard classroom equipment. Calling and writing for needed information is something students should know how to do. They should also leave school with the ability to obtain information through face-to-face conversations and interviews. We would like to see more opportunities made available for students to get off the school grounds and into the community to meet the knowledgeable people who are out there. We hope

Books

BROWN, C.S. 1988. *Like It Was: A Complete Guide to Writing Oral History*. New York: Teachers and Writers Collaborative. See Chapter 3, "Conducting the Interview."

MACRORIE, K. 1984. *Searching Writing: A Contextbook*. Upper Montclair, NJ: Boynton/Cook.

MOFFETT, J., AND B.J. WAGNER. 1992. *Student-Centered Language Arts, K–12*. Portsmouth, NH: Boynton/Cook. A short but useful section on interviewing beginning on page 383.

SHERWOOD, H. 1969. *The Journalistic Interview*. New York: Harper and Row.

Articles

CARWIN, M. 1990. "Developing Civic Identity and Kentucky Pride." *Civic Perspective*, 3: 1–7.

CHADWICK, D. 1991. "Future Perfect: Community Planning." *English Journal* 80: 69–70.

DOWNS, J.R. 1993. "Getting Parents and Students Involved: Using Survey and Interview Techniques." *Social Studies* 84: 104–06.

GANDESBERY, J. 1990. "Ordinary Lives Illuminated: Writing Oral History." *Quarterly of the National Writing Project and the Center for the Study of Writing and Literacy*, 12: 14–19.

HICKEY, G. 1991. "'And Then What Happened, Grandpa?': Oral History Projects in the Elementary Classroom." *Social Education* 55: 216–17.

HIRSHFIELD, C. 1991. "New Worlds from Old: An Experience in Oral History at the Elementary School Level." *Social Studies* 82: 110–14.

LAUGHLIN, J.S. 1992. "When Students Confront the Experts: Toward Critical Thinking." *English Journal* 81: 72–75.

PHELPS, T.O. 1992. "Research or Three-Search." *English Journal* 81: 76–78.

PUNTNEY, L. 1990. "Just Ask Me Anything. *Communication: Journalism Education Today* 24: 4–6.

SCARNATI, J.T. 1994. "Interview with a Wild Animal: Integrating Science and Language Arts." *Middle School Journal* 25: 30–6.

SEARS, A. 1990. "Enriching Social Studies with Interviews." *History and Social Science Teacher* 25: 95–98.

WHITLOW, F.R. AND D.J. SIDELNICK. 1991. "Integrating Geography Skills and Local History: A Third Grade Case Study." *Social Studies Journal* 20:33–36.

WONG, W. 1989. "The Three 'ings'—Reporting, Writing, and Interviewing." *Social Education* 53: 176–77.

FIG. 5–11 *Resources on the Interview*

that teachers will explore the possibility of developing chaperone systems, perhaps using teacher aides or other school staff to shepherd individuals and groups of students on mini field trips. This idea is appealing because, in the context of small-group or individual exploration, it allows students to make their journeys when the need arises. If students cannot be taken into the community, the option is to bring these community resources into the classroom. We have witnessed several projects where this has been done. In the water project we spoke of earlier, each group of students was responsible for bringing at least one guest speaker into the classroom and making all of the necessary arrangements for the visit.

Oral history projects such as Eliot Wigginton's Foxfire (1985) program in Appalachia and Marian Mohr's Snake Hill to Spring Bank (1984) project in Fairfax County, Virginia, illustrate how the opportunity to speak with people outside the classroom is a powerful way for students to develop interpersonal skills, to learn about people and the community, and to see how what is learned in school relates to the work of the community. A teacher we know in Oakland, California, Jan Matsuoka, asks her early elementary students, on their birthdays (or half-birthdays if they are summer babies) to bring one of the special adults in their lives so that this special adult can be interviewed by the children in the class. The students are given several lessons on interviewing technique prior to the visits. Figure 5–11 offers a list of publications that provide information on teaching the interviewing process.

There are, of course, people to contact for specific information needs, and learning how to find these people, contact them, and ask the proper questions are amongst the most basic and most important skills schools can offer students. How often do we struggle with the question of whom to call, or whom to go to when a problem arises? And how often do we find it difficult to say what we need to say in order to get the information we need? At one point during our research, with highways on our minds, we noticed of a series of bright blue signs strung along a two-mile stretch of a major Reno street. The first read, "SPS-3, Crack Seal, 32A330." Another was inscribed with a different set of numbers and the words "road test," followed by others with numbers and phrases such as "slurry seal" and "chip seal." We had a sense that what was being tested were road surfacing agents, and, sure enough, a glance at the roadbed showed changes in the coloration and texture of the pavement at every sign. We called the Nevada State Department of Highways to see if we could get more information about this project. The person answering the phone at the agency's headquarters in Carson City knew what we were speaking of and referred us to Rick Nelson in the Reno office. Rick seemed to be thrilled that we were interested and told us that the test sections were part of the Strategic Highway Research Project run by the Federal Highway Administration to collect information on the properties of various types of road surfaces and that this project was a part of an international testing program begun in the United States six or seven years earlier under the National Highway Bill. Nelson gave us the name of a firm of consulting engineers who have responsibility for the local part of the project. We now have knowledge and we have new leads. So simple!

A Look at the Classroom During Exploration

Well, perhaps not always so simple. To this point we have made only passing reference to the issue of management of classrooms involved in the kind of thematic interdisciplinary study we are proposing. We have suggested the use of student-developed research proposals and frequent calls for progress reports. But neither of these tools ensures that students will stay on task and the problem of classroom management is exacerbated by the fact that different groups of students are involved at any given moment in different types of work. Some students may not even be in the classroom but rather off to the library, to the telephone, to the computer lab, or out in the community to pursue their quest. How does one manage a classroom situation such as this?

We have reason to believe that in classrooms where students are involved in work that is of high interest, fewer management problems occur. So part of our answer to the question of management is given in the sections above concerned with theme selection. In Chapter 6 we address the issue of assessment and look at projects as an assessment tool. Projects are a management tool as they give students tangible goals to achieve. We have observed students involved in a number of project-based interdisciplinary activities in which groups of students work independently, the teacher acting as a facilitator who is called upon when the group finds itself in need of guidance. So too with the Lego-Logo project we have mentioned so often in this book.

We do not claim that the students in these situations always did what they were supposed to be doing. In each of the projects some groups sometimes were not working productively. In some instances teachers intervened. In others, students in the group found ways to get their colleagues back on track for the sake of finishing work that was necessary for achieving a desired goal. Those who write about cooperative learning often mention something called *positive interdependence*. Positive interdependence is an understanding that people working in certain kinds of group settings develop: that the success of the group is dependent on the success of individuals and that the success of individuals is dependent on others succeeding.

The complexity of tasks and students' understanding of the purposefulness of tasks has much to do with the development of positive interdependence, and much to do with the force positive interdependence will exert in keeping groups on track. Tasks have to be complex enough that they cannot be accomplished by one or two people; they have to be complex enough that they cause group members to turn to one another for help. And the project that students are working on has to be compelling enough so that students will turn to one another for help rather than give up when the going gets rough. Teachers working in such settings sometimes play the interesting role of the *complicator*, reminding groups that easy answers often will not suffice. The nature of the task and students' sense of their goals also act to avoid "taking the easy way out" as the easy way proves to be the unproductive way; it doesn't get them closer to what they want.

Teachers working in interdisciplinary teams have an advantage over those working on their own in their own classrooms since three or four teachers can be

Ash, B.H. 1990. "Reading Assigned Literature in a Reading Workshop."
English Journal 79: 77–79.

Farnan, N. 1993. "Writers' Workshops: Middle School Writers and
Readers Collaborating." *Middle School Journal* 24: 61–65.

Harte, D.V. 1989. "Fine Tuning the Learning Experience: An Information
Age Model for Excellence." *NASSP Bulletin* 73: 6–101

Kasten, W.C., and B.K. Clarke. 1993. *The Multi-age Classroom: A Family of
Learners.* Katonah, NY: Richard C. Owen Publishers.

Staab, C. 1991. "Classroom Organization: Thematic Centers Revisited."
Language Arts 68: 108–13.

Swift, K. 1993. "Try Reading Workshop in Your Classroom." *Reading
Teacher* 46: 366–71.

FIG. 5–12 *Workshops, Centers, and Multi-Age Classrooms*

in three or four places at once, supervising different groups of students involved in
different kinds of work. Teachers with aides are also at an advantage for similar
reasons. The use of interdisciplinary thematic exploration is incentive for cultivat-
ing pools of aides. We do know of schools that involve non-teaching staff in such
things as advisory groups and quiet reading time. Perhaps ways can be found to
make use of these people for supervising explorations. There is great potential in
this, we think, for bringing schools closer to becoming fully functioning instructional communities. There is also opportunity here for bringing parents and members of the outside community into the school.

For those teachers who are by themselves, we point to the single classroom
workshop models described in Nancie Atwell's *In the Middle* (1987), in Pappas, Kiefer,
and Levstik's *An Integrated Language Perspective in the Elementary School* (1990), and
in the other works listed in Figure 5–12. Again, our observations tell us that classrooms can be structured in ways that allow for different students to be doing different
things at the same time. One model for elementary schools that we are particularly
fond of is the multigraded interdisciplinary classroom where first, second, and third
graders, or fourth, fifth, and sixth graders spend three years with the same teacher.
In these rooms, older students, longstanding members of the classroom community,
shepherd the young, inculcating them in the norms of the learning community they
have entered. These classrooms work well for independent group activities as older
students are often anxious to show those who are younger what they know. Like
Atwell's middle school classroom, multigrade rooms are often organized into centers
set up for different kinds of work, each equipped with the materials needed for
completing certain kinds of tasks. For the kind of work we are suggesting, some
centers will be located outside the classroom but they can be attached to centers in
the room that inform students of procedures and rules for utilizing outside resources.

The exact configuration of classrooms for thematic interdisciplinary study is
something individual teachers and teams need to develop for themselves. We do

know that independent group work dedicated to exploration is possible and profitable, in terms of academic achievement and affective development, especially in regard to students' developing the skills, habits, and attitudes essential for lifelong learning and active participation in the society. Flexibility is a key concept here. Classrooms should be capable of becoming divided into many classrooms, and the classroom should be able to expand beyond its own walls.

As we said above and will say again in Chapter 9, exploration activities are not the whole of the curriculum. But they should be a central element in the curriculum. On some days, in the flexible classroom we are calling for, students are sitting at their desks in neat rows, all eyes to the front of the classroom for a lecture or a demonstration. What is different is that students are listening for information that may be useful in answering the questions that arise during the learning quest or in solving problems encountered as they work toward the goal of completing meaningful projects.

References

ARONSON, E., N. BLANEY, C. STEPHAN, J. SIKES, AND M. SNAPP. 1978. *The Jigsaw Classroom*. Beverly Hills, CA: Sage.

ATWELL, N. 1987. *In the Middle: Writing, Reading, and Learning with Adolescents*. Portsmouth, NH: Boynton/Cook.

BOEHM, E.H., ed. 1965. *America, History, and Life: A Guide to Periodical Literature*. Vol. 1. Washington, DC: American Bibliographical Center.

COHEN, E. 1986. *Designing Groupwork: Strategies for the Heterogeneous Classroom*. New York: Teachers College Press.

———. 1980. "Design and Redesign of the Desegregated School: Problems of Status, Power, and Conflict." In *School Desegregation*, ed. W. Stephan and J. Feagin, 251–80. New York: Plenum.

CLARK, J. 1994. "Pieces of the Puzzle: The Jigsaw Method." In *Handbook of Cooperative Learning Methods*, ed. S. Sharan. Westport, CT: Greenwood Press.

COLLINGS, E. 1993. "Curriculum History." In *The American Curriculum: A Documentary History*, ed. G. Willis, et al. Westport, CT: Greenwood.

DICKERSON, W.B., ed. 1973. *Historic Documents*. Washington, DC: *Congressional Quarterly*.

ELBOW, P. 1973. *Writing Without Teachers*. New York: Oxford University Press.

GLADDING, E.P. 1915. *Across the Continent by the Lincoln Highway*. New York: Brentano's.

HAN, H. AND R. STOUT. 1994. *The Internet Complete Reference*. Berkeley, CA: Osborne McGraw-Hill.

———. 1994. *The Internet Yellow Pages*. Berkeley, CA: Osborne McGraw-Hill.

HOKANSON, D. 1988. *The Lincoln Highway: Main Street Across America*. Iowa City: University of Iowa Press.

HUGGINS, E. AND J. OLMSTEAD. 1985. *Adventures On and Off Interstate 80*. Palo Alto, CA: Tioga.

JOHNSON, D.W., AND R.T. JOHNSON. 1979. "Conflict in the Classroom: Controversy and Learning." *Review of Educational Research* 49: 51–70.

JONES, D., ed. 1981. *Who's Who in Technology Today.* Pittsburg, PA: Technology Recognition Corporation.

KAGAN, S. 1992. *Cooperative Learning: Resources for the Classroom.* San Juan Capistrano, CA: Resources for Teachers.

KELLY, B. 1971. *The Pavers and the Paved.* New York: Donald W. Brown.

LEAVITT, H. 1970. *Superhighway—Superhoax.* Garden City, NY: Doubleday.

LINCOLN HIGHWAY ASSOCIATION. 1984. *The Complete Official Road Guide of the Lincoln Highway.* Sacramento, CA: Pleiades Press.

MILLER, N. AND M.B. BREWER, eds. 1984. *Groups in Contact: The Psychology of Desegregation.* Orlando, FL: Academic Press.

MILLER, N. AND H. HARRINGTON. 1994. "A Situational Identity Perspective on Cultural Diversity and Teamwork in the Classroom." In *Cooperative Learning: Theory and Research,* ed S. Sharan. NY: Praeger.

MOFFETT, J. 1992. *Harmonic Learning: Keynoting School Reform.* Portsmouth, NH: Boynton/Cook.

———. c. 1991. "Integrating Learning: The Rhythmic Curriculum." Unpublished paper.

MOHR, M. 1984. *Snake Hill to Spring Bank: A Classroom Publishing Project.* Videotape. Alexandria, VA: Association for Supervision and Curriculum Development.

NATIONAL COUNCIL FOR HISTORY EDUCATION (NCHE). 1993. "National Standards Project—U. S. History." *History Matters!* 5(6): 6.

PAPPAS, C., B.Z. KEIFER AND L.S. LEUSH. 1990. *An Integrated Language Perspective in the Elementary School: Theory into Practice.* New York: Longman.

ROSE, M.H. 1990. *Interstate: Express Highway Politics, 1939–1989.* Rev. ed. Knoxville, TN: University of Tennessee Press.

RUFFNER, J.A. AND F.E. BLAIR, eds. 1987. *Weather of U.S. Cities.* Detroit, MI: Gale Research.

SCHMUCK, R.A. AND P.A. SCHMUCK. 1992. *Group Processes in the Classroom.* 6th ed. Dubuque, IA: William C. Brown.

SHARAN, S. 1980. "Cooperative Learning in Small Groups: Recent Methods and Effects on Achievement, Attitudes and Ethnic Relations." *Review of Educational Research,* 50: 241–71.

SHARAN, Y. AND S. SHARAN. 1990. *Expanding Cooperative Learning Through Group Investigation.* New York: Teachers College Press.

SLAVIN, R.E. 1990. *Cooperative Learning: Theory, Research, and Practice.* Englewood Cliffs, NJ: Prentice Hall.

SLAVIN, R.E. AND N. MADDEN. 1979. "School Practices that Improve Race Relations." *American Educational Research Journal* 16: 169–80.

STEWART, G.R. 1953. *U.S. 40: Cross Section of the United States of America.* Boston: Houghton Mifflin.

VALE, T.R. and G.R. Vale. 1983. *U.S. 40 Today: Thirty Years of Landscape Change in America.* Madison, WI: University of Wisconsin Press.

WIGGINTON, E. 1985. *Sometimes a Shining Moment: The Foxfire Experience.* Garden City, NY: Anchor Press.

6

Let Me Show You What I Know
Putting Knowledge into Action

hat does it mean to "understand" something? What does it mean to "know" in the best sense of the word? David Perkins and Tina Blythe (1994) say that:

> Understanding is being able to carry out a variety of "performances" that show one's understanding of a topic and, at the same time, advance it. (7)

They explain that a performance can come at any time during teaching: It might develop as a response to questions asked by a teacher (the traditional mode of question-and-answer performance), or it might grow out of an active participation in small group discussion or through writing a paper. A "performance" in this sense is not a dramatic extravaganza or a place for artistically gifted kids to strut their stuff (although public performance can certainly be one outcome). To perform simply means to show your understanding in action.

In Chapter 7 we'll focus directly on questions of authentic *assessment* and *evaluation* for both individual classes and school curricula, but the linchpin of interdisciplinary assessment is having something to assess: meaningful student *productions* and *performances*. In this chapter we'll stress the *how to* of helping students translate their understanding into a variety of end products and performances. We'll want to lay to rest the old notion that newer approaches to education don't care about the quality of what students do, or that learning that focuses on process ignores real learning. We'll want to show that when kids are working to show what they know, they can use their knowledge to push beyond or (to use Perkins and Blythe's phrase) to "advance" understanding of a topic.

The Sharing of Knowledge

An eighteenth-century French philosopher and economist, Anne-Robert-Jacques Turgot, wrote in *Progress of the Human Mind* (Adler and Van Doren, 1977) about the shared pool of human knowledge:

> ...speech and writing ... have made a common treasure-store of all individual knowledge, which one generation bequeaths to the next, a heritage constantly augmented by the discoveries of each age. (1976)

In our own time, there is more to the "common treasure-store" than speech and writing, although as English teachers, we will argue for the centrality of those modes in student performances. Knowledge is stored on video- and audiotape and lodged in the memory banks of computers. Other kinds of electronic storage and retrieval will continue to revolutionize not only how human beings receive information, but how they package what they pass along to the next generation.

We don't mean to suggest that what students produce or create as end products will necessarily go down in the electronic annals of human knowledge-making along with the discoveries of a Marie Curie or a Lev Vygotsky; nor will their performances necessarily rival those of a Rudolf Nureyev, Georgia O'Keeffe, Auguste Rodin, or Shaquille O'Neal. However, within the microcosm of the classroom, each child has an opportunity to add something to the community store of knowledge, to produce and perform, and to receive the satisfaction that comes with public recognition.

The underlying premise of this chapter, then, is that *teachers must value student-generated knowledge as they do adult knowledge.* When young people learn for understanding, they have something important to share.

The Rhythm of Discipline and Generalization

In *The Aims of Education*, Alfred North Whitehead (1929) wrote about "the rhythm of education" and "the rhythmic claims of freedom and discipline." He argued that learners begin their inquiry in a stage of *freedom* or *romance* where they are drawn to a topic for the sheer joy of learning. This learning is initially unsystematic (or *apparently* unsystematic to the outside observer) as they poke into the nooks and crannies of a topic. Eventually, however, learners rhythmically begin looking for more, seeking order in their knowledge, and they enter into a stage of *discipline* or *precision*. Then, through disciplined study—the use of "discipline" in the best sense of the word (c.f. Chapter 1)—the learner eventually returns to a higher stage of *freedom* or *generalization* where he or she can continue to "play" in a field, but do so in original ways, backed up by disciplinary learning.

Test Whitehead's model against your own experience learning something new—something you have chosen to learn. This could be a hobby, a sport, an author whose works you admire, a language. You might even test the model against your love life! Whatever the topic, what first piqued your interest in it? Was it the sort of freedom and romance that Whitehead describes? Did there come a time when you moved into more disciplined learning or understanding? Did you reach the advanced stage of generalization (what Whitehead also calls "disciplined romance")? Have you experienced times when you failed to complete the cycle, when you abandoned an interest (or relationship) due to failure or disillusionment? What modifications, rules, or qualifications would you add to Whitehead's perception of the learning cycle?

We appreciate the Whitehead model because we've seen it operate successfully so many times: with kids playing with Lego blocks, learning about music, learning to ride a bicycle, and (all too infrequently) mastering a school subject. We also find that the cycle applies to learning in our own lives, including our own interest in interdisciplinary teaching.

To illustrate: We began exploring interdisciplinary teaching some years ago with a certain kind of infatuation as we discovered the joy of bursting beyond the confines of the traditional English classroom—"Wow, this is great stuff!" "This really has potential for our own teaching." We had some classroom successes, but there were failures, too. Romance wasn't enough for the tricky business of interdisciplinary teaching. So we engaged in a (self-)disciplined quest to learn more about interdisciplinary pedagogy, especially in disciplines outside our home base. After reading, experimenting, and teaching, our work is culminating (but by no means terminating) in the "performance" of this book, which we hope advances knowledge and understanding of this field (and also forces us to put our generalized knowledge to work).

In *The Aims of Education*, Whitehead was speaking broadly about development of competence in a traditional academic discipline, and he was writing principally about older learners who were going on to master physics, chemistry, history, or literature at the university. For the adult learner or the serious scholar, the cycle might occur over a number of years. Thus, we've taken a few liberties in applying the model to schools, but perhaps this is our way of advancing knowledge in the area.

In schools we see the cycle operating in both short- and long-term settings. One can "do" the cycle in as short a time as a single class period. For instance, one might begin a science lesson with a "teaser" opener—with romance. We've seen a science lesson begin with the teacher having students figure out how to float a penny on a sheet of aluminum foil in a container of water, both objects, as he pointed out, being heavier than the water. After the students learned to do this by making the foil into a boat, the class moved on to explore additional problems with the displacement of water—a "disciplined" phase of research. How many pennies can you stack on your boat before it sinks? Are there more or less effective ways of shaping your boat? Does a low-sided, large surface boat work better or worse than a deep small one? Finally, students moved on to the generalization stage by applying learning to other related situations. How would *you* get an Exxon Valdez off the rocks in Alaska?

More commonly, the cycle might take place over a month or longer. A unit on flight might begin with a romantic exploration where kids play around with kites, Frisbees, and balloons. At some point, the teacher would draw the class together for more focused discussions: So what questions do we want to answer about the nature of flight? Are some of you interested in aeronautical history? In space flight? In the aviation industry? Students would enter the discipline phase by reading more about flight, interviewing aviators, conducting experiments. Finally, at the generalization stage we envision a spectacular set of performances: Kids flying paper airplanes of their own design, showing off a modified model airplane, presenting papers and panels on problems associated with space flight, a hot debate over the (non)reality of UFOs.

One teaching approach, pioneered by British and Canadian educators, provides an explicit model of the Whitehead cycle in action. It's called the *jackdaw*. One commercially produced unit we've seen was based on Canadian labor problems in the 1930s (designed for advanced secondary school students). The jackdaw box included labor pamphlets from the era (reproduced in facsimile), copies of numerous newspaper articles from the '30s, several filmstrips reproducing photographs of labor disputes, and a series of taped interviews with labor leaders. In short, the jackdaw was stuffed with reproductions of primary materials. The instructions to the teacher were to equip the classroom with the necessary audio-visual equipment, to remove the lid of the box, and to give the students several days to explore the material. Another jackdaw on the Globe Theater included numerous charts and maps of the theater and its area, various books and pamphlets about the theater in Elizabethan England, facsimile theater programs, and copies of several Shakespearean plays. Again, the teacher was to allow the students to explore the primary materials at some leisure.

The instructor's manual for each jackdaw then called for the students to formulate research or study questions that they would answer using both the materials in the box and those they found at the library. Finally, the students would prepare projects or reports: freedom coupled with discipline leading to performance.

InterMusing

There's no reason why a teacher cannot produce his/her own homemade variations on the jackdaw theme; in fact, we have used the jackdaw for years in an adolescent literature course as a way to help prospective teachers learn to bring the widest possible range of reading materials into their classrooms. In creating one, take as your model the bird named the "Jackdaw"—the bird we in the U.S. call a grackle—a bird that hoards or collects stones, pebbles, and bright and shiny objects in its nest. When you're contemplating an interdisciplinary unit, begin looking for artifacts such as newspaper clippings, historically relevant brochures or booklets, and photographs copied from books in the library. When you have a rich collection of stuff in your nest, open it up for student exploration. Of course, you need to institute the usual crowd control procedures here. The students' browsing should be purposeful. After they have reviewed the materials, ask them to frame questions for more disciplined study and to think about performances that might grow from their research.

The Modes of Presenting and Performing

Where can production- or performance-driven learning lead? In describing her work with some Louisville, Kentucky, sixth graders, Gina Schack (1993) points out that talking about a research project in a typical class brings groans and the usual nonacademic questions like, "How long does the paper have to be?" "How many sources do we need?" "Do we have to do an outline first?" She had students identify topics they wanted to study, gather information from a variety of sources (not just the library), interpret data, and share the results of their work through slide shows, oral presentations, graphics, skits, photographs, videos, and debates. Does the approach work? Schack reports that students were enthusiastic about their projects, especially because they could see that results could have an impact on a real-world audience. "How different this is from the usual classroom view of research!" (31).

Her approach is just one of many variations on the idea of classroom performances. We'll now move on to discuss a host of classroom strategies and techniques that can lead your students to genuine and engaging projects, presentations, and performances.

The Research Notebook as Product

Yes, kids and teachers, a notebook can be more than a chore, more than a list of homework assignments, more than a set of scribbled notes on whatever is supposed to be on the next examination.

We have used a research notebook, or research log, as an integral part of our teaching by making the book itself an item for public display. As students are engaged in collecting materials and synthesizing ideas, we tell them:

> Save the good stuff you find during your learning quest. Put photocopies of articles you are reading into a three-ring binder; save pamphlets and brochures you locate while doing research; cut out newspaper articles and neatly paste them on notebook pages.

The notebook then becomes a display of supporting material for a project.

More importantly, we try to help our students see that notetaking should be more than a borechore, that a good set of notes will actually provide a readable, engaging record of their research:

> Make your notebook a conversation with yourself. Sure, write down the names and dates you want to remember, but also write down your thoughts. Who was this guy who invented vulcanized rubber and wore rubber clothing? Didn't Marie Curie realize she was killing herself with radiation? Write down reactions you have to your interviews. Write up the details of the trip to the interview, not just the questions and answers. Think of your notebook as the record of a voyage.

InterMusing

The idea of an inquiry notebook can also be adapted to your own teaching, especially as you explore interdisciplinary possibilities. Along with writing about your classroom experiments, your failures and triumphs, the notebook can also contain journal articles you find especially helpful, newspaper or magazine articles or brochures that have interdisciplinary connections, descriptions of conversations in the teacher's lounge, plans, outlines, and dreams for future interdisciplinary teaching, and photocopies of student work. It becomes the evidence of your performance as a teacher.

Teaching by Projects: A Basis for Purposeful Study

Our title for this section is taken from a book by Charles A. McMurry and is selected in his honor, for his book was written as long ago as 1924. A cutting-edge educator, McMurry wrote:

> At the present moment we need to be jolted out of our conventional, formal school phrases and to find terms better adapted to the educational needs and forces of the hour. The term *project* is a newcomer among educational phrases. It seems to suggest not the school but the shop, not the textbook but the busy mart, the industrial life, the unhallowed things of the schemer and the promoter. Perhaps this is its merit, that it forces attention upon things that have come to importance in life, things which need to break over the threshold into the school. (10–11)

Although readers might find his language a bit quaint, McMurry's educational aims are still valid today—schools and colleges do need a jolt of precisely the sort he describes. He felt that projects in schools should be of two general sorts:

> First, the child's project undertaken at his own behest when he is pressed by a felt desire or need, e.g., the bird house, the rabbit trap, a homemade telephone.
> Second, the projects of others which the child appropriates, into which he is easily drawn, and to which he gives his undivided attention . . . (1)

The second kind of project was, in effect, the school- or teacher-sponsored unit. McMurry felt that projects could grow out of any school discipline, not only the obvious starting point of the shop class or workshop, but from geography, history, literature, and the arts. He also clearly invited interdisciplinary connections.

Like many progressive educators of the twenties, McMurry was concerned with providing students with practical, manual skills. In reacting against what he perceived as the uselessness of traditional school education in the classics, he may have gone a bit overboard in proposing such projects as

> . . . concreting a basement floor; papering and decorating a family living room; building a tree house; making a tool chest; supplying the kitchen with running water; building and hanging a gate; constructing a corn crib; planning and laying a tile for drainage; planning and building a chicken house; putting in an asparagus bed; the construction of a fireplace and chimney; building a silo. (20)

On the other hand, we and our kids could do worse than to master some of those skills!

McMurry's projects also moved into conventional academic disciplines, offering alternatives to textbook study that still look pretty good three-quarters of a century later. He proposed, for example, a study of "The Great Migration of 1849," an era when some forty thousand emigrants crossed the Midwestern plains and the western deserts and mountains en route to California. Projects emerging from this work included maps and models, dramatizations, and monographs on many aspects of the California migration. (This topic, by the way, is one that we have found equally valid today and have used in our summer institutes on "Reading and Writing the West" for teachers.)

McMurry articulated three principles for project teaching:

- "the inductive-deductive thought-movement" (85), quite similar to Whitehead's stages, actually: *data gathering* followed by *synthesis* and *application*

- the "progressive assimilation and use of knowledge" (88), where students not only accumulate information, but think about ways of putting it into action

- "the big project, a gateway to freedom and self activity" (93), a culminating activity that might be a whole class project or a series of individual projects

We don't want to dwell on McMurry, but we do want to point out that he and his contemporaries of the 1920s had a bead on some teaching concepts that are quite modern. His book also included ideas on structuring projects that are not very much different from those of our contemporary Marsha M. Sprague (1993), an education professor at Christopher Newport College in Newport News, Virginia. She shows her student teachers the value of "production-driven learning" covering topics "from newspapers to circuses." She first saw the value of having students produce concrete projects when she was teaching high school journalism (a course that has traditionally been production-driven), but she came to see the applications across the curriculum. The most spectacular example Sprague presents is that of a first grade circus. After a study of circus traditions and literature, the children invited their parents to an evening performance.

> Children dressed as circus performers were in and out of three rings. They read while on a "high-wire," told circus stories on the "flying trapeze," juggled while calling out numbers, and counted out bareback riders and elephant riders sweeping around the room. (69–70)

Another powerful project involved turning a fourth grade classroom into a simulation of a rain forest. Still other projects sponsored by Sprague's students centered on a "living biography" event (with youngsters dressed up as historical figures), an American history puppet show, and a poetry reading of children's works.

Sprague has four criteria for quality, production-driven learning units:

1. "There is a visible, although not always tangible product." That is, there may be a product (such as a newspaper) or a performance (such as a poetry reading) at the end of the unit.

2. "An audience other than the students themselves views the product." It may be parents or other students, Sprague says, but the project needs a true external audience. [We would modify, based on our own experiences, that students can work on individual projects and find a very satisfactory and satisfying audience among their classmates. But we strongly agree that outside audiences are desirable.]

3. "The entire class is involved in the production." [Again, in our experience this can be handled at least two ways. In one, all the students team up to work on a single, coherent performance; in another, students work on individual projects and bring them together for display or audience reception.]

4. "Most of the production occurs during school time." That is, she makes this an in-school project, thus enhancing the students' feeling of classroom community. (68–69)

An Australian language arts teacher, Geoff Ward (1988), has written the best contemporary book we've seen on the project method. He says,

> The term "project" is generally used to describe tasks which people undertake when they seek to achieve something substantial or personally satisfying. . . . [The] project task may be to accomplish something never done before, where the means to the end are not necessarily known, or it may involve the use of materials already prepared to perform a task done successfully by many before. Whatever the form of the project, it is likely to incorporate a level of challenge which induces interest but is capable of being met. (1)

☐ Topic selected and accepted by teacher.
☐ "What I know/What I want to know."[1]
☐ Reasons for study understood.
☐ Parents informed of project topic and deadline.[2]
☐ Sources of information identified.
☐ Gathering of information commenced.
☐ Format for project report accepted by teacher.
☐ Study of relevant library files completed.
☐ Letters to outside sources of information drafted.
☐ Letters edited and sent.
☐ Interviews arranged and proposed questions prepared.
☐ Information-gathering completed.
☐ Headings for report selected.
☐ Outline of sections drafted.
☐ Introduction completed.
☐ Section 1, etc., completed.
☐ Illustrations selected or produced.
☐ Summary completed.
☐ Assembly of project completed.
☐ Oral report prepared.
☐ Reports presented.[3]

From Ward, G. 1988. *I've Got a Project On*. Rozelle, NSW: Primary English Teachers Association.

_____

1. The student makes a list of his/her background knowledge on the topic and the questions to be explored through the project.

2. An especially good way of securing parental involvement and approval, it seems to us.

3. Ward's projects obviously emphasize written and oral reports rather than some of the projects we've described earlier in the chapter. Obviously the same sort of checklist would apply if the final product or performance is a play, musical composition, or architectural creation.

FIG. 6–1 *Project Procedure Checkpoints*

Ward emphasizes that project teaching must be done carefully, using the best managerial techniques the teacher can muster. His "Project Procedure Checkpoints" list (Figure 6–1) gives a clear idea of the methodology he employs and can be adapted by any teacher working by the "projects" approach.

In our experience, project or production-driven learning is genuinely engaging to students. It creates great pride and satisfaction among them, and the hands-on nature keeps their attention. Above all (as we will reiterate in Chapter 7), a concrete product or project leaves no doubt as to what has been learned. One cannot roleplay a high-wire walker without having thought, read, and learned something about the circus!

Creating "Objects"

Here is one of our fantasies for project-centered education: We imagine an elementary or secondary school class, probably from about fifth grade on up, that would take a whole year to build a *boat* from the ground up, including researching various kinds of boats, finding and learning to read boat plans, locating materials (or at least a kit), and building the craft. Along with boat-building, students would explore the history, literature, art, and music of the sea, and they would quite naturally master the science and math of basic boat-building. In our dream, this would be a small sailboat (since this sail introduces additional mathematical and science problems, including the age-old problem of how you get a boat to sail into the wind). Toward the end of the year, we would haul Das Boot to the nearest reasonably sized body of water, and sail it into the wind, with the wind, from shore to shore, from nor'east to sou'west, perhaps while singing sea chanties. This would be our object lesson on boats.

Far-fetched? A wild dream? Not altogether.

We know of high school shop classes that have built houses with materials contributed by local merchants, houses turned over to Habitat for Humanity, and we see such projects as a superb demonstration of what project learning can be all about—creating real objects, real things, like the following.

- At the Dalton School in New York, a progressive institution with roots back to the early part of the twentieth century, elementary school girls began their education by learning to make a smock, a protective garment worn during their art class.

- The relatively new school subject of materials science (which, in some schools, is replacing general science), has students explore a wide range of properties of materials and, as a final examination, create objects from those materials as evidence that they know their properties and qualities. The claim of materials science advocates is that learning through this hands-on approach, like our boat project, actually covers much of the basic school science curriculum in ways that will stay with students for a long time to come.

InterMusing

With your students (or with a group of adults at a party), try some project activities such as:
- Who can build the strongest bridge using only glue and a specified number of toothpicks?

- Who can build the longest bridge from the same materials?
- Using only cardboard, foil, plastic wrap, and string, create something "interesting and maybe useful" (Jacobs n.d.).
- Using cardboard, Saran wrap, string, toy rubber tires, and any items that you can recycle, create a model for an exciting new roller coaster ride at an amusement park (Winnett 1993).

  After the fun part, discuss:

  a) What did you learn about the math and science of materials, including the properties of materials?

  b) What did you learn about design and architecture?

  c) What would be required to move your model or project from the design stage into real-life production?

- In science, students can create objects to test out a particular hypothesis. The National Aeronautics and Space Administration has a wonderful booklet of hands-on experiments one can conduct on microgravity, the gravity of a small environment (e.g., inside a spaceship). Using common materials and supplies, kids can construct a free-fall demonstration, an experimental device to show how free-fall eliminates gravity effects, and create tests showing the behavior of candle flames within a microgravity environment (NASA 1992).

In "object lessons," students can build telescopes and electronic equipment; they can cook experimental recipes or recreate the foods of different cultures; they can grow plants or trees; they can build a bridge over a schoolyard creek or gully; they can write, print, and bind a book.

InterMusing

Muse on the term *object lesson*. What does it mean in your lexicon? What do parents mean when they plan to give a child an object lesson? What object lessons have you learned in your own life? The term actually originated in the pedagogy of the nineteenth century, when teachers were first exploring ideas concerning what we now call hands-on learning. An object lesson would literally be centered on an object: apple, pen, pen knife, book. Students would explore the object, name its parts, consider its functions. Entire curricula were built along the principles of giving students an increasingly sophisticated set of objects to study. We don't propose to go back to the nineteenth century object lesson. Nor do we advocate pedagogy based on the popular view of an object lesson being a harsh lesson in reality. Nevertheless, we believe that teaching-by-objects, especially the creation of objects, is an especially rich learning approach. Take an object to class tomorrow and see what comes of, from, and through it.

The Boy Scouts and Girl Scouts do a good job of teaching kids through the production of *objects* in their interdisciplinary, extracurricular program. For example, the Webelos Cub handbook for boys 10 and 11 (Boy Scouts of America 1991) includes projects on such topics as *aquanaut, athlete, communicator, engineer, scientist,* and *traveler,* always with solid objective outcomes: demonstrating water rescue methods, building a piece of athletic equipment, making a Morse Code telegraph, building a model bridge, designing an experiment, collecting and displaying travel information. The kid who has been through any of the Boy or Girl Scout programs graduates with some solid object lessons in a range of interdisciplinary fields.

Another good resource for projects with objective outcomes, now, unfortunately out of print, is *The Great Learning Book* (Bogojavlensky et al. 1977). The authors describe school and home projects for kids eight to eighteen, including such outcomes as pillows, paper airplanes, a magic show, a loaf of bread, an origami zoo, crossword puzzles and other games, safety posters, safe bikes and cars, a ghost story-telling festival, comic books, a "believe it or not" book, kids' own Emmy awards, and a student-made film festival. The book is a glorious testimony to the fact that kids can create things—stuff, goodies, knick-knacks—and learn in the process.

While one might not want to devote a curriculum exclusively to the generation of material objects, one could do worse than to focus the curriculum in this direction.

What did you learn in school today, little boy, little girl?

Learn? Let me show you what I *made!*

Objets d'Art

We want to make a modest distinction between product-driven education that leads to concrete objects and that which leads to the creation of a work of art. Objects are functional, while works of art have meaning that goes beyond the combination of molecules that someone has assembled. At the same time, we don't mean to create a distinction among levels of achievement (where art is traditionally ranked high, shop class low) or to regenerate the distinction between the humanities (which generally side with the arts) and the sciences (that favor technology and functionalism). We value both.

The elementary art teachers of the Poudre School District, Fort Collins, Colorado, phrased it well when they said, "Art is a process that involves thinking, talking, and research—as well as producing art itself. It is an extended effort to make a message clear" (Colorado Department of Education 1992). They could have said much the same of *any* project that leads to creating something interesting and useful.

Some of the Colorado art teachers' imaginative art projects for children are shown in Figure 6–2. Although not every student in the school will necessarily be highly skilled in graphic arts, almost every kid can use art either to enhance presentation and performance of an idea or as a means of expression or recording of final results.

In the Artist badge for Webelos Cub Scouts, kids are taught some fundamentals of drawing and sketching (including perspective and "action lines"), the nature of acrylic and oil paints, the color wheel, how to make a picture frame, some ele-

Animated clay movie or filmstrip	Mural
Puppet show combined with narration	Charts
	Flip books
Posters	Postcards
Advertisements	Sidewalk drawings
Pictionary illustrations of words	Stitchery
Diorama	Pop-up books
Cartoons—may be political	Window-wheel book
Story boards	Paper dolls
Illuminated manuscript	Slides
Greeting cards	Filmstrip
"Blown-up" postage stamps	Origami
Printmaking	Illustrated letters
Cut paper art	Rebus stories
Stencils	Mobiles
Banner	Found objects
Quilt	Sculpture
Flannel board	Mask
Wear art = wearable art	Individual large painting
Photos	Woodcuts
Ceramic tile	Tissue paper/watercolor/ink
Forms rather than flat (bas-relief, 3 dimensional)	Billboards

(Colorado Department of Education, 1992. Reprinted by permission.)

FIG. 6–2   *Ideas for Art as Process*
(Brainstormed in an elementary art teachers' workshop, Poudre School District R-1, Fort Collins, CO)

ments of good design, how to draw a profile, how to make a clay sculpture, how to make a mobile, all "tested" through creation of *objets d'art*.

How do we integrate or employ art in the interdisciplinary classroom? We're not artists or art teachers, but we've plunged in to use art and photography frequently in our teaching.

For example, we often adapt an idea we first saw at professional conferences: the poster presentation. At conventions where the program is packed with great sessions, people often want to get the gist of a presenter's ideas without sitting through the presentation, or they'd like to have a sample before committing themselves to the presentation. In poster sessions, professionals hone their main ideas, print them neatly on a poster board, and then place the poster in a conspicuous place for review by passers-by. Sometimes the presenter stands by his/her display to answer questions.

We added an artistic twist to our adaptation. When students are summing up their work, we will frequently ask them to display it on a poster, complete with complementary graphics. (Note that we say *complementary*, not *decorative*, which is quick to raise the ire of any art teacher.) Students can use collage techniques, "rub off" or computer lettering, clip art, graphs, or their own illustrations or diagrams to highlight a point.

One of the most successful of these projects is our "Word Museum," conducted in an introductory language class. Students are to pick a word that they find interesting or amusing—*skulk, ballad, north, witch*—read about its history in the *Oxford English Dictionary* and look it up in various quotation indexes and poetry concordances to see it in use (Anderson 1991). We also ask students to interview others to determine its modern usage. They are then to squeeze all of their findings onto a poster board and, as much as possible, do a concrete "rendering" of the word. We saw "grass" rendered as green fur (and once, to our dismay, as a plant material of dubious legality), and "skulking" was portrayed as a silhouette of a skulker. (One student came close to fulfilling our boat-building dream by bringing in a reconstruction of a Welsh coracle—a tiny boat flying a banner with the Welsh word for boat—that he almost successfully paddled across our campus lake.) These are words that students take away with them, and in the process, they learn a great deal about the history of the English language, a subject we've found is difficult to teach straight on as information.

In our program at the Pyramid Lake Paiute Reservation, we invited community elders to tell traditional stories about the land: from creation myths to reminiscences of how that land has changed within the elder's lifetime. We then equipped the students with Polaroid cameras and sent them out to photograph the land: mountains, lakes, sagebrush, lizards, and lizard tracks. Finally, they retold the traditional stories, wrote poetry about their own observations of the land, and illustrated their work with both photographs and original drawings.

Carolyn Petty (1988) has argued that the dimensionality of some art projects adds to the intellectual learning that goes on in the classroom.

> To a young child, the world is three-dimensional. His toys, family, and environment come in shapes and sizes with widths, heights, and depths. So, why is it that when a child starts school, he is expected to translate his exciting world onto a flat sheet of paper? (32)

Petty specifically indicts art teachers who insist that in elementary school, drawing must precede sculpture and pottery. But, metaphorically, hers is an indictment of the flat world of textbooks as well; kids should be able to learn and demonstrate learning in multiple dimensions. She goes on to describe how she has children model an Australian koala from Play-Doh and create models of snowflakes, atoms, molecules, and mobiles of the solar system. Molding in plaster of paris not only creates 3-D *objets d'art*, but shows students the nature of endothermic reactions, since plaster gives off heat as it solidifies. As it is with materials science, students explore

FIG. 6–3 *Calvin Creates Objets d'Art. Calvin and Hobbes by Bill Watterson. 2/15/94, Copyright ©️ 1994 Watterson. Distributed by Universal Press Syndicate. Reprinted by permission.*

the media of art and sculpture even while using those media to display their learning and understanding.

Nor should we omit music as an *objet d'art.* Curtis Lichtmann and Barbara Lewis (1985) remind us:

> The ballad has always been a primary medium for the reliving of historic events, allowing the singer to become involved uniquely with past people and situations. Song heightens the impact of storytelling, adding a vitality missing from mere textbook description. (37)

One of their high school history units begins with such songs of the Civil War period as "The Battle Hymn of the Republic," "Deep River," "Swing Low, Sweet Chariot," and "Dixie." From there, students go on to create ballads surrounding historical events. Some student writing teams create their own tunes, while other groups write lyrics to mesh with classical ballad tunes or contemporary songs.

Fairs, Displays, Collections, and Exhibits

The science fair seems to us an especially good way of translating student learning into a concrete form and sharing learning with others. Often the fair is a school-wide project, and everybody from kindergarten on up conducts a science project and creates a display. Kids display gumdrop-and-toothpick models of molecules, lima beans growing hydroponically, the migration habits of worms in earthworm farms, the effects of catch-and-release programs on fish health (Gordon 1994). When kids prepare for the science fair, they are *doing* science, and as parents/veterans of innumerable science fairs over twenty-plus years, we can testify to the learning that takes place. We only wish that more science teachers used this approach day-in and day-out, rather than returning to the textbook once the fair is over.

We often end classes with something we call "The Country Fair." Students display whatever they have been doing over the term or unit, as always, making it graphically interesting. A fair might find some students exhibiting written work, others enacting a skit they have written (see next item), still others showing a videotape or a collection. When visitors come to the fair, we give them a fistful of blue ribbons (actually, rectangles of blue paper) and have them create prize categories (e.g., Best Poem on the Death of a Goldfish, Weirdest Video). The visitors then attach these ribbons to projects they find especially interesting, and as it turns out, all students go home with some prizes that explain what was good about their work.

Drama as a Way of Knowing

From these sorts of demonstrations and displays, it is but a short leap to drama. The value of a dramatic approach has been brought home to us through our connections with the Great Basin Chautauqua (sha-*taw*-kwa), a humanities program in Nevada for which we supply a teacher institute. The original chautauqua took place at the upstate New York lake of the same name; it was an extension of the Sunday school and featured a summer tent show with lots of preaching, singing, and educational lectures. The chautauqua movement spread, both in content and geography, and until well into the 1920s, roaming the rural areas of America, bringing learning and entertainment to people. After dying out because of the competition of radio, the chautauqua has been revived, but with a new twist: Humanities scholars learn about an historical character's life and "become" the character, performing the person under the tent show.

Two of the students in our summer institute program, Diane Beebe and Launie Gardner of Sparks (Nevada) High School, thought the chautauqua idea could work in their urban school, where kids are known for being unexcited about American history and literature. Under their leadership, kids at Sparks High selected Western American characters—from the famous Annie Oakley to the infamous Julia Bulette, a legendary prostitute in historical Virginia City—and had students work up dramatic performances. The students performed under the chautauqua tent to rapt audiences. They also entered a Nevada History Day competition. As Launie has written:

> I have to say that for the first time in my teaching career students have been actively responsible for their own learning. My teaching partner and I played only a minor role in guiding students to resources, checking to make certain they followed formats, and stayed within the limits of our theme. I can think of no better way to teach students than to bring the subject alive and to make each student active participant. (Gardner 1993)

During the time this book was being written, fifth grader Chris Tchudi joined the chautauqua program and developed the character of the young Kit Carson. Chris researched Carson's life and prepared a dramatic presentation that told the story up to Kit's twenty-first year. The contrast between Chris's interest in his regular school work and his chautauqua scholarship—yes, the chautauquans call it "scholarship"—was remarkable. Not content with simply learning about the facts of Carson's life as one might in the usual history class, Chris raised difficult and interesting questions: Did the Louisiana Purchase come before or after Kit Carson's birth, and what did that have to do with his desire to leave his Missouri home and move west? Where can we get a map that shows the locations of western rivers when they had different names—the "Salida" instead of the "Salt," the "San Francisco" rather than the present-day "Rio Verde"? Chris performed successfully under the chautauqua tent and fielded a series of difficult questions with aplomb. His performance led to an invitation to perform again at the Nevada State Fair and to participate in performances and discussions in area schools.

Charles LaRocca (1993), a teacher in Pine Bush, New York, writes with enthusiasm of his work in having students do Civil War reenactments. His classroom drama is based around the 124th New York State Volunteers, "the famed 'Orange Blossoms,' an historic regiment recruited in Orange County in the summer of 1862." For over a decade LaRocca has encouraged his students to conduct research using newspapers, letters, diaries, and photographs leading to presentations for schools and civic groups. In a follow-up survey of a decade's worth of former students, LaRocca found that his students had a high degree of agreement that the project improved their attitude toward social studies, and that they believed it enhanced their school achievement.

Drama is by no means limited to history/English/social studies classes and has an extraordinary range of applications in interdisciplinary settings. Students can:

- roleplay historical figures in the sciences.

- present science articles and even textbook chapters as reader's theater, with students taking parts to talk their way through their understanding of key concepts.

- write one-act plays that highlight important ethical questions underlying scientific problems or achievements: "Now that we know the underground waste chamber is leaking, Mr. Industrialist, what do you suppose we should do about it?"

- improvise alternative solutions to problems such as the one immediately above: What happens if the Industrialist says, "Sit on it"? Or, "It's our responsibility to clean up the mess"?

- do puppet plays with atoms, molecules, microbes, viruses, and other wee beasties.

- create a series of "two-minute mysteries," where students roleplay discussions of problems or "mysteries" in a field or (inter)discipline: the death of dinosaurs, who really "discovered" America, whether or not there is a greenhouse effect. Let audience members interact with the players or suggest appropriate endings to these minidramas.

Games and Simulations

From drama, it's just a hop over the floodlights to the area of game and simulation design. Any game, after all, is a minidrama: *Clue* recreates a mystery and acts out the answer to a dramatic question, "Who killed whom with what weapon and where?" *Monopoly* simulates tycoonery and the competition for hotel space.

Moreover, games can (and do) both *teach* and *measure* learning. Your students can develop games centered on classroom topics that will be fun to play and will demonstrate mastery of a topic in several ways: The game *designer* must know the area very well in order to be able to create a game; the *player* must have done his/her homework in order to play it successfully.

English teacher Barbara Warren (1988) writes,

> My students have been designing games as an alternative to writing term papers for the past three years. While three or four per year admit they had rather have completed the research papers, the rest are overwhelmingly in favor of the games, which range in content from vocabulary to figures of speech, from mythology to grammar, from listening skills to literature. (12)

In helping students design games, she has them consider:

- *overall design* (her students mostly do board-style games like Monopoly)

- *time limits*

- *the clarity and coherence of directions*

- *questions and tasks,* in particular, considering whether problems or questions are within the grasp of fellow students

- *answers, with emphasis on fair, impartial judging*

- *mechanics* (meaning mechanics of language and the overall correctness and thoroughness of the game and its rules). She also has the students do a careful self-evaluation.

We see games as very closely linked to *simulations*, the main difference being that a simulation does not require elaborate points, rules, and winners and losers. Like a good game, a simulation will be a reasonably accurate portrayal of an authentic situation or problem; it will engage students in critical thinking about solutions; it will require an understanding of the (inter)discipline in order for a student to play.

We've offered game or simulation design as a form of presentation and performance for years and have had students develop some ingenious products: *The Daily Newspaper Simulation* (selecting and choosing stories, creating the first page of a tabloid); the *Student-Teacher Game* (involving the survival skills of the new teacher); *Nuclear Disposal* (a simulation of the nuclear waste problem); and a vari-

When designing a simulation or a game, consider:

1. What is the core knowledge or the core concepts on which the game will be based? Be sure you *know*. (Example: For a game called *Origins*: "What are the major theories of the origins of life?")

2. You can't have a game without *conflict*. What are some competing or conflicting ideas that create tension for your game or simulation? (For *Greenhouse Effect,* a central conflict will be the need for economic growth versus preserving ecology.)

3. How can you represent reality? Can you squeeze it onto a playing board? Can you squeeze it into our classroom-as-stage? (For *The Automobile in American Life*, one could represent the acquisition of driving skills as a series of stopping points on the trail of a board game, or you could simulate it by having students go through various steps in order to get a license to balance an egg on their noses.)

4. Set up rewards and penalties. For a game, this will usually involve points. For a simulation, you try to build in simulated consequences. (In *Doctor, Doctor,* a board game version might have a "chance" card that kills a patient. In the simulation, failure to call for a vital test means that the patient dies, and the simulation is over.)

5. Develop your game or simulation through pilot tests. It is almost impossible to get either one right the first time. So develop the game or simulation by playing it yourself.

6. Write extremely clear rules. Read them critically looking for loopholes (your players certainly will!). Commit yourself to writing early in the process; do not depend on memory or conversation to get the rules into good shape.

FIG. 6–4 *Gaming and Simulation Gambits*

ation on the commercial game of *Authors*, where students not only have to identify a writer's work, but provide a response to it.

Virtually any of the interdisciplinary topics we've suggested in this book can be turned into a game: fast food, ecology, the economy, geography, outer space exploration, dinosaurs. Figure 6–4 summarizes some of the rules and suggestions we review whenever our students create a game or a simulation.

Oral Language as Performance

"Talk is cheap," goes the old saying. We prefer to say, "Talk is inexpensive and fundamental." Oral language is an extraordinarily useful mode of presentation, one that has been underused in schools. Too often "instruction in oral language" is taken to mean "speeches," where kids prepare five-minute talks and are criticized for their lack of eye contact. Without devaluing these oral reports (clearly several of the productions we described earlier in this chapter rely on oral presentations), we want to invite the reader to think of all the ways in which knowledge and understanding is transmitted through talk.

InterMusing

Keep a one-day record of the role of oral language as an information-bearer in your life. Split a page into two columns:

Type of Talk	Information Conveyed

For example, if you get your news by radio, write down the programs and the information provided.

| 6 a.m. "breakfast club" | local news, sports |
| 9 a.m. Rush Limbaugh | conservative viewpoint |

If you are a phone-in junkie, list that as well, along with what you pick up from listening to the phone-ins and the host's responses.

List other media, conversations, lectures, presentations, and so on, then consider the classroom implications of the list you've developed. Most of these real-world uses of talk can be turned into modes of presentation or performance for your class.

As our InterMusing on this topic suggests, you can pretty quickly come up with a long list of oral discourse forms that will work in your classroom.

In addition to the oral report we recommend the use of:

- *Debates.* You can follow formal rules for debate with timed speeches and rebuttals, or you can do a less formal debate where students take turns. You can score a debate formally, have students vote on a winner, or (perhaps most useful) have other students talk about how a debate has shaped their view of a topic. In our experience, most kids love debates, and almost any interdisciplinary topic you can name lends itself to phrasing in a question that will initially split your debaters along two-value lines but eventually allow them to talk of consensus and agreement or synthesis.

- *Soap Box Oratory.* At Speakers' Corner, Hyde Park, Londoners traditionally gather on Sundays to hear tub-thumping speeches on political and social issues. The classroom adaptation is to offer the soap box at one-minute intervals from time to time for students to get out ideas that are really important. At Hyde Park, audience members are free to heckle. We discourage that in schools, but we think that soap box orators ought to be willing to defend their positions or respond to people with differing views.

- *Talk Shows.* This is the national media rage. The talk show format invites a variety of classroom approaches. Your class expert on a topic can be the talk show host, skillfully interviewing others who have learned something about it. Or your host can be somebody in the class who knows nothing about the topic but can raise good questions. Students can be themselves on the show, or they can roleplay important people in the field.

- *Telephone Conference Calls* or *Interactive Video Conferences.* Although these electronic conversations can also be used at the information gathering stage of a project, they also make good culminating activities. After your students have researched an issue of statewide importance, get the governor or an aide on the line for a discussion via the school's video hookup; after your students have researched automobile recalls, get the public relations person for an auto company on phone via a conference call.

- *Questions and Answers.* Instead of having kids do reports, let them field questions.

- *Panel Discussions* or *Seminars.* At the college level, we find that very few students are highly skilled at participating—truly participating—in discussions. Often they merely take turns making statements or assertions or broadside rebuttals, rather than building on the previous speaker's remarks. Panels-as-performances require students to do more than recite in turn. Help your students focus panels on orally solving a real problem: "Who did write Shakespeare's plays?" "Would reform of the welfare system put more people back to work?" "What is the best hypothesis about the death of the dinosaurs?"

- *Interim Reports.* Although we've been stressing *final* products and performances, oral language is an especially useful tool early on and midway through a unit. Have students talk about their knowledge-in-the-making, what they're learning and not learning, what's becoming clearer or murkier, what they plan to do next. Have them answer in-process questions from fellow students, questions that will give direct hints as to what needs to be done in future research.

- *Dramatic Readings.* There *is* drama to be found in writing about the arts, the sciences, literature, history, social studies, and even physical education and home improvement. Even the dustiest of knowledge can be turned into powerful drama. (Look what Christopher Marlowe did with a scholar's scholar, Dr. Faustus of Wittenberg U.) Students can dramatically read the writing of others—say, a good Loren Eiseley or Annie Dillard essay—or their own writing, with vim and vigor. Because all writing involves interaction between an author and reader, it all has an element of drama to it. Kids need to overcome their shyness about oral reading to do it well, and one way to do that is for teachers to stress the content of the reading, rather than (as often happens) using oral reading as a test of reading skills. What we're advocating then, is a sort of reading-across-the-curriculum approach where you use oral, dramatic reading to accomplish genuine instructional ends and—in the process—actually help kids learn to read better.

Technology and Media

The availability of inexpensive, easy-to-use visual and audio media in our time gives the teacher a rich arsenal of alternative ways of having students present information and ideas. What's particularly important, we believe, is that teachers consider ways of using classroom media not simply as ways of transmitting information passively, but as ways of synthesizing and communicating ideas, of presenting them *persuasively*.

Among the positive, presentational uses of media that are well suited to the interdisciplinary classroom are:

- *Video production.* Make no mistake about it, to create a *good* video using amateur or school video equipment is a demanding task. Any tourist can take a camcorder out in the street and shoot some stuff and play it back; the results of such casual video are predictably boring and uninformative, no better than Uncle Winslow's summer vacation slides. To be successful, student videos need to be carefully planned and edited. Aside from technical matters of planning shots, a *designed* video also requires students to organize and synthesize their learning prior to production. The first question is not "What pictures should we take?" but "What have we learned?" From a carefully designed project, an outline or shooting script grows, leading, in turn, to precise and careful editing.[1]

- *Photography.* Video and TV have taken some of the lustre off photography, but the technological advances in this area have been every bit as fantastic as they are in TV technology. New cameras—from point-and-shoot to sophisticated single-lens reflex models—make it relatively easy for students to get professional-looking results from their photographic forays. Films get faster every year with even more saturated colors and fine grain prints. One-hour or overnight development services make it possible to put together photo or slide exhibits in a day or two. Students can also transfer their slides and prints to CD-ROM units for computers, getting gloriously colorful shots on the screen. Many feel that in the not-too-distant future, film will be largely replaced by electronic cameras, basically "still" video recorders.

  We are partial to a form of presentation called the "slide tape," with 35 millimeter slides—still the most dramatic form of color photography, in our opinion—shown with an accompanying tape-recorded commentary (or done

---

1. It is beyond the scope of this book to go into production techniques for the various media productions we describe in this section. Help is available for the teacher who wants to go the media route that ranges from school media specialists to salespeople to how-to books in the library. Our own experience suggests that one must be relatively fearless in tackling a new medium. There's much to be learned by just doin' it.

live with a script). The same approach can also be a computer "slide" show. We also like a display of photographs—color or black and white—as a measure of student work. In science, students can do dramatic closeup works of experiments in progress; in history, they can photograph local sites or rephotograph portraits and maps from history texts; in art they can photograph their own work to avoid carrying it around; in geography they can turn field trips into photographic reports.

- *Computer Presentations.* Increasingly computer hardware and software includes multimedia capabilities. Scanners can turn photographs or drawings into computer images; video signals can be fed into a computer, frozen on the screen, turned into pictures, and be electronically pasted into a newsletter, making the phrase "up-to-the-minute news" a literal reality. Draw and paint programs let students create attractive diagrams; spreadsheets and databases allow them to array research information easily and even to calculate basic statistics on the screen. Hypertext programs—multidimensional, "interactive" texts—allow a reader to browse through and receive supplementary information on items of interest, creating a wealth of opportunities for presentations.[2] In computer work, as with perhaps no other area in education, students are often way ahead of teachers in thinking of possibilities. While writing this book, we attended a dazzling display of computer wizardry by high school students from Norfolk, Virginia, using a hot new program called a Video Spigot to pour images into their computers and from there into slick presentations about their interdisciplinary work and interests. But that technology will be dated by the time you begin thinking about applications for your own class.

- *Computer Networking.* We also think of computer nets as a form of performance—output as well as input. While browsing the Internet, we came across a description of what some call a "virtual university," an institute that would exist not in a physical location, but along the intersections of the electronic highway. Not only would this university provide instant access to a richer variety of information sources than is presently available in any library, it would also be a source of collaboration among scholars, a pooling of discussion of experiments and research, an outreach center getting new ideas to people who need them, an archive of papers and ideas produced by its members, and feature an on-line, real-time series of seminars and colloquia. Increasingly images as well as words will be part of the virtual university. The World Wide Web branch of the Internet creates hypertext presentations that combine many media and give students a global audience. Students can cre-

---

2. Here, too, the rapidly changing nature of computer multimedia makes it unwise for us to comment in detail about specific products. What is cutting edge as of this writing may be old-fashioned or obsolete by the time the book sees print. Computer magazines do a good job of keeping you up on what's available for your own machine. So do catalogs of computer hardware and software. If you're not a computer junkie, a browse through a computer catalog every six months or so will keep you up to date.

ate web pages growing from specific thematic units or from their work in various (inter)disciplinary classes. One web site we visited electronically, an on-line display of young people's writing, reported receiving over 65,000 "hits" or log-ons. Few professional print writers have that size audience for their work. In the future, your students will have an audience for their work beyond any that we have imagined: They will be able to perform, not only for you and their fellow students, but for kids in all areas of the world.[3]

■ *Using the Media and Media Literacy.* "Media literacy" is a phrase that has been around schools for a couple of decades, and most teachers would agree that "media literacy" should be a part of education. However, as so often happens with new trends and fads, many educators have taken a somewhat narrow look at the concept. Computer literacy, for example, often means little more than an introduction to keyboarding skills and computer terminology. Film literacy means the mastery of some technical terms about filmmaking, or maybe knowing what a "key grip" (always acknowledged in the credits) actually does. We want to argue that true media literacy is represented by what students do, often on their own, when they confront a new product, gizmo or program: push it to its limits. Whenever you give kids a new electronic game to play, they figure out how to beat it most efficiently. If you give them an interesting new educational program, they figure out how to use it for some purpose other than it was intended. Thus we'd like to suggest that when it comes to performances and presentations, you give students the challenge of pushing the media to their limits. See how you can have your students express their knowledge and understanding through:

• *xerography*, black-and-white or color, machines that shrink copy and enlarge it

• *electronic chalkboards*, those great devices that record and photocopy what you write on them

• *the overhead projector*, dependable and potentially dramatic; and don't forget the good old *opaque projector*, that projects images of any object or piece of print

• *computer programs*: word processing, databases, spreadsheets, outlining programs, graphics programs, computer "movies," CD-ROM archives

• *flip charts*, those old-fashioned but still interesting sheets of paper

• *bulletin boards*

• *the school P.A. system*

. . . and so on.

---

3. Here again news is breaking very rapidly. Just a few years ago, "cutting edge" teachers would have students mail computer disks to other kids in other parts of the world. Now such a technique seems Stone Age. As we write, all over the country youngsters are tapping into the Internet, working with one another through commercial networks such as CompuServe and America Online. A hot new program called "Netscape" goes beyond the text bias of the Internet to permit integration of sound and graphics. Our advice: Stay tuned.

The Second 'R: Writing

We've saved writing for near the end of this catalog of presentational modes, in part because this is one of our areas of provincial interest, but principally because even in this media-centered, talk-oriented world of ours, writing remains a mainstay of the school curriculum. Writing, like talk, is cheap and effective, and the writing-across-the curriculum movement of the past two decades has persuaded many people that writing is a best way of synthesizing and exploring learning. Kids simply learn more when they write about what they have explored and accomplished.

Many teachers outside the area of the English/language arts initially balk at becoming writing teachers. First, they say, it's the English teacher's job to correct spelling and grammar. Second, they add, they don't have *time* to include writing because of the theme grading required. Third, they continue, they were not trained in writing instruction and feel perplexed and frustrated by it.

This is not the place for us to go into an in-depth exploration of the teaching of writing. (See Tchudi 1984, 1986 for a discussion of content-area writing.) But we do want to offer some suggestions for the interdisciplinary teacher who is not an English major on how to use writing successfully for interdisciplinary projects:

1. *Have students write in "real" writing forms.* Don't just have them write papers or or reports. Figure 6–5 provides a long list of just some of the writing forms that students can use, ranging from informal notes to and through creative or imaginative forms. You can assign particular forms (e.g., "Write about your history project as a magazine article") or give students a choice (e.g., science fiction, magazine article, or proposal). Being specific about the form of the writing also helps with the next item.

2. *Have students write for audiences other than the teacher.* Even if it is only fellow students in school—your class or another—help students see that their writing should be read by someone other than the teacher. In interdisciplinary work, community audiences are often possible, so look for places beyond the classroom where students can send their writing.

3. *Teach writing by stages.* Don't assign a paper, wait for it to come in, then tell the students what they did wrong. Rather, provide time for students to discuss their ideas before they write, to exchange and discuss rough drafts, to give a copy to you for review before they put the project to bed. Although time consuming, actually this planning time is *learning time*, and by treating writing in stages, you are working to ensure not only that the writing is good, but that the learning is secure. It also cuts *way* down on theme grading time.

4. *Put correctness and mechanics in context.* Good spelling and standard English are important, especially when papers are being sent to audiences outside the classroom. But don't become obsessed with surface correctness. When students are drafting, have them work first on the content: what they want to say

Edited notes or journal	Song
Field notes or learning log	Essay or commentary
Notebook/scrapbook	Editorial
Reading report	Telegram
I-search paper	Bulletin board
Micro-theme/postcard essay	Poster display
Letter	Satire
to editors	Advertisement
to classmates	Commercial
to e-mail pen pals	Guerrilla theater
to elected officials	Reader's theater
Community forum	One-act play
Newspaper article	TV script
Biography	Cable TV show
Proposal and proposition	Slide tape
Feature article	Collage or montage
Question and answer column	Photo essay
Critical review	Magazine
Monologue or dialogue	
Radio interview	And writing in support of projects, e.g.:
Fiction	Community project
Fantasy	Museum collection
Adventure tale	Painting or photograph
Science fiction	Dance or mime
Historical fiction	Invention or gizmo
Books for young readers	
Collaborative novel	Or personal projects, writing:
Riddles	Leisure plans
Jokes	Future scenario
Poetry of all sorts	Finding a career

FIG. 6–5 *Writing as Performance*

and how they say it. Focus your responses on the content as well—is the paper *working*, are the ideas *coming through*, does this *make sense*, does it *tell the truth*? Then, just before papers come in, have students carefully polish their work. They should use the computer spell-checker if they have one or another reader if they don't. They should read their paper aloud to themselves (a sure cure for myriad errors). They should ask questions if they are uncertain about language use. Most kids have better control of English than we think, but they don't always apply it.

5. *Focus grading and evaluation on content.* Don't become a Mr. or Ms. Fidditch and deduct points simply for grammar or spelling. Rather, focus on the ideas of the writing. If the student's language interferes with comprehension then you have to take that into account. For the most part, however, focusing on the content of a paper automatically requires the students to use their best language. What else could you want?

Don't be buffaloed by writing. Get help from the English/language arts faculty if you have questions. But know that your understanding of your (inter)discipline makes you a natural teacher of writing, especially if you're focused on the principal idea of this chapter: that knowledge and understanding developed by students shouldn't be kept in a vacuum; that it should be shared in the most effective ways possible.

Ethics, Understanding, and Decision Making as Performance

In the past several decades, schools have increasingly taken on new areas of instruction in response to public demand. Sex, once a taboo in schools, is now seen as an instructional responsibility, coupled with discussion of teenage mores, restraint, and decision making. Critical thinking is seen as an important skill, so units and lessons are developed to be squeezed into overstuffed curricula. The government declares war on drugs, and teachers become the foot soldiers carrying the students to the battle lines through instructional programs. Students are seen as deficient in their culture, so we teach cultural literacy. They allegedly lack moral and ethical convictions, so courses in ethics and values education spring up. Computer literacy a problem? Let's set up a lab and send the students to it once or twice a week. Students are said not to be able to apply their learning, so faculty members attend workshops on "teaching for understanding" and are told to weave that into the curriculum. Your kid can't get a job? We'll add careerism to the school curriculum.

One of our British friends once chuckled about an American trait: "Every time you discover a bit of new knowledge, you invent a course around it." His alternative possibility, one with which we are naturally sympathetic, is to seek new ways of integration rather than adding each new element in its own isolated box.

As we draw this chapter to a close, we want to argue that the worthy ideals described two paragraphs ago can not only be included in the curriculum, but can be handled comfortably within the (non)confines of an interdisciplinary classroom, *especially one that values student performances as an outcome.* Following are some possibilities for your classroom.

Volunteerism

Increasingly across the country secondary and even elementary schools are finding an outlet for student understanding and knowledge through volunteerism. Our own students at the college level, in addition to serving as tutors and teacher aides, have volunteered their time to a host of public service agencies. This work can be linked to a variety of courses from "Science and Society" to "Childhood and Adolescence." Wesleyan University has created a fellowship program that rewards high school students who engage in public service programs in their area and provides financial support for their college work (Sommerfield 1993). Kids in Detroit have developed a seven-acre nature and fitness center as an outgrowth of their school science work (Raymond 1988). One of the kids in that project turned portions of it into a science fair presentation, won the grand prize, and earned himself a trip to Stockholm, Sweden, to sit in on the Nobel Prize ceremonies.

In our age of generally restricted town budgets, communities are crying out for volunteers. Local libraries often maintain lists of public service organizations (in addition to needing volunteer help themselves), and we guarantee that in any community, you can find agencies that will not only be seeking help, but can provide a proof-of-learning for your teaching: a hands-on, real-world, applied experience that most students will find superior to any term paper or exam they have ever written.

Ethical Questions

Susan Downie (1989) of the Virginia Beach schools poses ethical problems for her students to consider:

> Jane's father is dying. Should she authorize life support for him or allow him to die? Cindy works for a cosmetic company that tests its products on a large number of animals. Is this testing justifiable? Joe works for a large chemical company that dumps its wastes into a canal near residential property. Despite his excellent salary and a large family to support, can Joe ethically continue his career? (28)

She describes an interdisciplinary program involving teachers of English, social studies, physics, and calculus who taught eleventh and twelfth graders about decision-making processes. Community members came in to discuss issues; students wrote, researched, presented, and defended their beliefs in public. Our only quarrel with this unit is that, once again, it seems to isolate ethics rather than treating ethical questions on a daily basis. What happens after the unit is over? Why not include these ethical issues in daily work?

The *Science, Technology, Society* movement seems to us to be at the forefront of bringing ethics questions into the classroom, not as contrived units on "doing the right thing," but by supplying students with real-world problems. Ethical questions are then linked to scientific and technological wisdom and discovery. "What should we do with nuclear waste?" "Do we have an obligation to end the increases in carbon monoxide emission?"

Ethical questions can evolve from any field or (inter)discipline. Your students can ask questions about economics ("What are we doing to future generations if we don't balance the budget?"); history ("Does history repeat itself, and if so, what does our history tell us about U.S. involvement in the current 'brushfire' war?"); literature ("What do Jay Gatsby's values tell us about how our society lives?"); the arts ("Does pornography degrade women and children?"); and education ("Do creationism and evolution deserve to be treated as intellectual equals?" "Are tests fair?").

Other ethics-centered topics reported in professional literature include "Education to Live in a Nuclear Age" (Sagor 1991), "Racism in America" (Molnar 1989), and "Understanding Must Begin with Us"—a look at multiculturalism, including the topic of the incarceration of Japanese-Americans during World War II (Higuchi, 1993). Some of these issues are sensitive, and one must proceed with great caution in many schools and communities—we don't want ethics tossed out because of a community uproar. Nevertheless, we want to make the case that a discussion of ethics, or even more important, a change in kids' ethical systems, is not only a desirable but necessary end product of education.

Global Issues and Multicultural Concerns

Barbara Levak, Merry Merryfield, and Robert Wilson (1993) centered their work around developing global awareness in Reynoldsburg, Ohio, a city of 25,000 people. Pooling specialties in art, biology, social studies, mathematics, and English, the teachers developed a unit on "global connections." They looked at biological ecosystems, literature reflecting cultural differences, art depicting cross-cultural awareness, and literal and figurative bridges (this last leading to construction of "a full-size rope bridge in the school courtyard") (74). Their work led to a variety of products and presentations and the students saw that,

> For once, schoolwork relates to their out-of-school learning experiences. They now see themselves as part of a larger world, where their lives touch and are touched by the myriad lives of others. (75)

Obviously the products and performances by these teachers are similar to those we've already discussed in this chapter: A global or multicultural unit might lead to writing, drama, video production, computer displays, and miscellaneous projects. Our point is that the outcome is actually much broader and much more fundamental than a mere product that demonstrates learning. There's a good chance that the final product is a changed attitude toward other people, an awareness of people, issues, and concerns beyond one's immediate neighborhood. We're talking about lifelong learning here, and application of knowledge well beyond the traditional goals of schooling.

In discussing teaching units with ethnic or multicultural content, James Banks (1994) describes four "evolutionary" levels for including multiethnic or multicultural content in the curriculum:

1. The contributions level: with focus on the contributions of various cultures to our life, especially through holidays, ethnic foods, etc.

2. The additive approach: where concepts and content are added to the curriculum systematically.

3. The transformational approach: where materials are so fully integrated that courses represent diverse perspectives, not simply multiculturalism from an American or western perspective.

4. The social action approach: which leads students to take action or make decisions reflecting their understanding.

While we applaud all four levels in any curriculum, clearly level four and, to some extent, level three are the ones that move in the direction of performance as an outcome.

Decision Making and Problem Solving

In *The Young Learner's Handbook*, Stephen Tchudi (1987) developed a series of models to help youngsters see how they can apply knowledge and information that they have acquired themselves. Students can use their learning to:

- *reach decisions* by weighing facts and evaluating pros and cons.

- *solve problems* by systematically identifying possible solutions and predicting the probabilities of success as well as estimating negative or unanticipated outcomes.

- *create applications and inventions* by assessing what they know and projecting the principles involved into new areas or settings.

- *set and achieve personal goals* by figuring out what they know, what they need to know, and how they can move toward completing specific projects that they value.

- *predict the future* by studying the past and present and making intelligent prophesies.

These applications and extensions of learning are *not* the sort of thing one treats in isolated units. They are processes that ought to be built into every unit, and we see the culminating stage—the stage of performances and products—as the place to make certain they are included.

Theory Building and Systematic Doubt

Lastly, we want to touch on the value of having students construct theories, not only as a guide to inquiry, but as a final product. We admit to having fallen into some jargon as we talk of "the creation of knowledge," a phrase that makes learning sound deceptively like a nicely stacked ice cream cone or a tower of blocks.

As we know, knowledge is slippery stuff. It is based on the gooey substratum of personal belief. It is buffeted by winds of intellectual fashion. It is warped by the pressures of selfishness and personal gain (and even subject to the distortion of mixed metaphors!). "Pure" knowledge is a very rare commodity, and so is its cousin—knowledge unbiased by personal perspective.

So we want to suggest that to draw an interdisciplinary unit to a close, the final performance might be construction of theories that move toward the *unexplained* and *unanswered*. Students can generate new questions to be explored and investigated, even questions that they suppose may never be answered. At the close of a doctoral dissertation defense, it is traditional for the committee to quiz the candidate about his or her perception of unanswered questions. We suggest a similar application at the close of interdisciplinary units. After appropriate praise for the students' accomplishments—that rope bridge across the playground, the play that we've just put on for school—students should spend some time answering questions like the following:

- What have we overlooked in our study?

- Are there still areas where we are uncertain?

- What do we suppose will happen next as this (inter)discipline develops?

- What additional questions have come as a result of our study?

- Where would we like to go next?

The very last of these suggests the recursive nature of lifelong, interdisciplinary learning. When students offer imaginative ideas about what to ask next, the teacher begins to fade into the background and kids take over their own learning: a bravura performance on the part of both the students and the teacher.

References

ADLER, M. AND C. VAN DOREN. 1977. *A Treasury of Western Thought*. New York: R.R. Bowker.

ANDERSON, G. 1990. "I-Search a Word." *The English Journal* 79(1): 53–58.

BANKS, J. 1994. *An Introduction to Multicultural Education*. Boston: Allyn and Bacon.

BOGOJAVLENSKY, A.R. AND D.R. GROSSMAN, WITH C.S. TOPHAM AND S.M. MEYER III. 1977. *The Great Learning Book*. Menlo Park, CA: Addison-Wesley.

BOY SCOUTS OF AMERICA. 1991. *Webelos Scout Book*. Irving, Texas: Boy Scouts of America.

COLORADO DEPARTMENT OF EDUCATION. 1992. "P.A.W. Process of Art and Writing." Denver: Colorado Department of Education.

DOWNIE, S. 1989. "Ethics, a Choice for the Future: An Interdisciplinary Program." *The English Journal*. September 1989, 28–31.

GARDNER, L. 1993. "The Chautauqua Approach in the High School." *Silver Sage* September.

GORDON, S. 1994. "Science Projects Push Imaginations to the Limit." *Reno Gazette-Journal* 31 January 1994. 6B.

HIGUCHI, C. 1993. "Understanding Must Begin with Us." *Educational Leadership* 50(8): 69–71.

JACOBS, M. n.d. "Our Material World: Resources in Technology" (Handout at the 9th Technological Literacy Conference, Arlington, VA, January 1993).

LAROCCA, C. 1993. "Civil War Reenactments—'A Real and Complete Image'." *Educational Leadership* 50(7): 42–45

LEVAK, B.A., R.C. WILSON, AND M.M. MERRYFIELD. 1993. "Global Connections." *Educational Leadership* 51(1): 73–75.

LICHTMANN, C. AND B. LEWIS. 1985. "A Composer Teams with Student Lyricists to Make History Live." *Music Education Journal* (October 1985). 37–38.

MCMURRY, C.A. 1924. *Teaching by Projects: A Basis for Purposeful Study.* New York: The Macmillan Company.

MOLNAR, A. 1989. "Racism in America." *Educational Leadership.* 47(2): 71–73.

NATIONAL AERONAUTICS AND SPACE ADMINISTRATION. 1992. *Microgravity: A Teacher's Guide with Activities.* Washington, DC: NASA Office of Human Resources and Education.

PERKINS, D. AND T. BLYTHE. 1994. "Putting Understanding Up Front." *Educational Leadership* 51(5): 4–7.

PETTY, C.A. 1988. "3-D Potpourri." *Science and Children* April 1988. 32–34.

RAYMOND, R. 1988. "From Stumpsitter to Stockholm." *Michigan Natural Resources Magazine* January/February 1988, 5–9.

SAGOR, R. 1991. "Educating Students to Live in a Nuclear Age." *Education Digest.* 56(8): 3–7.

SCHACK, G.D. 1993. "Involving Students in Authentic Research." *Educational Leadership* 50(7): 29–31.

SOMMERFIELD, M. 1993. "To Promote Service Habit, Wesleyan Creates Award for High School Students." *Education Week.* 29 September 1993, 9.

SPRAGUE, M.M. 1993. "From Newspapers to Circuses—The Benefits of Production-Driven Learning." *Educational Leadership.* 50(7): 68–70.

TCHUDI, S. 1987. *The Young Learner's Handbook: A Guide to Mastering Skills, Thinking Creatively.* New York: Charles Scribner's Sons.

TCHUDI, S., et al. 1984, 1986. *Teaching Writing in the Content Areas.* 4 vols.: Elementary, Middle/Junior High, Senior High, College. Washington, DC: National Education Association.

WARD, G. 1988. *I've Got a Project On.* Rozelle, NSW, Australia: Primary English Teaching Association.

WARREN, B.L. 1988. "Designing Games." *Gifted Child Teacher.* 11(2): 12–14.

WHITEHEAD, A.N. 1929. *The Aims of Education and Other Essays.* New York: Macmillan.

WINNETT, S.J. 1993. "Technology for Fun." *The Technology Teacher.* 53(2): 13–21.

7

What's Going On in There?
Assessment, Evaluation, and Grading in the Interdisciplinary Classroom

athy Mathers (1993) writes: "One of the nicest compliments I ever received came from a visitor who popped into my classroom one day, watched my students hard at work on a wide variety of projects, and asked, 'Just what is it that you teach, anyway?'" Cathy explains that her students were variously working on a public service advertising campaign, making a video, writing a letter to the editor, and developing a community service project. She continues, "there were so many things going on that this could have been a science or social studies class just as easily as English." (65)

Cathy takes great joy (as do we) in the range of activities in her classroom, but one can also anticipate hearing a less joyful voice, that of a parent or school administrator or other visitor saying, "Just what *is* going on in that classroom? How do you know all this chaos is leading to learning? How do we know this isn't just fun and games? How do we know . . . ?"

We'll turn down the volume on that skeptical voice for a few pages to take up a discussion of how assessment and evaluation in the interdisciplinary classroom can answer those tough questions. But it is important to listen for a voice (and to a similar voice within every responsible teacher) that sounds a note of deep concern among community members and educational leaders when it comes to non-traditional instruction. What delights us interdisciplinarians and may seem like a highly successful project may be largely incomprehensible to the outsider not schooled in interdisciplinary approaches. Before you reach the end of the chapter, we hope that you can turn up the volume, listen to that outsider's voice and then (as we know Cathy Mathers can) reply clearly and articulately, with evidence: "Well, to begin with, what we are learning in here is . . ."

What is *Evaluation*?: Making Distinctions

It is vital to offer some definitions and discuss distinctions among the three key terms on which this chapter is founded: *assessment*, *evaluation*, and *grading*. These are summarized in Figure 7-1.

Assessment is the broadest form of measurement, using the greatest range of techniques and strategies. It has to do with describing what's happening generally and with figuring out what's going on. If your automobile stops on the freeway, common sense dictates that the first thing you do is *assess* the situation by a variety of measures: You look at the gas gauge first to see if there's fuel in the tank; you turn the ignition on and off in an effort to restart the car; you look at the warning lights on the dashboard to see if any unfamiliar ones are lighted; you flip through the owner's manual to the troubleshooting chapter to see what the experts advise; you pop the hood and stare into the engine looking for an obvious solution. You also assess a variety of circumstances: How far am I from the nearest exit? Is that gray cloud going to rain or snow on me? Can I recall seeing an emergency phone box in the past several miles? How soon will it be dark? Have I seen police cars cruising the highway?

In deciding what to do, you would compile these assessments, consider them, and reach a decision: "I'll leave the hood up to attract attention." "I'll walk back to that exit two miles back." "I'll hitch a ride to the next exit." "I'll sit here and wait for somebody to stop."

Assessment, then, is multifaceted. As Figure 7–1 shows, it involves a great deal of describing ("What's going on?") rather than the making of judgments. It can use formal data (represented by the owner's manual) and informal (common sense about whether it's worth the walk to the exit). Above all, we see assessment as being *functional*, *practical*, and *applied*, dealing with problems of the moment and asking: "What works?" "What will work more successfully?"

We believe that assessment is a natural facet of the human thought process, that most people assess their own performance without a great deal of prodding and poking. People also seek the assessments of others. When people do something in school or elsewhere—conducting a science experiment, rebuilding an engine, making a Hallowe'en costume—they ask themselves and others, "How's it goin'?" They assess at all stages of the process, and they apply what they know and are learning as they go along. Communications theory talks of "feedback loops," where the data people collect alters their performance as they proceed. This learning is *functional*, or applied, meaning that people tend to use it instantly to improve their performance: The last egg you separate goes easier than the first; the fortieth time through Mozart's clarinet concerto sounds a lot better than the first. In school, good teachers often set up a variety of assessment tools and feedback loops so that instead of plunging into projects and failing, kids get help along the way and push their way toward successful completion.

In this book, we're four square in favor of *assessment* in the classroom.

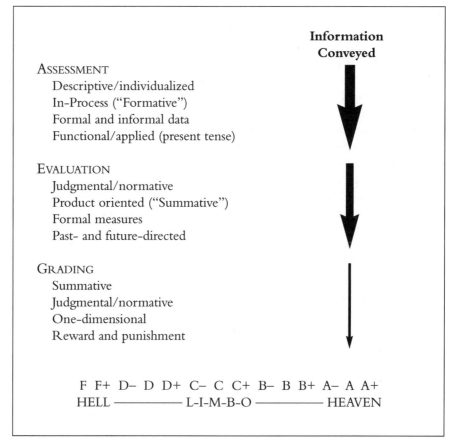

Information Conveyed

ASSESSMENT
Descriptive/individualized
In-Process ("Formative")
Formal and informal data
Functional/applied (present tense)

EVALUATION
Judgmental/normative
Product oriented ("Summative")
Formal measures
Past- and future-directed

GRADING
Summative
Judgmental/normative
One-dimensional
Reward and punishment

F F+ D– D D+ C– C C+ B– B B+ A– A A+
HELL ——————— L-I-M-B-O ——————— HEAVEN

FIG. 7–1 *Classroom Measurement*

Evaluation, as we define it, is a subset within assessment. It's extremely important to keep the two terms separated in one's talk about teaching, for evaluation narrows the spectrum of information supplied and the range of applications of that information. For instance, we left out part of the story about the broken-down car. The odds are pretty good that even before you even started your rational assessment of the problem, you did some evaluating, perhaps with ire. "%^& &★$%^&★ piece of ★()$#%!" you say, kicking the tires. "Why'd I ever get rid of my faithful '83 truck?" "I knew I should have had a tune-up before I left on this trip."

Evaluation introduces a judgmental or normative dimension to the discussion. As Peter Elbow (1993) has pointed out, much of what teachers do in the classroom traditionally involves *ranking*: "a single scale or continuum or dimension along which all performances are hung" (187). Evaluation moves from examining individual performances toward placing them in collective context, from data that are based in the moment ("My car has stopped") to those that are linked to other assessments over time ("This car isn't as good as my old one"). Because it is concerned with ranking and ordering, evaluation tends to focus on "summative" or product measures, and instead of being functional (applied to the present), it looks to the past (what you and others have done) and the future (what you should do differently to improve your performance next time). For instance, in the classroom, a science experiment might be *assessed* by a number of criteria—How is it working? What are you learning from it? What should we do next?—whereas it would be *evaluated* by narrower measures—Did you get the expected outcome? How well does this compare to the work of other students in the class?

Evaluation, like the larger concept of assessment, is perfectly natural in life and learning. It seems to be human nature to want to rank and sort things and to see where one stands on the scale (especially, we might add, if one finds oneself at the higher levels). But as that last parenthetical comment implies, evaluation also adds a dimension of negativity and competition that is not altogether helpful. As soon as we shift from assessment to evaluation, comparisons enter in, and people start feeling bad about where they stand on the scale, worrying about how to get higher.

Further, assessment in its broadest sense is more pragmatic, more useful than evaluation. Where does it get you to conclude that your present car is worse than your old one, or that you'll never buy one of *these* clunkers again? It's assessment, not evaluation, that will get you back on the road.

Although we're four square in favor of this thing called *evaluation,* as you can pretty much tell, we find the umbrella concept of *assessment* to be far more important and useful.

InterMusing

Monitor your intuitive assessment strategies for a familiar task: doing the dishes, brushing your teeth. What sorts of assessment and evaluation strategies do you employ (by now on automatic pilot)? When do you decide that you have brushed or flossed *enough?* How do you decide between putting the dishes in the cabinet or washing that spaghetti pot over again? Then, as you undertake a new problem—dealing with a parent complaint, figuring out why your car won't go—keep note of how you assess the problem or work your way to a solution. Consider the implications of the fact that most kids come to school with many of these same assessment strategies already under control. Also mull over how it is that kids' assessment strategies differ from those of the mature adult.

Next there's *grading*, which we'll describe to you as a subset of evaluation (which, if you recall, is a subset of assessment). Grading essentially reduces all judgments and analyses to a single symbol: A+, D−, A/B. It is summative (talking about final judgments) rather than formative (in process). Because a grade is such a concentrated symbol, many important distinctions and assessments are left out of the final tally. Where assessing your car's problems may help you figure out how to get back on the road, "grading" it gets you nowhere. You might just as well call AAA (How's *that* for a grade?) as waste time grading your car. ("Lemon." "Junk pile." D−.)

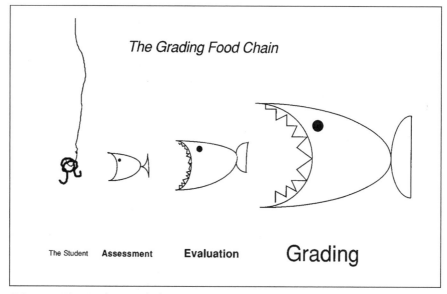

The Grading Food Chain

The Student   **Assessment**   **Evaluation**   Grading

FIG. 7–2   *The Grading Food Chain*

With Dave Majesky (1993), we believe "Grading Should Go":

"As at the Last Judgment, students are sorted into the wheat and the chaff. Rewards of *A*'s and *B*'s go out to the good, and punishments of *F*'s are doled out to the bad. "Gifts" of *D*'s (*D*'s are always gifts) are meted out, and *C*'s (that wonderfully tepid grade) are bestowed on those whose names teachers can rarely remember. (88)

He goes on to review his children's negative history with the grading system, including the story of a daughter who once earned an F "because she had used too much paste as she laid out the cut-outs on her paper" (88). Of course, one needs to discriminate among appropriate uses of grades and separate them from the abuses of a grading system (as a source of fear, punishment, or artificial motivation). But we're four square with Majesky when he argues that "the grading system is not only educationally unsound, but it is also the source of some degree of evil" (90). We go beyond "some degree" to suggest that grading is, in fact, a system that has swallowed up evaluation and assessment. (See Figure 7–2, "The Grading Food Chain.")

Grades make it extraordinarily difficult for teachers to engage in substantial and multidimensional assessment. It seems that no matter how carefully a teacher has assessed the students' work, the kids will just look for the grade, smile if it's good, frown at the teacher if it's bad.

"As we re-think the way we educate our future generations," Majesky says, we should "cast aside our grading system and focus, instead, on the process of learning" (88).

What was your personal history with grades in school or college? Did you ever get a grade you thought was unfair? What did you do about it? How did it alter your attitude toward the teacher and the class? Were grades a motivator for you? A threat? Did teachers ever punish you with grades? How might your performance have changed if you had not been under pressure to achieve good grades? In what aspects of your life today do you perform pretty well without grades?

Presently, grades are a fixture in the educational system, and it would be naive for us to ignore grading in this chapter. Before we're through, we'll discuss the grading problem, arguing that *if* teachers develop a thoughtful umbrella system of assessment and evaluation, it's possible to arrive at grades in ways that at least partially compensate for the kinds of problems Dave Majesky has so articulately identified.

Before we get to the nuts and bolts of assessment, evaluation, and grading, however, we need to make one other distinction and point out a phenomenon, like grading, that extraordinarily complicates classroom life for the reflective teacher. This involves an *us* versus *them* dichotomy: *us* being teachers and students; *them* being people outside the classroom. For the past several decades, assessment for *them* has assumed paramount importance in schools. Where assessment should be something that teachers and students primarily use to improve performance and measure true learning, assessment (or, more accurately, *evaluation*) has increasingly been used as a measure of "accountability," of bringing teachers "to account" for their successes and failures. Education has seen a proliferation of mass testing and standardized testing programs and instruments at the local, state, and national levels. It is common in many schools for kids to spend the whole first week of school taking a battery of pretests only to be halted in their learning again at the end of the year to retake those tests as a way of demonstrating learning.

There are numerous problems with this external testing movement. Lorrie Shepard (1989) laments that "political pressures exaggerate the inherent flaws" in many large-scale testing programs, leading to a "narrowing of content," "multiple choice" formats," and "teaching to the test" (5). Arthur Costa (1989) points out that many mass testing measures are in direct conflict with new directions in the classroom including the new emphasis on learning processes rather than fixed content and right answers:

> If we are to change education to meet the demands of the information age, we must overcome our habit of using product-oriented assessment techniques to measure process-oriented education. We need to redesign assessment techniques to fit the goal of the restructured school to prepare students for the complexities of the post-industrial era. (5)

But again, as much as we would like to see the death of the external testing movement (at least as it is presently constituted), mass assessment, accountability programs, college entrance exams, exit exams, and sundry other *them*-type teaching measures will continue to be imposed on schools.

Roland Case (1992) notes that "there is a common saying among educators: 'What is counted counts.'" He means that testing, grading, and assessment measures have a way of driving curriculum. Tests developed and constructed outside the classroom have a powerful influence on what teachers will choose to teach, perhaps almost as powerful as that of the conventional, adopted textbook. Teachers come to know what counts in the minds of parents and administrators, and often shape their teaching in that direction.

The material in this chapter is intended to bridge the gap; it will provide you with numerous ways of producing solid evidence of professionalism that anticipates and responds to the needs of *them* for information about what's going on.

Toward Authentic Assessment in the Classroom

"What is counted counts" within the classroom too. Students have an uncanny knack for figuring out not only what's on the test but also discerning any hidden agendas that the teacher may have in mind as well. Many readers of this book have developed that skill themselves, giving a cynical wink to a friend when a professor said, "There are no right answers on this test." You and your pals had already figured out the real meaning of that statement: "You don't have to regurgitate the text, but you'd better include lots of references to my lectures." What is counted counts.

Much traditional assessment (driven as it is by a grading system) has resulted in trivializing education. Instead of asking students to prove the best of what they can do, educators engage them in gamesmanship: figuring out what the teacher wants. For example, one of our children was recently assigned the task of learning the abbreviations of the fifty states and being able to pair them with the outline of a state on a map. (We don't justify that assignment; we've merely reporting it.) In an effort to contextualize his child's homework learning, the father pointed out connections between the child's experience and various states: "Look, here's Washington state, 'WA.' Your grandma and grampa live about there, in Richland. And here's Oregon, 'OR.' Your uncle John runs his river guide service out of Camp Sherman, about there on the map." The child waved off the paternal pedagogue: "I don't want to know about that. All I have to know is the abbreviations." What is counted counts.

There is an alternative to the approaches we have been criticizing. It's called "authentic assessment." This concept argues that instead of trying to judge students through tests and grades, teachers should look at their performance in authentic settings. In other words, what students *do* should be counted. Roland Case notes that this approach is variously called "alternative assessment," "whole assessment," "outcomes-based assessment," "performance assessment," and "naturalistic assessment," and it has been an emerging concept in education over the past two decades (15). Of course, there is a bit of doublethink involved in claiming that any *school* learning and assessment can be truly labeled "authentic" or "naturalistic," since, after all, the students are required to be there, the teachers are required to work with groups of thirty or more students, and the curriculum is, to some extent, mandated. But in its best sense, authentic assessment says that if student work is reasonably motivated, the work itself provides the necessary evidence of what students can do.

Rob Tierney (1993) of Ohio State University explains that he wants to break down the distinction between learning and assessment. The two, he argues, are the same, taking place concurrently.

> Can you imagine an assessment system that developed evaluations that were grounded in evidence, allowed for multiple perspectives, catered to individuals pursuing unique interests and alternative learning routes, and afforded judicious interpretation of the advances and achievements as well as processes? (1)

He explains that authentic assessment not only measures real achievement, but also reflects what scholars and learners in the disciplines do. In his summer institute for history teachers, participants engage in historical research of their own, creating a portfolio that includes notes, in-process commentaries, articles they have read, and discussions or monologues of the evolution of their ideas preparatory to formulating and reporting their conclusions. Tierney likens the students' portfolios to the material an archaeologist might collect while trying to recreate an ancient civilization. In the history academy, students are recreating or documenting their own intellectual journey.

In our own teaching, we have students create a notebook that contains a similar record of their researches. As we noted in Chapter 6, when students present their papers they also display their notebooks, which we tell them, is the paper trail, showing where they have travelled intellectually. A typical notebook will contain copies of articles, responses to readings, newspaper clippings, brochures and pamphlets picked up here and there, notes from interviews or conversations, and perhaps the draft and final copy of a survey or poll (along with tabulation of data). The notebook will also contain student self-assessment and a place for the instructor to record comments, interpretations, and judgments. As Tierney has suggested, we find that such an assessment tool becomes integral to the students' learning. The proof is in the pudding; what has been accomplished counts.

Doug Archbald and Fred Newmann (1988) explain that authentic assessment is not easily defined or encapsulated, and offer three criteria for recognizing it in action. Authentic assessment, they explain, is based on:

- "Disciplined inquiry" that "reflects the kinds of mastery demonstrated by experts who create new knowledge." In other words, authentic assessment invites students to perform as scientists, writers, historians, artists. Further, it should emphasize in-depth knowledge rather than surface facts, and it should allow students an opportunity to generate and synthesize ideas that are new for them.

- "Integration of Knowledge." Students are asked to pull together their learnings rather than to display bits and pieces separately.

- "Value Beyond Evaluation." That is, projects, displays, demonstrations, even examinations are designed so they are intrinsically valuable as learning exercises beyond evaluation.

To some extent, the development of authentic assessment is eclectic, meaning that because it is performance based, the measures and criteria will grow from and be integral to the project itself. How you assess brushing your teeth will obviously differ from how you assess your recalcitrant automobile. Thus authentic assessment of a field trip to an art museum will differ considerably from that of a students' scrapbook of fallen autumn leaves. What both of those projects have in common is an examination of student work for indicators of deeper things: knowledge of the subject matter, ability to apply knowledge in new settings, ability to synthesize, ability to interpret, assess, and evaluate. In Figure 7–3, Grant Wiggins (1989) lays out what he sees as the crucial features of this approach.

Keeping in mind our essential distinction between assessment, evaluation, and grading, we'll now move on to present a number of strategies for making the interdisciplinary classroom a site for authentic assessment.

A Catalog of Authentic Assessment Techniques

The Project Approach

In the previous chapter we outlined a number of ways in which school learning can lead to projects of one kind or another. We've argued for learning that leads to concrete achievement. The project method has a long and distinguished history in schools, and part of its appeal for students and teachers is that it leads to accomplishments that are of value or use to the student inside or outside of schools. In interdisciplinary classes student projects might create a pond for a wildlife center, a plan of action for a new set of city bicycle paths, or a set of letters written to (inter)national leaders outlining solutions to particular problems. The connection with authentic assessment is probably clear: The projects themselves are "what counts." The trick is to codify and systematize the measurement for the satisfaction and edification of students, teachers, and others.

In authentic assessment of projects, the teacher looks first and foremost at the *final outcome* as a measure of achievement. Did the pond actually fill with water? If so, the students' preparatory research and calculations demonstrably paid off;

A. Structure and Logistics
1. Are more appropriately public; involve an audience, a panel, and so on.
2. Do not rely on unrealistic and arbitrary time constraints.
3. Offer known, not secret, questions or tasks.
4. Are more like portfolios or a *season* of games (not one-shot).
5. Require some collaboration with others.
6. Recur—and are *worth* practicing for, rehearsing, and retaking.
7. Make assessment and feedback to students so central that school schedules, structures, and policies are modified to support them.

B. Intellectual Design Features
1. Are "essential"—not needlessly intrusive, arbitrary, or contrived to "shake out" a grade.
2. Are "enabling"—constructed to point the student toward more sophisticated use of the skills or knowledge.
3. Are contextualized, complex intellectual challenges, not "atomized" tasks, corresponding to isolated "outcomes."
4. Involve the student's own research or use of knowledge, for which "content" is a means.
5. Assess student habits and repertoires, not mere recall or plug-in skills.
6. Are *representative* challenges—designed to emphasize *depth* more than breadth.
7. Are engaging and educational.
8. Involve somewhat ambiguous ("ill-structured") tasks or problems.

C. Grading and Scoring Standards
1. Involve criteria that assess essentials, not easily counted (but relatively unimportant) errors.
2. Are not graded on a "curve" but in reference to performance standards (criterion-referenced, not norm-referenced).
3. Involve demystified criteria of success that appear to *students* as inherent in successful activity.
4. Make self-assessment a part of the assessment.
5. Use a multifaceted scoring system instead of one aggregate grade.
6. Exhibit harmony with shared schoolwide aims—a *standard*.

D. Fairness and Equality
1. Ferret out and identify (perhaps hidden) strengths.
2. Strike a *constantly* examined balance between honoring achievement and native skill or fortunate prior training.
3. Minimize needless, unfair, and demoralizing comparisons.
4. Allow appropriate room for student learning styles, aptitudes, and interests.
5. Can be—should be—attempted by *all* students, with the test "scaffolded up," not "dumbed down," as necessary.
6. Reverse typical test-design procedures: they make "accountability" serve student learning (attention is primarily paid to "face" and "ecological" validity of tests).

Thanks to Ted Sizer, Art Powell, Fred Newmann, and Doug Archbald; and the work of Peter Elbow and Robert Glaser for some of these criteria.

FIG. 7–3 *Characteristics of Authentic Tests*
From Grant Wiggins (1989), "Teaching to the Authentic Test," Educational Leadership *48(4): 45. Copyright © 1989 by the Association for Supervision and Curriculum Development. Reprinted by permission.*

they showed that they know that water runs downhill and that you can slow that downhill pace by creating a dam. Of course, they learned 1001 other things along the way. One problem with authentic assessment of projects is that virtually any project can show literally thousands, possibly millions of discrete achievements. For example, one could itemize and number the subskills and knowledges shown in just the understanding that water runs downhill and discover that, for practical purposes, the number is infinite, encompassing myriad concepts that lead to the ideas of gravity and properties of liquid. Where does one draw the line?

Some of the following procedures can help you order the process:

- *Carefully review the original project goals.* These may have been centered in a single multidisciplinary area. Create a "yes–no" criteria for evaluation of each major goal. Did the students look up the dimensions of an official baseball diamond? Did they lay out a new baseball diamond with 90-foot base paths? This gives you a "bottom line" of assessment.

- *Describe the conditions under which the learning took place.* Perhaps the ball diamond project was designed by a group of kids who wanted a real field to play on. As a result of this desire, they read up on the baseball rules, figured out a method for creating a proper diamond, and did the deed. Describing the conditions is essentially a measure of authenticity. (It's a different project if students come up with the right answer based solely on paper and pencil response to a math story problem.)

- *Document or detail the underlying principles.* OK, they laid out the baseball diamond. What mathematical concepts were required along the way? What principles of measurement were involved? Look for nested accomplishments: Before the students placed first base they had to measure a ninety foot rope; and before they did that, they had to discover that nylon rope stretches and sisal rope doesn't; and while measuring the ninety feet, they discovered several different ways of multiplying lengths (e.g., using yardstick vs. 25-foot steel rule vs. measuring a ten-foot length of rope and folding the rope nine times), each involving different margins of error; and afterward, they had to verify their measurements.

- *Seek alternative ways of assessing achievement.* Student notebooks and log books for the baseball project can supplement the teachers' observations. Perhaps the gym teacher can stop by to check out the new baseball field. Perhaps the students could find a second way to measure employing the Pythagorean theorem instead of lengths of rope.

- *Document additional achievements and learnings.* Here's the real payoff for authentic assessment and teaching. What did the students learn that *wasn't* part of the original objectives? What did they learn in the baseball project about grass, lime, drainage, or the history of baseball? Often your list of supplementary achievements may be longer than your original list of goals, providing ample evidence that interdisciplinary project teaching generally delivers more than the modest minimums demanded of teachers by the public and the press.

"Why did you have your students lay out a baseball diamond?" asks a concerned parent. "Well, from the perspective of math," you reply, "we learned X, Y, and Z. Of course, this was an interdisciplinary project, so in addition to math we learned baseball history concept Q, agricultural process R, not to mention S, T, and U, that the students picked up in their reading and writing."

What we've described above is assessment of group projects. Assessing individual projects is more complex. Charles built a birdhouse; Charlene built a bird feeder; Ramona charted a list of the birds that used both. How do we assess? Frequently one can identify *common learnings* in a series of related projects (how birds live, what they eat, how they choose habitat) and then go on to identify *individual achievements* as well (Charles learned to drive a nail; Ramona can use binoculars).

Careful bookkeeping is important for both students and teachers in this form of assessment. The sort of checklist shown in Figure 7–4 provides one systematic way of approaching the task.

Performances and Presentations

We discussed performances and presentations in the previous chapter, but in terms of making learning concrete rather than in terms of assessment. One is the hand, the other is the glove.

Presentations to a class can be a lively display of achievement: a talk or speech, show and tell, a reading of a paper. We especially like to have students do presentations with props or in costume. We've had kids cut open old snow tires to show how they work; we've had adults roll in a slice of a ponderosa pine to show history in the making through the counting of rings; we've had presenters show up dressed as mimes. A presentation is one step beyond the authentic learning of a project: Where the project itself demonstrates learning, a presentation also demonstrates the student's ability to articulate that learning and to share it with others.

In our classes we work hard to avoid a parade of presenters. That is, instead of having kids march to the front one after the other to do their bit, we try to weave in presentations as work is completed and as it might contribute to other students' learning. For example, in a recent college class we asked a student majoring in graphic arts to present his knowledge to the class prior to a classwide poster demonstration later in the term.

The Bongo Program (1987), a team-taught interdisciplinary project in New York, engages students in a wide variety of programs and projects with a strong emphasis on drama. Students prepare a scripted presentation to the whole school, usually a docudrama that lays out issues, problems, and an agenda for action. The program coordinators have a background in so-called "guerrilla" or "street theater," a combination of drama and public persuasion, so that in the case of Bongo, even the dramatic presentations have authentic outcomes: They *move* the audience toward action of its own.

Although grading a performance or presentation is fraught with the usual difficulties, assessment of student achievement is not. With the use of a checklist or score card, a teacher can easily identify important ideas and concepts that have been developed.

Recorded Performances

We have for years drawn on electronic media for students to demonstrate their learning. Back when the phrase "media literacy" was first echoing in the halls of learning, we had kids do eight millimeter movies of their work. The ease and portability of home video equipment has now made those early efforts look pretty crude, but the principle remains the same: Students can document their learning and reach expanded public audiences by taking advantage of electronic and audiovisual media. Students can, for example, record each stage of a project on video or with slides or photographs, leading to a photo essay, slide-tape, or video presentation. Many schools have fairly sophisticated video production facilities, so the production of polished videos is possible. Cable TV systems are required to have a public access channel, and we've had students have their work shown over community television. As guys who grew up with radio drama, we also have our students write and tape record scripts, dramatic or documentary, making their learning public. Is this work assessable? You bet. In fact, recorded presentations and performances offer the advantage that the teacher can view and *re*view the work under consideration, a luxury that is not always possible in a live theatrical performance or presentation.

The Portfolio

In recent years, few topics in education have attracted more attention than portfolio assessment. "Put 'portfolio' in the title of your speech," observes a friend of ours, "and you've guaranteed a slot for yourself on any conference program in the country." Much of the enthusiasm for portfolios is warranted because they offer a form of alternative assessment that is both pedagogically sound and relatively manageable by the busy classroom teacher. Portfolios were first developed in the world of the arts, where it is common for artists to create and display a portfolio or collection of what they regard as best or representative work.

Dennie Wolf (1989) observes that portfolios provide a "real-world" experience in that they are drawn from the approaches used by "experts—artists, musicians, and writers" to "sample and judge their life's work." Typically a portfolio will include a "range of works" (where the creator/student reveals the breadth of accomplishment), "biographies of works" (discussion of how a particular work or project came into being), and "reflections" (where the student/artist discusses perceptions of the work (38).

When first introduced to portfolios, many students see them as comprehensive, not necessarily selective collections of *everything* done for a class. We call this the "portfolio as catch-all." In our own teaching, we have actually used that concept to our advantage: "At first," we say, "save everything you do for this course: your notes, drafts, exams, works in progress, *everything*." But at assessment time we add, "Now winnow your collection down so that it shows off your accomplishments." We usually have students include the first and last things they've done in a class, plus a selection of materials in between. (We allow students to exclude some material that they think doesn't represent their best work. Everybody is entitled to a bad day.) The work in the portfolio is ordered or sequenced—often with the student's best work on top—and the students must write a careful analysis of the work done to date. We spend a good deal of time helping students write those assessments in class, and we help students see that portfolio self-assessment is *not* a place simply to justify all the goofs and blunders of the semester, to put on a display of false modesty for the teacher, or to beg for a grade. Rather, it is the place for students to offer their own best effort at explaining what they have done in the class.

Portfolios are now being used in virtually every discipline across the curriculum. In science, students include write-ups of experiments, copies of examinations, answers to essay questions, notes, even photographs of projects completed that are too large to include in the portfolio. In history (as Tierney has pointed out), a portfolio includes notes analyzing original source materials, in-process observations as students work their way to judgments about historical events or themes, notes on interviews, sketches of artifacts, and so on.

Wolf reminds us that portfolios are "messy." They require considerable work from students and careful reading and response from the teacher. They take much more time than checking a batch of multiple choice answers. They are, however, a form of *authentic* assessment because they measure and count what students actually do. Most portfolio users believe that they provide better measures than other forms of assessment because of their inherent focus on the processes of learning and on student growth and development over time.

Checklists of Skills and Competencies

As we have stressed throughout this book, we recognize that teachers will almost invariably be faced with curricula that must be followed or with lists of minimum or maximum skills that must be demonstrated by their students. At the same time, we know that most interdisciplinary lessons and units go far beyond core minimums and actually teach most of the skills and competencies required by the core or basic curriculum. To demonstrate this phenomenon, we recommend that the teacher carefully study the curriculum guide or prescribed text and prepare a series of checklists on the basic ideas that are presented. Let's say that an art curriculum requires that students (a) know the color spectrum, (b) demonstrate the use of a variety of artistic tools, (c) know some of the differences among art papers and

Subject or Class: _____
Interdisciplinary Unit: _____
Principal unit activites: _____

Students' names (enter below)	Major Unit Concepts			
	Color spectrum	Use artistic tools	Compose in medium #1	Compose in medium #2
Abrams, Juliana	11/6	11/8	11/20	11/26
Blanchette, Bill	11/6	11/10	11/10	11/26
Cosgrove, Mary	11/6	11/12	11/12	11/14

FIG. 7–4   *Curriculum Concept Checklist*

their uses, and (d) compose works of art in at least two different media. Let's say, further, that the teacher is teaming with the science teacher to have students put their understanding of molecules into a visual form. Unless something goes terribly awry, the odds are pretty good that each of the core objectives a through d will be achieved not just once, but on a number of occasions. As students prepare paintings and models of molecules, they will certainly compose in different media; as they paint, they will necessarily show mastery of the color spectrum. The teacher, then, merely enters into the grid the date of observation of these competencies. Figure 7–4 shows one way of setting out such a grid.

InterMusing

Consider how projects, presentations, and portfolios could be used, separately or together, to assess student work in an interdisciplinary unit you have been planning. (Don't worry about grades at this point; simply focus on collecting data that would reliably document what you want the students to gain from the unit.) Draw up a grid, using Figure 7–4 as a model, that displays the core learnings of the unit and provides a mechanism for you to record their achievement neatly in your grade book.

Other Documentation of Learning

These various approaches to authentic assessment—projects, portfolios, presentations, checklists—may seem cumbersome initially, but it is important to recall that authentic assessment refuses to accept a distinction between assessment and learning itself. The data gathering takes place as students learn, and much of the data is a direct outgrowth or even a part of that learning. The following methods and approaches further enrich the assessment process.

- *Journals and learning logs.* These are not simply collections of student notes, but emphasize interactive or responsive learning. The child keeping a science journal or log not only records observations and experiments, but reflects on them as well. John Dixon's *Growth Through English* (1967) contains a charming series of diary entries of a British lad, Nigel, who has been collecting newts and keeps them in a jar in his room. The reader delights in Nigel's puzzlings about newtdom, and one even discovers poetry in his descriptions. The reader also becomes convinced that Nigel knows a lot about newts. Dixon's point: A journal or learning log is a record of inquiry that crosses many lines, allowing for personal response and reflection as well as scientific data gathering or diary-like recording of names, dates, and events.

- *Teacher anecdotes.* Many advocates of authentic assessment now keep journals themselves. Pausing from time to time in their work (or perhaps writing while their students are at work on their own learning logs), the teacher jots down specific examples of student learning: Marilou did a nice piece of work thinking about the historical causes of race relation problems; Katy had a light bulb moment in figuring out how tides work; Jacob studied and studied the globe and can now explain why there is an international date line. Often these anecdotal records can go home to parents to supplement other forms of reporting.

- *Conferencing.* Holding formal or informal conferences with students may be the most efficient form of assessment we have. Where many assessment strategies require paper and pencil which in turn implies documents for the teacher to read and assess, conferencing relies on conversation. In *formal conferencing*, the teacher usually gets the whole class started on some sort of independent project or reading, then meets with students one at a time. A student might come to the conference with a portfolio of work, an assignment or project in process, or simply arrive ready to discuss a current activity or project. One can also employ *informal conferencing*, where the teacher circulates through the classroom while students work on projects or experiments. In a thirty- to fifty-minute time block, the teacher can chat briefly with each student, make a suggestion or two, and gain a good sense of what's happening. Formal and informal conferencing often leads directly to teacher anecdotes as well. After the class, the teacher takes a few minutes to jot down observations about specific students and/or problems observed in the class or to fill in a checklist of the sort shown in Figure 7-4.

- *Mastery learning*, *outcomes-based education*, and *competency-based learning.* These three approaches are often described in professional literature as dealing with authentic assessment, for they place strong emphasis on measuring what it is that students do. In *mastery learning*, a series of tasks of increasing difficulty are set for the students (Martinez and Lipson 1989). These could be mathematical problems that reflect a hierarchy of skills, science experiments that show acquisition of more and more complex procedures, or a series of writing assignments of increasing breadth and sophistication. Students complete the hierarchy by demonstrating the skills in question. In a similar vein, *outcomes-based education* concentrates on the final product: Can the student solve a problem or write the paper? Carefully designed enabling outcomes present intermediate tasks that lead the student toward successful completion of the final outcome (Brandt 1993). Likewise, *competency-based education* centers its aims on achievements rather than global skills or concepts: It's the students' demonstrated competencies under authentic conditions that count.

We want to offer a strong warning, however: Although we very much favor the emphasis on a demonstrable product in these three approaches, we feel that as practiced in many schools, they are too often reduced to coverage of minimums or an accountability model. In literacy education, for example, they often emphasize so-called "fundamentals"—spelling, phonics elements, library skills—rather than holistic language use. Further, these approaches presume that the educator can know precisely the sequence of skills and knowledges that competent performance requires. We think it is presumptive, as well, to assume that having mastered the hierarchy, students will *ipso facto* demonstrate holistic or synthetic competencies. The sum of many parts does not necessarily add up to a whole, and too often, the parts that constitute a whole lose their authenticity when detached from that whole. Mastery learning, particularly as practiced by its generally acknowledged popularizer, Madeline Hunter (1982), often trivializes learning by breaking mastery into a series of rote or routine projects or tasks to be completed by the students. Thus, much of the authenticity goes out of learning, and little has changed from old-fashioned basic skills instruction. Nevertheless, teachers pushing for authentic assessment and interdisciplinary studies might find some allies in the proponents of these approaches to assessment.

- *Questions answered.* In earlier chapters we have stressed that inquiry-based units generate long lists of questions to answer. It follows that a very simple form of assessment is to find out whether or not questions have been answered. Did we, in fact, learn how to estimate the number of board feet of lumber required to build a house? Did we learn why the French impressionists liked to use all those dots in their work? Did we learn the origins of the universe?

Now, that last question raises some interesting complications. In the first place, probing the origins of the universe might well lead to a fight over religious values, even to discussion of creationism versus evolution. But aside from that, we have to acknowledge that, creationists aside, nobody knows the answer for sure. Students might well conclude that their question cannot be answered at the present time. Or they might find that the Big Bang theory involves so much mathematics and advanced physics that they are not qualified to answer the question. Does this mean that the teaching unit has failed? Of course not. A valuable byproduct of this assessment would be that some questions are not easily answerable (at least at the present) or that the original question was naive. Students can, as a form of assessment, spend time revising their original questions or even generating a new set of questions for exploration. If our "failure" to pin down the origins of the universe leads, say, to a class visit from an astronomer, further reading, or even to a debate between a creationist and a scientist, the authentic purposes of learning have been served.

- *Self-assessment.* Last on our list, but perhaps most important in terms of the long-range aims of authentic assessment, is the assessment students do themselves. If the aim is to produce students who are independent learners, critical thinkers, and capable evaluators, teachers need to be helping them learn to assess their own work from kindergarten on. Indeed, one of our great objections to the grading system is that it operates counter to the development of self-assessment skills, tending to make students dependent learners, waiting around for what the teacher had to say. Of course, professionally, the teacher *is* the person in the classroom best equipped to appraise students work. But it is often useful and frequently surprising for the teacher to break the teacher-dependence cycle by having students describe, carefully and honestly, what it is they think they have done and how well they have done it.

At the close of interdisciplinary projects (and as a standard part of portfolio assessment), many teachers will have students review the goals of the project, describe what they did to meet those goals, and what they see as the strengths and weaknesses of their performance. The importance of the teacher in this process is not to tell the students whether they came up with the right answers, but to help them develop their abilities at coming up with answers that are right for them.

The biggest problem we've encountered with self-assessment is first, that students have often been trained to think of themselves as failures and thus to undervalue their own accomplishments and, second, that they confuse self-assessment with grading. "Do you mean I get to pick my own grade?" is the common question. "No," is our reply, and we carefully outline the differences among assessment, evaluation, and grading with which we began this chapter.

InterMusing

For an interdisciplinary unit or project that you're interested in conducting, consider how these additional forms of assessment—journals and logs, conferencing, self-assessment, questions, and even mastery learning—could be employed as tools for measuring what students have accomplished. What new information would each style of assessment give to a teacher? Which would be your preferred forms? Which would be least labor intensive for the busy teacher?

From Authentic Assessment to Evaluation: Alternatives to "the Test"

FIG. 7–5   *Copyright © 1993. Reprinted by permission. Tribune Media Services.*

Near the cash register at our campus bookstore, right next to the breath fresheners, the cheap pens, and today's newspaper, all available for impulse-buying or last-minute shopping are the Scan-Tron sheets: computer-readable forms printed with blanks all ready to be filled in with #2 pencil. University students are required to purchase these sheets in preparation for the multiple-choice tests that are given in a great many of their classes. Obviously enough professors use this approach that the bookstore gives prominent shelf space to them, more prominent, for instance, than *Omni* or *The Atlantic Monthly*.

We all know the ease of multiple-choice evaluation: Teachers write out a set of questions and four or five answer stubs. Tricky teachers throw in clever language designed to get presumably less knowledgeable students to fill in the wrong bubbles, and occasionally all the answer stubs are wrong or right, allowing for the "all of the above" or "none of the above" response. The answer sheets are scanned at the computer center, and scores come back alphabetically by student, showing scores, means, standard deviations, rank orders, or just about any compilation of data the teacher wants to request. In this form of evaluation, all of the student's work and energy is reduced to a single number or rank in class.

We'll let the scan sheets represent our worst view of *in*authentic evaluation: Learning is evaluated out of context, the students are not required to synthesize their learning in any significant way, and the assessment is utterly divorced from the learning process.

To our encouragement, next to the Scan-Tron sheets, our bookstore also stacks up the traditional "blue books" used for essay exams. We'll let the blue books represent a middle ground in the push for authentic evaluation. On the one hand, we're encouraged that many professors on campus still do give essay tests, enough that the bookstore puts blue books in the checkout lane, in preference, say, to *Muscle and Fitness*, *Garfield on the Warpath*, or condoms. Nevertheless, as most of us know, essay tests—at least as practiced on many university campuses—are seldom a particularly authentic form of evaluation. Crowded into a room, writing over a limited period of time on carefully phrased topics, students know full well that the real purpose to the essay is to persuade the prof that they've studied the course material. Essay exams obviously invite a great deal more synthesis and integration than is possible with the multiple-choice test, but there are trade-offs. Essays are also subjectively graded and depend on writing skills. Many grade-hungry students would actually prefer the trivia of the multiple-choice test to the essay exam, which is a more informative, data-rich form of evaluation.

Keeping in mind that an "examination" or an "evaluation" does not necessarily have to lead to a grade, each of the following is an alternative to testing of the Scan-Tron *or* essay sort that comes closer to the aims and values of authentic evaluation.

- *Rites of passage.* Most societies have rites of passage that may involve ritualistic or actual performance: The young man kills an animal to show he is an adult; a young woman creates her bridal costume to show she is ready for the duties of housewifery. In our society, obtaining a driver's license is an important rite of passage, bringing with it a certificate of adulthood (the picture ID) and new privileges (the freedom of the road). A "rites of passage" examination is an authentic assessment version of the final examination or diploma exam. Archbald and Neumann (1988) describe the ROPE (Rite of Passage Experience) at Walden III High School in Racine, Wisconsin, where all seniors are required to "demonstrate mastery in fifteen areas of knowledge and competence by completing a portfolio, project, and fifteen presentations before a ROPE committee consisting of staff members (including the student's homeroom teacher), a student, and an adult from the community" (23). Students prepare for the presentations throughout the year by accumulating materials in a portfolio that include an intellectual autobiography, self-assessment of their school performances, letters of recommendation, a reading record, an essay on ethics, and various reports and polished projects on art, media, ethics, science, math, American history and government, geography, English, physical achievement, and social and life skills. Now that's a mind-boggling list, and we have not seen the program in action, with the network of presentation scheduling that must be involved. Nevertheless, the list of areas used at Racine gives evidence that the rite of passage concept can be used in almost *any* school area. If one purpose of science is to teach laboratory skills, let the students demonstrate their ability to design an experiment as an exit task. If the intent of music instruction is to teach some skills of unison singing, let the student sing in tune with chums in a mini-choir as a rite of passage to the level of two-part harmony. A rite of passage we have proposed, only half facetiously, is that the candidate for a diploma from high school or college would be required to pose, justify, and answer a single question he or she sees as being of major importance

THE FAR SIDE   By GARY LARSON

"It's OK! Dart not poisonous ...
Just showin' my kid the ropes!"

FIG. 7–6   *FAR SIDE copyright 1993, 1994 FARWORKS, INC.
Distributed by Universal Press Syndicate. Reprinted with permission. All rights reserved.*

in the world during the coming half century. Rite-of-passage evaluations should
not, we think, function chiefly as "gatekeepers," as ways of catching sly students who have somehow managed to pass their courses without learning anything. Rather, these should be times of celebration, where young people get to
strut their stuff before advancing to the next level.

Students should be well prepared for these examinations, and if there is
a great discrepancy between their performance in authentic settings and their
previously graded course work, one might want to ask some careful questions about the validity or authenticity of classroom instruction.

- *Oral examinations.* An oral exam does not have to be the feared pop quiz where
an instructor grills students with oral questions on the text material. (A TV
pizza commercial satirizes this learning-motivated-by-fear, showing elementary kids literally sweating and shaking in their boots as a teacher asks, "If you

can get three toppings for $10.99, how much will six toppings cost?" The answer turns out to be $10.99. Who would have guessed?) A more authentic form of the oral examination is for the teacher to pose a discussion question and to invite the students to explore it. The teacher explains beforehand that full participation is expected, that part of the evaluation is to determine whether or not every student can join in. Topics can range from science to humanities, and the questions usually ask the students to synthesize knowledge from the unit and to apply it in new settings.

- *Roleplaying.* In this approach to evaluation, the teacher identifies an issue or problem related to course content. In small groups, the students assume roles and act out solutions. For example, in auto shop: "The four of you are driving on the highway when your car suddenly stops. Roleplay how you would go about assessing the problem." The teacher's evaluation can range from whether the students remember to check for traffic before stepping out the door to whether they follow standard diagnostic procedures. To add to the complexity of the problem, the teacher can "side coach," introducing additional data: "As you open the hood, a cloud of white vapor emerges. How does this change your approach?"

- *Problem solving and brainstorming.* Here students are given a real problem, perhaps something clipped from the daily newspaper: "Nation's Economy Needs Long-Range Cure," "Athletes: Good Sports or Spoiled Brats?" Based on information supplied by the teacher (or the newspaper article), students identify the problem itself and show possible solutions, with justifications that demonstrate their mastery of content and skills.

- *Student-created problems and tests.* Wiggins (1989) gets at an ancient problem in education by advocating "Teaching to the Authentic Test." That is, if the purpose of an examination is to reveal students' understanding (rather than to confuse, befuddle, or trick them), it makes perfect sense for the teacher to teach to the test, to provide the kind of support students need to get the job done. (Such teaching to the test is also a form of teaching toward accountability; that is, the "test" of the teacher's skill is whether or not the teaching to the test is successful.) Further, there's no reason why students cannot be involved in designing the problem themselves. We've frequently used an examination review period to have students design questions or problems. "What would be a good question to test your mastery of this class?" "What criteria would you use in evaluating your own work?" "How could you best prepare to show your mastery?"

- *Computer simulations.* "Where in the World is Carmen Sandiego?", a popular computer game, draws on students' knowledge of geography and provides a model of what we might call simulated authentic assessment. Students never have to leave the classroom, nor the computer console, yet are able to go on a search that requires them to use creative and critical thinking and a solid knowledge of places. Simulated problem/games have been developed in other disciplines and are being/will be developed at an increasingly rapid pace as computer sophistication and interactivity continue to grow. With programs that integrate computer functions, video, and sound, the limits of the classroom will be infinitely expanded.

One warning about computer simulations (or, for that matter, *any* game that simulates reality): Someone (the game designer) has made judgments, possibly simplistic ones, about what that "reality" entails. For instance, if you were developing a game to explain the personalities of your family, you would have to write almost an infinite set of rules in order to characterize those folks fully. For simplicity in the game, you'd reduce everyone's character to dominant traits, leading to stereotyping. So it is with computer games, which sometimes invite oversimplification of reality. Even at their best, computers are less real than reality.

As we discussed in the last chapter, students can devise games that represent the core concepts of whatever you're teaching. Can they design a game that reasonably simulates the risks of nuclear waste disposal? Or the care and feeding of animals? Or the nature of life in a pond? Or the causes of any war in history? If the game works, the test is "passed."

InterMusing

Keeping in mind that we're still talking about *evaluation*, rather than grading, think about the kinds of judgments that a teacher can make about students' work from the various examination alternatives we've listed. What does it prove if a student can roleplay a scientist solving a problem or an historical character presenting his/her views? So what if a kid can design a game that does a pretty good job of simulating life in South America prior to the arrival of the white people? Or if a student is able to articulately defend his/her view in a discussion? And what is shown if students can't perform these tasks? For a unit or project of your own design, develop an evaluation (not grading) system that would employ diverse forms of measurement. What criteria would you develop for yourself to evaluate the students' work?

From Assessment to Grading

We hope at this juncture you're convinced of the value of authentic assessment in the classroom and its myriad applications in interdisciplinary teaching. But if you're at all like us, the idea of grades lurks at the back of your mind. "All these alternatives are sound and interesting and probably better than old-fashioned tests," you say. "But grades have to be given. Administrators want to see grades in grade books. Parents want to see grades on examinations. How do we grade in an interdisciplinary, authentic classroom?"

Damned good question. We freely confess to having felt a lifetime of conflict between the pressures exerted by the grading system and our own aims as educators. And we confess to not having solved the problem completely. Every time we teach we find ourselves compromising, to some extent, our own vision of what the course or unit could be with what the demands of grading systems will allow it to be.

To be sure, there are those who sharply disagree with our view of the problems induced by grading. One of our colleagues at the University of Nevada, for example, has spoken out strongly not only in favor of grades, but in favor of system-wide grading standards. "What should be most important," writes Professor Grant Stitt (1993) of the criminal justice department, "is that we have a set of academic standards to which we are committed and which should be enforced on a university-wide basis." Not only does he see it possible to arrive at such standards, but he maintains that "we have an obligation to our society to maintain a system of quality control so that society can benefit from those with true talents and high levels of achievement . . ." (4). Uniform grading standards, grades based on careful discrimination among levels of quality, grades not inflated by instructors' desires to be "nice"—all these are a part of Professor Stitt's view of evaluation and grading.

Predictably, we're doubtful about the ability of teachers at any level to describe levels of achievement with such accuracy, precision, and confidence. Indeed, we'd like to be shown that grading can be done consistently and without subjective bias for anything except rote skills or basic factual information, the very sort of teaching that interdisciplinary, inquiry-centered, authentic learning seeks to avoid.

There is a middle ground in this debate, of course. Or perhaps more accurately, there are middle *grounds* that push toward solving three major problems that we see with grades:

1. Grades are often highly subjective, awarded without clear-cut criteria, especially criteria stated in advance so that students can know what to achieve to earn a grade.

2. Grades convey little information of substance that allows students to improve their performance.

3. Grades are destructive to the teacher/student or mentor/novice relationship.

Now we will discuss some options that we've explored and recommend for interdisciplinary teaching.

Pass/Fail Grading

Many pro-grading people would immediately reject this middle ground solution, saying that it begs the question by not giving "grades." But such systems are increasingly being used in the elementary schools and have been used for years in a few areas of college teaching. (High schools and the middle schools seem more deeply locked into alphabetical grading, in no small measure because of college entrance expectations and the alleged need for grade point averages for use by selection committees.) Pass/Fail (P/F) systems are ideal for authentic assessment programs, because the bottom line is the effectiveness of a project or piece of work: "Did the student perform authentically and successfully?" "Did she demonstrate that she has control of enough math to design a footbridge?" "Did he know enough materials science to design a new use for recycled plastic?" Although there are seldom yes/no answers to such questions (there may have been flaws in the footbridge design or the student's use of plastic bags may have been based on naive assumptions about recycling costs), P/F grading allows for clear-cut identification of criteria for success, and it invites the use of many forms of assessment and evaluation so that students know what they have done well, what they have done less well, or what steps they need to take to receive credit for a project. Indeed, as we see it, P/F systems can actually be used to raise standards: There is no "gentleman's C" under P/F—mediocre work is simply not credited. Collaboration between teacher and student is assured, and the thrust is toward production of high-quality work, rather than the annotating or labeling of gradations of poorness and failure. In practice, the final P or F is based on a number of projects or works completed over a term or marking period: A series of Ps in the grade book add up to a P for the class. Some systems also include an "honors" or "high credit" option that permits teachers to acknowledge particularly well-done work. The introduction of P/F systems across the board would, in our judgment, do much to solve educational problems that are literally induced by alphabetic grading.

Analytic Scoring

As we have suggested, perhaps the strongest argument against conventional grading systems is their failure to articulate criteria for success. Too often children are faced with vague expectations or are simply surprised at the grade they receive because criteria were not made clear. Analytic scoring can be used to grade performance on individual pieces of work over the school term.

Figure 7–7 represents an effort at making criteria clear in advance of what will be scored, in this case, for an entry in the school science fair. Whether students built a hot dog cooker or did a project raising seedlings, their authentic achievement can be evaluated by numbers that can be entered into the grade book. Note that the form includes a breakdown of the features of the project to be evaluated, a range of scores, and a weighting system that allows the teacher to make it clear how much the various aspects of the project will be counted. It is important to recognize that there is plenty of room in analytic scoring for the teacher to enter in his or her own values. Suppose you want to find a way to reward more ambitious projects: You want to give extra credit to the kid who builds a cold fusion device as opposed one who slaps together the relatively easy hot dog cooker. In this case, you would create a category that would award points for what you value, say:

Science Project

1) (20%) Project follows the steps in "the scientific method."
    Low 1 2 3 4 5 6 7 8 9 10 High   x 2 = _____
Teacher comments:

2) (30%) Quantity and quality of data collection.
    Low 1 2 3 4 5 6 7 8 9 10 High   x 3 = _____
Teacher comments:

3) (30%) Explanation of your findings and conclusions.
    Low 1 2 3 4 5 6 7 8 9 10 High   x 3 = _____
Teacher comments:

4) (20%) Neatness and clarity of your display.
    Low 1 2 3 4 5 6 7 8 9 10 High   x 2 = _____
Teacher comments:

Total score   _____

Grading Scale: Below 60 = failing
                60–70 = D or poor
                70–80 = C or adequate
                80–90 = B or good
                90–100 = A or excellent

FIG. 7–7 *Analytic Scoring Sheet*

Difficulty of the attempted project
Low 1 2 3 4 5 6 7 8 9 10 High

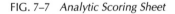

And you would weight it appropriately in your scoring system. In a world where what is counted counts, analytic scoring leads teachers—forces them to force themselves—to be explicit about what's counted. Although the distribution of "low" and "high" grades is still subjective, we find that many students rather like the feeling of security that having the analytic form gives them. In fact, when we use this system, we pass out the grading sheet at the beginning of the assignment so students will know the score in advance.

Primary Trait Scoring

Many educators argue that analytic scoring alone is not sufficient. It's not enough to say, "20 percent of your grade comes from following the scientific method, 30 percent from data collection, 30 percent from interpretation, and 20 percent for the pre-

The Science Project
Interpretation of Data

Score	Explanation
Below 6 (Fail)	Does not present or attempt to explain the data. Merely presents the data as self evident.
6 (D)	Presents conclusions without any discussion or assumes that readers can figure it out on their own.
7 (C)	Presents conclusions or interpretations and makes a good effort to explain why these are valid.
8 (B)	Goes beyond simply explaining data to show how they do or do not support the hypothesis. Gives some indication of looking for alternative explanations.
9–10 (A)	Does an extremely thorough analysis of data, including discussing and rejecting alternative hypotheses. Discusses limitations of the findings.

FIG. 7–8 *Primary Trait Scoring*

sentation." Students will inevitably ask, "How do I know whether I've followed the scientific method well enough? How do I get a ten rather than a seven? And what about 'interpretation'? Tell me, teacher!" This, again, is the problem of subjectivity.

To some extent, criteria for any grading system will be unclear about some criteria due to the fact that any human endeavor involves a certain amount of working things out as one goes along. What makes a good interpretation of a poem or a piece of scientific data? Well, it depends, in part on the poem or data, who analyzed it, and for what purpose. Nevertheless, primary trait scoring attempts to describe levels of achievement, and research has shown that if levels of criteria are spelled out in advance, students find them a helpful guide and teachers are more inclined to grade following the stated criteria. Figure 7–8 shows a set of criteria for just one part of our science project, the interpretive section. These criteria would be explained to the students *before* the project begins. You'll note that there is still some vagueness of description (the teacher cannot prescribe in advance what would be A-level performance in, say, discussing the limitations of a set of conclusions), but the students who receive such a list of criteria have a pretty good idea of what will score well. Where do these criteria come from? It's important that they *not* simply represent the teacher's fantasies or dreams or a set of expectations developed without regard for students' developmental levels. The best primary trait scoring systems, in fact, emerge from *observation of students' work over time*: What last year's kids did helps the teacher think more realistically about what this year's ought to/might/should be doing.

Portfolio Grading

As portfolios have gained in popularity as assessment tools, many teachers have found that they can be linked to grading systems as well. The advantage to grading a portfolio (as opposed to individual student works) is that the focus becomes growth and development, rather than a single final product. Further, portfolios can engage students deeply and thoughtfully in the assessment process (although the final determination of the *grade* is left up to the teacher). Usually a portfolio will be graded on such criteria as completeness (fulfilling basic assignments), the quality of work turned in, evidence of growth, and even the quality of the student's self-assessment. Analytic scales and primary trait descriptions can easily be combined with portfolio assessment so that students know explicitly and in advance how their portfolio work will be judged and translated into grades.

Merit Badges

Here we'll advocate adapting a system that, to our knowledge, has not been directly tried in schools but has a seventy-five year history of success with young people. As we've noted, in both Girl and Boy Scouts (and in their programs for Cubs and Brownies), kids themselves select levels of achievement, and work toward those by way of mastering particular skills or projects. To earn a forestry badge, you perform several authentic tasks: identify trees, learn about prevention of wildfires, talk to a forester, or read pamphlets distributed by the forest service. Many options are provided so a child can select from a variety of tasks that are directed toward common learning or mastery goals. Further, scouting gives boys and girls a choice of levels of achievement. The greater the range, diversity, and quantity of activities completed, the higher the rank or award. Although there are obvious problems inherent in this merit badge system—quality control and uniformity of criteria of merit are among them—scouting programs do a pretty good job of distinguishing among levels of performance (the basic goal of a grading system) and placing responsibility for those levels on the child, rather than on the teacher/judge.

Actually, there *are* variations of this sort of approach linked to school grading systems. In middle schools, in particular, teachers have had good success with point systems where basic and supplementary tasks in the classroom carry point values and students have a degree of choice or in selecting which tasks they will undertake. Although teachers using these systems point out that some students—usually high achievers—pay more attention to points than to the substance of the project (just as, in the scouts, there are some kids who pile up merit badges mainly for the sake of getting to the next award), generally the point system offers a legitimate middle ground that identifies levels of performance without the negativity of direct grading. The teacher creates an array of activities that can be taken up for extra credit, each one linked to a particular set of point values. Students might receive 25 points for reading and reporting on a book, or 50 points for a longer book. They might receive 25 points for each lab experiment completed; 50 points for successfully passing a science exam; 75 points for designing an independent lab experiment. The range of point values is arbitrary: depending on the system, a lab experiment might be credited one point or fifty or 250. One middle school we know creates astronomically high point values—a thousand points or more per project—because "kids like lots of points." Integral to the point system is setting up a scale that shows how many points will be required for a C, B, or A.

Contract Learning

Contract grading is a particularly attractive alternative approach to grading, one that is well suited to authentic learning and assessment. In a course or class that is graded by means of contracts, the teacher begins by describing the range of levels of performance he/she has in mind for a class activity, similar to the descriptors for a primary trait scoring system. In art, for example, a C or minimum level project might involve completing a painting successfully, while B- and A-level work might involve painting the same subject from several subjects or in different media, or could involve the students in doing supplementary reading or going to an art museum. The students get to design their projects and—this is especially important—choose the level of grade they seek and to describe the criteria that should be used to determine whether or not they have reached it. Contracts also include due dates, interim deadlines, and dates for progress reports. The student writes a contract, which is approved or modified in discussion with the teacher, allowing for negotiation of curriculum (see Boomer 1982). Most teachers who work with contracts also build in escape clauses or provisions for students to change the contract once it's under way. For an especially detailed discussion of contract grading see Malcolm Knowles' book on the topic (1986). Figure 7–9 is freely adapted from that book and merges his notions of what a good contract includes with several of the authentic assessment, evaluation, and grading strategies we have discussed in this chapter.

InterMusing

This is a test. A reasonably authentic one, we hope. The assignment is this: Develop a grading system for an interdisciplinary unit you plan teach. Build it on the hierarchy we have suggested in this chapter:

A Strong Assessment Base
leading to
Ways of Evaluating Work
leading to
The Grading System

The criteria for evaluating our "examination" are based on your own self-assessment: Can you come up with a system that is fair to students and one that you can live with in your own teaching?

---

1. Objectives
   Instructor (course minimums)
   Student (individualized)

2. Criteria for quantity
   Points
   Projects (merit badges)
   Individual negotiation

3. Ground rules/regulations
   Assigned work/attendance
   Details of requirements
   Proposal forms
   Interim deadlines/conferences

4. Criteria for quality
   Assessment measures/criteria
   • student
   • instructor
   Evidence of achievement
   Reflection/self-assessment

Adapted from *Using Learning Contracts* by Malcolm Knowles. San Francisco, CA: Jossey-Bass, 1986.

FIG. 7–9 *Contract Grading: Common Characteristics*

On Beyond Zebra

There are, of course, many other options and wrinkles to the messy business of assessment, evaluation, and grading. The growth of authentic assessment programs is encouraging, we think, because despite the limitations of grading systems, it is axiomatic that *the better the assessment system, the more just and fair the grades.* Analytic scales, for example, give much more information and are a truer measure of student performance than, say, multiple choice tests; grades growing from portfolios are better than those originating in essay tests.

In his charming book, *On Beyond Zebra*, Dr. Seuss (1955) introduces us to a narrator whose friend has just learned the alphabet:

Said Conrad Cornelius O'Donald O'Dell
My very young friend who is learning to spell: . . .
I know all the twenty-six letters like that . . .

So now I know everything anyone knows
From beginning to end. From the start to the close,
Because Z is as far as the alphabet goes.
(Excerpts from On Beyond Zebra. *Reprinted by permission of Random House, Inc.)*

Not so fast, says our narrator. He tells young Conrad that there is an undiscovered world, an alphabet that goes past Z:

So, on beyond Zebra!
Explore!
Like Columbus!
Discover new letters!

He takes Cornelius on a tour of a land of fantastic new animals described by letters like "Wuzz" and "Yuzz-a-ma-tuzz." And, he concludes:

There are things beyond Z that most people don't know.

And so it is with assessment, evaluation, and grading. Interdisciplinary teaching, linked to authentic assessment, promises new worlds of learning. In the twenty-first century, we predict, the old-fashioned letter-grading system and what it represents in testing and assessment may well prove to be as conventional as the animals in the traditional alphabet book.

"On beyond zebra!" we say, knowing that it will be people like the readers of this book who will push us into new realms of assessment, evaluation, and grading.

References

ARCHBALD A., AND F.M. NEWMANN. 1988. *Beyond Standardized Testing: Authentic Academic Achievement in the Secondary School*. Reston, VA: National Association of Secondary School Principals.

THE BONGO PROGRAM. 1987. *The Bongo Workbook*. La Guardia Community College, NY: The ECHO Project.

BOOMER, G., ed. 1982. *Negotiating the Curriculum: A Teacher-Student Partnership*. Sydney: Ashton Scholastic.

BRANDT, R. 1993. "On Outcome-Based Education: A Conversation with Bill Spady." *Educational Leadership* 52(1): 66–70.

BROWN, R. 1989. "Testing and Thoughtfulness." *Educational Leadership* 48(4): 31–33.

CASE, R. 1992. "On the Need to Assess Authentically." *Holistic Education Review* 5(4): 14–23.

DIXON, J. 1967. *Growth Through English*. London and Urbana, IL: National Association for the Teaching of English and National Council of Teachers of English.

ELBOW, P. 1993. "Ranking, Evaluating, and Liking: Sorting Out Three Forms of Judgment." *College English* (55)2: 187–206.

HUNTER, M. 1982. *Mastery Learning*. El Segundo, CA: TIP Publications.

KNOWLES, M. 1986. *Using Learning Contracts*. San Francisco: Jossey Bass.

MAJESKY, D. 1993. "Grading Should Go." *Educational Leadership* 52(7): 88–90,

MARTINEZ, M., AND J.I. LIPSON. 1989. "Assessment for Learning." *Educational Leadership* 48(4): 73–75.

MATHERS, C. 1993. "When Decades Collide: An Interdisciplinary Approach to Research and Technology." *The Astonishing Curriculum: Language in Science and Humanities*, ed. S. Tchudi, 65–75. Urbana, IL: National Council Teachers of English.

SEUSS, DR. (GEISSEL, T.). 1955. *On Beyond Zebra*. New York: Random House.

SHEPARD, L.A. 1989. "Why We Need Better Assessments." *Educational Leadership* 48(7): 4–9.

SLAVIN, R. 1989. "On Mastery Learning and Mastery Teaching." *Educational Leadership* 48(4): 77–79.

STITT, G. 1993. "Winning at Any Cost Unacceptable." *The Sagebrush* 100(20): 4–5.

TIERNEY, R. 1993. "Pursuing Assessment, Pursuing History: Trying to Make Them the Same." *History Matters!* 5(8): 1, 5.

WIGGINS, G. 1989. "Teaching to the Authentic Test." *Educational Leadership* 48(4): 41–47.

WOLF, D.P. 1989. "Portfolio Assessment: Sampling Student Work." *Educational Leadership* 48(4): 35–39.

8

Developing and Defending Interdisciplinary Curriculum

I n preceding chapters we have explained our conception of interdisciplinary thematic instruction, emphasizing throughout that teachers must loosen the structures within which they plan courses and daily lesson plans to allow for the contingencies of exploration. We have said that exploration often leads into the unknown, creating a degree of uncertainty that teachers must contend with in their planning and teaching. Teachers, we have suggested, must follow at times, taking direction from students as their explorations cause them to ask questions that lead to quests for new understandings.

Simultaneously, as students are engaged in their quests, teachers find ways to interject the curriculum, offering within the context of the quest disciplinary knowledge and aid in the development of the skills that allow for more effective learning. Among those skills are the use of structures and processes employed by the various disciplines to make knowledge.

As we have said before, this is no mean trick. It involves the creation of a learning environment that looks different from what most are used to, a more fluid environment in which, at most times, many things are taking place at once. Somewhat chaotic, yes, but with good reason, because students are wrestling with information rather than receiving it in neat packages. Chaotic but most definitely goal oriented. And it is this we want to stress: Good interdisciplinary thematic teaching is tightly bound to clearly defined goals and objectives. Teachers still provide direction, but the path to goals and objectives is *of necessity* less clearly defined than with more traditional modes of instruction. Teachers and students, under the best interdisciplinary exploratory conditions, blaze paths together, the teacher serving as the seasoned guide, the one most capable of recognizing and pointing out the signs that mark the trail. Essentially, curriculum must come to be understood as a process that allows methodology to evolve from interaction with students. Curriculum, in a sense, becomes something less than a blueprint, and something more like a set of intellectual procedures that allow one to read, interpret, and act upon what one observes to be happening as students act and interact to make sense of their world.

This is not "far out" stuff. Indeed, it is chiseled from some of the bedrock principles of curriculum development first espoused by Ralph Tyler in his book *Basic Principles of Curriculum and Instruction* (1949). Tyler posits that curriculum must emanate from a sense of the "educational purposes" that a school should "seek to attain," and these purposes must be derived from "studies of the learners themselves" and "studies of contemporary life outside the school." Once the purposes are understood, broad curricular goals can be set, which will govern the objectives that schools seek to help students attain (3–25).

A most sensible template, we think. In fact this book has called upon teachers to study their students and the communities in which they live to discover themes relevant to the student's world. The questing we hope to inspire is not, as we said before, directionless. But it is less direct and more loosely directed than what has arisen from Tyler's maxims. Let us put it this way: The purpose of learning can be understood to good ends in Tylerian terms by schools and teachers *if* it is understood also that students learn for reasons other than those that guide the formal curriculum. While schools operate, we would hope, for the sake of helping individuals and society achieve necessary and meaningful goals, these long range goals are not the potent incentives that cause students to learn. Students learn for the sake of satisfying more immediate needs and desires. This does not mean that the long range and lofty need to be sacrificed for the immediate. Rather, it means that good curriculum helps students advance toward the achievement of long range goals by allowing them to learn for the sake of satisfying immediate needs and desires.

The curriculum we envision, the curriculum that some are now using with good results, is one that places the student first, not in a selfish or self-serving way, but in a way that brings immediacy to the learning that is taking place so that learning comes to be understood as a response to the circumstances of life. Learning becomes something other than a means for passing school-based tests. It becomes a habit, a tool, a means for discovering viable truths upon which to base action. Those actions may serve self, but because they are *thoughtful*, there is potential that they will serve others as well. The student is at the center because the student is ultimately the decision maker. The ultimate purpose of a socially sound, future-minded curriculum is for individuals to attain the ability to make informed and wise decisions.

Curriculum aimed at strengthening decision-making ability is bound to look different from curriculum designed to inculcate students in particular contents. And we would contend, despite acknowledgment in recent years of the importance of critical thinking as an instructional objective, most of the curricula we see today, and most tests of achievement, are indeed content based. Now, we do not argue against the importance of content and knowledge. We do not want to be misunderstood to be promoting a contentless process model of instruction. Instead, what we seek is a true fusion of process and content, knowledge taken in and properly evaluated so that actions are based on sound understandings.

The constructivist perspective we have come to adopt causes us to understand that knowledge, no matter how common, is never understood by all in completely the same way, that different people looking at the same objects or events inevitably will see things differently. And cognizance of this difference in the way things are seen is an essential element of critical thinking—an understanding of the possibility of many perspectives that can change the meaning of the phenomenon being considered. Vygotsky (1989) makes the point that the ability to wrestle internally with multiple perspectives *is* the engine of critical thought. Further, Vygotsky tells us that the critical mechanism results from interaction with those who do not think as we do, who place their *constructions* in contention with our own. The external manifestation of critical thinking is *dialectic*, and dialectic is dependent on the existence of *knowledges* rather than commonly held knowledge.

This theoretical perspective does not preclude the teaching of particular bodies of content to all students. And it does not argue against the possibility of commonality of thought, of minds converging to agree upon the existence of certain truths. However, it does dispute the efficacy of instruction as indoctrination. "Cookie-cutter curricula," one method, one answer, one *shape* for all learners, is not only an impediment to healthy intellectual development, it is also a major obstacle to social progress, for it eliminates the possibility of students participating in dialectical activities that lead to thoughtfulness and rigor in decision making.

Though we strenuously contend with the notion that lists of common knowledge (à la E.D. Hirsch 1987) will bind together a fractured society, we do see value in attitudes held in common that allow for good judgment in matters of personal and social significance. These attitudes are bound to a willingness to enter into and the ability to become *truly* engaged and active in the learning process, the desire and the capacity to find the *real* meaning of things, and the gumption to cope with the uncertainty that the quest for real meaning, for truth, is bound to produce.

Attitude and will are personal attributes and are often ignored in systems of mass education. So are the motives that lead individuals to learn and to consider the meaning of what has been learned to guide action. Motive has much to do with willingness and attitude, and the three much to do with the *quality* of the learning that takes place.

InterMusing

Test the theory. Have you learned anything of value lately? How to use a personal computer or a new piece of software? Something about how children think, or how they can be taught? How to properly use the gears on a mountain bike, or how to turn clay into rich soil? Something about human nature? Describe for yourself what gave you the will to pursue this learning. Compare learning in this instance to learning in another, say learning in preparation for an examination of some kind, the Graduate Record Exam or a driver's license test. Do you detect differences in your attitude toward the learning, in the nature of your willingness to learn? Consider how the factors of motive and attitude affect the quality of the learning experience.

A Hierarchy of Motives

As motive drives the learning process, so too does motive drive the process of curriculum development. We mentioned above that curriculum should be viewed as a process for evolving methodologies that are responsive to the needs of students and society. Assessment of these needs produces the motives underlying the creation of curriculum. These motives, in turn, serve to produce the criteria by which determinations of the soundness of curriculum and the instructional moves it promotes are made. Judgments of what is good or bad, what should be discarded or retained, must be made in reference to these motives. And to this end we offer Figure 8–1, a *hierarchy of motives* for instructional planning.

The hierarchy of motives is a framework for thinking about curriculum, a framework for deriving both the principles of instruction and instructional practices. The hierarchy, properly employed, will not lead to a single best curriculum for all teachers and all students. It will not even lead to a one best curriculum for any individual teacher over a period of time. Instead, it is intended to generate

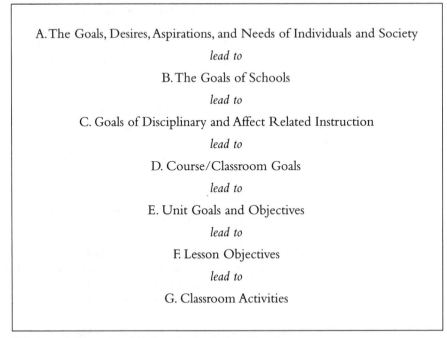

A. The Goals, Desires, Aspirations, and Needs of Individuals and Society

lead to

B. The Goals of Schools

lead to

C. Goals of Disciplinary and Affect Related Instruction

lead to

D. Course/Classroom Goals

lead to

E. Unit Goals and Objectives

lead to

F. Lesson Objectives

lead to

G. Classroom Activities

FIG. 8–1   *A Hierarchy of Motives for Curriculum Planning*

student-appropriate curricula, to illuminate for teachers the many paths available to them for moving students toward something understood to be an *ultimate* curricular goal. For ourselves, we have defined the ultimate goal as competence in decision making. Others may find different beacons to guide instructional decisions. In fact, establishing sound beacons probably should be the issue of foremost concern for a dialectic of educators. We cannot know what to do until we know what we are about.

The existence of contending ideals based on contending notions of what the beacon goals of education should or must be is a healthy thing. It should constantly remind us of the legitimacy of constructivist theory and the true meaning of knowledge—that individuals are not handed what is real and what is right. Somehow they make those determinations for themselves. Education does not produce agreement, nor should it. Instead, it should lead one to know when to agree, when to disagree, and how to deal with disagreements, be they with other persons or intra-personally. Through such intra-musings and inter-musings, honestly enjoined, we become more thoughtful, and get closer to the truth.

Teachers and the Hierarchy of Motives

Throughout the book we have asked readers to become engaged in InterMusings. These exercises are intended to produce the *feel* of authentic learning in hope that the sensation will put teachers in touch with what students feel when they are engaged in learning that is authentic. We place the responsibility for curricular decision making in the hands of teachers for they are able to monitor the sensations and feelings students are experiencing at any given moment in response to curricular moves. Responsive teaching, "reflective practice" as Donald Schon (1983) refers to it, calls for regular adjusting of curriculum in light of the teacher's assessment of how students are reacting to the methods being employed.

This procedure of reflection and response has its guidelines, and echoes some of the principles of curriculum development advocated by those who followed Tyler. Goals govern objectives, and objectives govern the content and methods employed in lessons. Outcomes are evaluated to establish whether the methods employed have achieved the desired effect. This sounds very mechanical, and, in the context of the textbook, standardized-test-generated curriculum so prevalent today, they are mechanical. They dictate curriculum that is static, that tells teachers that the starting point of their work is the lesson. The goals and objectives are set. When things do not go well, it is the methodology that is adjusted, not the objectives, not the goals, not the notion of what it means to truly learn what is important to learn. The curriculum comes from outside and as such cannot be responsive to the learners inside a particular classroom at a particular point in time.

For reflective teaching to take place, we hand the whole of the hierarchy over to the teacher. It a tool for teachers to use to develop curriculum models, to determine what should be taught, when it should be taught, and how it should be taught. It should also help in defending decisions made and in determining how far out on a limb one should go.

The basic elements of curriculum are the lesson and the activities of which it is composed. The primary occupation of teachers is designing lessons, which is dictated by the elements A through E in the hierarchy in Figure 8–1. Lessons are shaped by deliberations concerning what instruction is supposed to accomplish. Lessons and lesson activities take place, under the best conditions, when it is understood that participation in certain activities is the best possible way for students to accomplish legitimate lesson objectives. Somewhere along the line, determinations are made as to which objectives are the best, based upon some understanding of how achievement of these objectives aids in the attainment of broader goals, such as unit goals. Unit goals are determined to be worthwhile if they move students toward the goals of courses; course goals are validated in relation to the goals of disciplines; and discipline goals are validated in relation to the goals of schools. Ultimately, the goals of schools are justified in terms of how their achievement aids students in accomplishing goals related to the desires, aspirations, and needs of individuals and society.

An Example

To demonstrate how the hierarchy is to be used, we will use the U.S. Constitution as an example. In looking at the Constitution as something to be taught, somewhere along the line a determination has to be made as to what about the Constitution *should be* or *needs to be* taught. To discover the best answers, one climbs up the hierarchy of motives' ladder, ultimately basing what is taught on what will best serve the goals, aspirations, desires, and needs of individuals and society. The question is really one of "Why the Constitution?" If there is good reason to teach the Constitution, it is that reason that provides the guiding light for decision making.

If the answer to "Why the Constitution?" is that the Constitution is the basis for all law and conduct in the United States, and law and conduct as suggested by the Constitution provides guidelines for the proper social and political behavior of individuals in the United States, then the teaching of the Constitution must be aimed at helping individuals develop an understanding of the Constitution that will allow them to use it as a guide for social and political behavior.

Such an understanding is something other than knowing when it was written, by whom it was written, why it was written, and the exact words of which it is composed. All of these aspects of "knowing the Constitution" may play a role in developing an understanding that leads to decisions regarding how one behaves in a country governed by such a document, but knowing these does not necessarily lead to that end. Such facts can, however, be taught *for* that end. The framers' lives, for instance, can be studied in such a way as to get at their motives for placing particular statements in the document. These motives can be studied in relation to their significance, for the meaning of the statements can be studied to determine how they are meant to guide the conduct of individuals.

At the lessons and activities level, this notion of knowing the Constitution would mitigate such things as simple memorization of passages and dates. But a profitable lesson might be one that asks students to understand the conditions of life in eighteenth century America and the concerns of eighteenth century Americans such as Jefferson, Hamilton, and Franklin as they drafted the document. A unit might consist of a project recreating a colonial village based on readings from period literature and newspapers and discussions of how this life influenced thought and the shaping of the Constitution. This could be made to lead to questions of the relevance of elements of the Constitution for governing social and political life of twentieth and twenty-first century societies. Such activities would be consistent with the societal and individual goals we have stated that give reason to the teaching of the U.S. Constitution.

This process of reflection can be used to assess the meaning and value of any piece of curriculum. And we would wager that when so analyzed, the teaching of almost any content benefits by being taught in the context of interdisciplinary activities. If the Constitution is to be understood as a guide for social and political behavior, then so too must its relevance to the conditions of modern life. These conditions cannot be adequately understood without reference to mathematical, historical, literary, and scientific knowledge and procedures. Today, decisions are being made in the Supreme Court, the nation's Constitutional arbiter, on such things as recombinant DNA research, moral issues related to surrogate motherhood, automobile safety, automatic firearms, and the rights of gay people, none of which is mentioned specifically in the document. Understanding the Constitution in a *relevant* and *useful* manner calls for application and integration of multiple disciplines.

InterMusing

Choose a piece of curriculum from the discipline, or one of the disciplines you teach and consider what, for yourself as a learner, it means to *have understanding* of it. If you have learned what that piece of curriculum can or should teach, what is it that you would know or be able to do as a result of having *successfully* received *effective* instruction? Then consider how the piece of curriculum would have to be taught if instruction were to be effective.

Flexibility and Quality

In checking out objectives and activities in light of the higher order instructional goals on the hierarchy of motives, we become honest about what has to be done to promote *meaningful* learning. Such reflection might cause us to question why we do some of the things we regularly do in our teaching. Now, goals and objectives and all the talk with which we've surrounded them makes it sound as if with enough thinking a right or a "one best" curriculum can be fashioned. The individual and the particular circumstances under which certain groups of students learn provide the ringer. There is no one best if the individual is the focus of instruction; good curricula must be able to accommodate for individuals and individual groups of students. Not all students need to or care to achieve the same ends. All do not come to the curriculum with the same predispositions, knowledge, or attitudes.

This does not mean separate curricula for each students, or for each group of students. Rather, it calls for curriculum that is flexible enough to suit their needs, take advantage of predispositions, knowledge, attitudes, and the rest. And we think that most practitioners can have a flexible curriculum even in the face of seemingly rigid administrative prerogatives. We say this because most curriculum directives are most concerned with content. Our concern is more with the quality of learning that takes place. We do not suggest that anyone abandon the teaching of the Constitution, the legislative process, or cubic measures. We do not argue against the teaching of facts. Our concern is that these things be taught so that they are meaningful for the student, relevant to the individual and beneficial in terms of how the individual operates within society.

In a booklet titled *Social Studies Guidelines* published by our local school district, one stated goal of the curriculum is for students to "understand the development of the American Constitution." Listed under the heading, "To demonstrate this, students will," are listed the following items:

- list and explain the weaknesses of the Articles of Confederation

- describe areas of agreement and disagreement among the framers of the Constitution

- identify major areas of compromise in the Constitution

- identify contributions of major political philosophies to American constitutional government

These are definitely content-related outcomes. But each has within it the potential to help students develop decision-making skills if the methods by which they are taught allow for such.

The goal we stated above for the teaching of the Constitution was to allow students to utilize the Constitution as a guide for proper social and political behavior. To this end, the "weaknesses" of the Articles of Confederation could be discussed as they pertain to the contingencies of life today, and from this perspective, they could be contrasted with the "strengths" of the Constitution that replaced them. At the same time, the decision-making process that led to the replacing of one document with another could be studied in a manner consistent with our Constitution goal. So could "agreement and disagreement among the framers" and "major areas of compromise."

All of this could be taught in the context of several of the interdisciplinary units we have described. The U.S. Highway 40 project, for instance, might, as we have suggested, involve exploration into federal legislation surrounding the construction of interstate highways. Through insights gained by students into the role of Representative Baring in the legislative process, they could look at Constitutionally mandated legislative processes, their facility and their flaws. And, we would argue, taught within this context, the objectives are made relevant to the broader goals of schools as they relate to the betterment of individuals and society.

Certainly, we would like to see the "objectives" in the *Social Studies Guidelines* rewritten to better reflect what we believe to be more relevant and useful ends for instruction. But we do know that these guidelines are much like those many teachers are handed. We use the Washoe County School District guide to show that even when faced with such mandates, teachers need not retreat from finding ways to make learning meaningful.

InterMusing

Find your beacon, one that you can rest with, however tentatively, for now. Define it. Consider its implications for individuals and the society in which they live. Take a piece of the curriculum you teach and the methods you use to teach it and examine your instruction under the light of the beacon goals. If our beacon were your beacon, how well would the manner in which you teach the structure of the DNA molecule, the Constitution, cubic measurements, or English grammar work to help students become better decision makers? If confined to a curriculum imposed from outside, find a dictum that you believe may be on the "cheap" side and consider how you might comply without dimming for yourself or your students the light cast by the beacon.

Time

As we write we hear the voices of readers pleading the case of limited time. We have listened carefully to that case. Curriculum has much to do with time, and as one can see in curriculum guides, curriculum organization is often cast as a more or less rigid sequence of instructional events. At certain moments in their careers, students are to learn particular things. Tests are administered at "strategic" times to determine whether those things have been learned.

The sequences of learning are sometimes based upon developmental theory, sometimes upon someone's sense of the structure of the disciplines in line with conceptions of a hierarchy of knowledge and skill: One cannot learn to divide until he or she has learned how to add, subtract, and multiply. One cannot learn to write until he or she knows the letters of alphabet and can use them to spell words. And one cannot do research until he or she knows how to use the library. These are seemingly logical assumptions, but they sometimes get in the way of good instruction. While we are not so certain as to whether the sequence of mathematical processes can be changed, we do know of students who write before learning to spell through the Language Experience Approach by dictating their words to adults for transcription (see Lehr 1991; Watson 1987; Brown 1991). In programs based on exploration, we can see students beginning research before being given lessons on how to use the library, beginning their research, discovering a *need* to know how to access materials, then being given the instruction their situation calls for. We can imagine a *need* for division arising prior to lessons in the "earlier" math functions in the context of exploration projects, for example, children needing to know how many people will be working in each exploration group when the class is evenly divided.

Time plays another role in curriculum planning. Floyd Robinson, John Ross, and Floyd White in *Curriculum Development for Effective Instruction* (1985) explain it in this way:

> A fundamental starting point for a definition of curriculum in terms of formal public education is the recognition that curricula have clearly designated time periods associated with them. Schools have available to them a relatively fixed amount of student time. Consequently, naturally occurring or artificially created time periods provide a dominant framework and set of constraints for curriculum planning by professional educators. (2)

No doubt, this is true, and we know that time constraints must be dealt with. On the other hand, hyper-awareness of time constraints, coupled with sequence pressures made all too real by testing programs, sometimes cause teachers to back away from truly good curricula or from following pedagogical instincts that allow curriculum to be shaped by teachers' recognition of individuals' needs.

Some reading this book will back away from thematic interdisciplinary teaching for these very reasons, because even if they do buy what we have been selling, the methodologies we have argued for are time consuming and may preclude certain things being covered by the appointed times. Chapter 2 offers a critique of the coverage mentality, and we reiterate Richard Paul's claim that coverage often stands in place of depth of understanding (1994).

It is easy for those on the outside to pontificate on the importance of depth in relation to coverage. We do not have to suffer the slings and arrows. But we will continue to pontificate nonetheless, taking a slightly different tack, one we have implied throughout discussion of the hierarchy of motives. We think there are legitimate ways to reduce the number of pieces that *must* be covered. Some bits of content, as the standards documents discussed in other chapters indicate, can justly be ignored. Others can be covered adequately by integrating them with more essential chunks of learning and by making the argument that those pieces need not be touched upon directly, or that students, given essential knowledge and skill will be able to find and make use of this information when they need it.

In every curriculum, those we use at the university included, there is *stuff* that can be ignored, and by being ignored will not diminish the *quality* of the learning that takes place. In education courses, for instance, Bloom's Taxonomy inevitably shows up. Some would think it criminal to allow graduates to leave education programs without being able to recite the six elements of Bloom's scale. The taxonomy may be helpful, but instructors should wrestle with the question of whether it needs to be taught as a discrete piece of information. Perhaps time can better be spent analyzing cases of teaching and discussing the kinds of learning to which the observed teaching might lead. This could be considered a covert or inductive way of teaching the *principles* of Bloom's, but there need not be any expectation that students know specifically the Bloomian categories, even if they have been encountered in text or classroom discussion. If some curriculum guide existed for these courses and demanded that students be able to recite the names of the categories on the taxonomy, and instructors had no time to fight for curricular revisions, then perhaps one could introduce a clever mnemonic device to get students through the test.

What we are suggesting is that teachers and curriculum planners work toward a leaner sense of content by weighing the pieces to determine whether they are essential to student attainment of the real goals of the disciplines, schools, individuals, and the society. To test the criticality of a piece of information, run it up the hierarchy of motives and try to prove its essential nature. Our bet is that many pieces of content deemed to be essential will be found not to be so essential and that the *essence* will be picked up, taught either directly or indirectly at some point in the course of the student's life as a learner.

InterMusing

Make a list of items taught as a part of your curriculum. List at least one hundred of them. Go through the list and check off those that are essential bits of learning and justify the check by explaining how students, in light of goals at the upper reaches of the hierarchy of motives, will be worse off if they do not receive direct instruction on these items. How many essentials are you left with? And how much time can be saved if you forgo the teaching of those that your list shows to be non-essential?

We could say, after going through our list, that in line with our highest order or *beacon goal* of decision making, students do not have to know the names of the signers of the Constitution to understand the essential principles for which its teaching is intended, though it is probable that students will bump up against these names as the essential principles are being taught.

Awareness of what is essential leads to another economically sound practice, noticing where the essence is taught *across the curriculum*, within the different curricula. Many essential principles related to the Constitution, for instance, are taught through studies not directly related to the Constitution. Such things as laws, compacts, negotiations, contracts, and compromise can be taught as students attempt to

Discipline	Concepts Laws	Negotiation	Contracts
Math	Algorithms, theorems	Bargaining activities	Bargaining activities
English	Grammar, poetic form, metrics	Collaborative writing projects, Jack and the Bean Stalk	Faustus, Huck, and Jim
Music	Rhythm, chord progressions	Improvisation	Composer to player, player to player (harmony)
Social Studies	Civil law, constitutional law	Legislative process, labor/management	Constitution, treaties, agreements
Science	Laws of physics, laboratory rules, chemical bonds, scientific method	Methods of proof	Scientific method, methods of proof
Physical Education	Rules of games	Strategy sessions	Teams, cooperation

FIG. 8–2 *Essential Principles Across the Curriculum*

work with one another on projects and attempt to govern themselves in groups. Games taught in physical education have rules that function to serve all players in important ways. Laws are rules. A physical education game that has students playing without rules will most likely be a very unenjoyable game. Given time, players will negotiate a compact, a set of rules that most certainly will restrict action, compromise their "rights," but make the game a more enjoyable one to play. Figure 8–2 is a rough conception of a chart that might be used to map essential concepts across the curriculum. A similar map could be developed to show how these essential concepts are taught across the grade levels. In the earliest grades, in very concrete ways, laws, negotiations, and contracts are a part of the everyday lives of children. As they grow older and become better able to understand abstractions, their early encounters with the *forces* of these concepts can be used to make the abstractions more comprehensible.

Economies of Redundancy

The *economy of redundancy*, if studied by teachers, not only leads to better use of time, but to a more realistic sense of what quality learning is. A concept learned as it applies to one set of phenomenon but not recognized when it applies to others is a concept not well understood. Another example: If one were to properly and adequately *know* the double helix, what is it that would be known? That Crick and Watson discovered it? That it defines the structure of the DNA molecule? Or is it important that our conception of knowing concern itself with the relationship of that structure to function? It is, after all, the relationship of form to function that gives Crick and Watson's discovery explanatory power. The structure of the DNA molecule allows it to function as a DNA molecule. A curriculum that spends time moving students toward an understanding of form/function relationships as they apply to the DNA molecule, even if *time consuming,* is more economical than a curriculum that leaves off at Crick and Watson and the name of the structure.

Interdisciplinary curriculum is potentially the most economical of curricula, if it causes teachers to examine carefully what it is that is essential in the *contents* they teach, and to recognize where across curricula these same essentials are being addressed. The principle of form/function relationships, once learned in biology or physics, for instance, can be applied by students, with some nudging from teachers, to form/function relationships in literature and art. On a more abstract plane, understanding of form/function provides an explanatory base for cause/effect relationships. This is the economy of redundancy.

Interdisciplinarity and Economy

Redundancy teaches only if one recognizes similarities between occurrences, understands that *A* is another or *other* occurance of B, and takes advantage of the relationship. Teachers free up time by making these connections. There is more time for exploration. And students benefit through the improved quality of the learning that results from understanding the broad application of the concepts they encounter. To recognize that ratio and proportion are constructs that have relevance outside mathematics is to truly understand the essence of ratio and proportion and to know of and be able to take advantage of the cross disciplinary relevance of concepts is to know the power of those concepts as explanatory tools, as tools for making decisions across the spectrum of situations one will encounter in a lifetime.

Economical Versus Cheap

What we are looking for and want to offer are tools for deriving lessons and classroom activities that are essential, possess essence, and are economical in the best sense of the term. The distinction between economical and cheap is a critical one. As a curriculum planner, one is constantly forced to make decisions as to how to use time and resources and how to *argue for* time and resources. Economical means that one is doing what needs to be done and doing it so well as not to squander time or resource. Cheap, on the other hand, implies sacrifice of quality, goals diminished to fit a budget. Cheap approaches get something done, but not well.

Lesson Objectives: Students will understand the concept of cubic measurement and the usefulness of such measurements. They will understand the concept of cubic measurement in relation to squared and linear measurements. Students will apply their understanding of the cubic yard to the problem of purchasing sufficient material to cover a five-mile segment of road and be able, using price lists from actual road materials suppliers, to calculate the cost of the materials they will need.

Activity: Students will be given cubes scaled to represent a cubic yard. They will be asked to examine the cube and to describe its properties to show that width, length, and depth measure one yard. The cubes are hollow so that material can be loaded into them to show how a cubic yard may be used to measure quantities of certain kinds of material such as gravel, rock, and cement, or asphalt. The students will then be asked to consider the problem they, as road planners, must deal with: How many cubic yards of particular materials they need to cover the five-mile segment of road they are responsible for planning. Groups of five are asked to consider what must be done to calculate first, the quantity of material needed, and second, the price they will have to pay for those quantities. As much guidance as necessary will be given to help students determine that at some point cubic yards must be translated into square feet. Using specifications found in regulatory documents for highway construction, students will find the depths to which various materials must be poured (according to Sargious 1975 "less pavement structure thickness is required" for asphalt). Students will, with what help they need from the teacher, find that the surface area of the top of a cubic yard is nine square feet. The depth of the cube is three feet and, if one needs to use material to a depth of one foot, a cubic yard will cover twenty-seven square feet (nine square feet multiplied by three). Students will then be asked to find how many cubic yards of material they will need. To do this they will have to find the number of square feet to be covered. To do this they will need to know the standard width of traffic lanes and paved sidings and the number of lanes the road will have. With their knowledge of the number of feet in a mile and the formula for calculating area, they will be able to determine the surface area. They will then have to translate their findings into cubic feet. Lastly, students will be asked to calculate the cost of purchasing particular materials for their road segment. The prices will come from suppliers' catalogs or from price quotations obtained by phone.

FIG. 8–3 *Lesson Plan: Cubic Yards*

Perhaps the single most difficult obstacle to implementation of interdisciplinary curricula, especially the kind of exploratory interdisciplinary curriculum we advocate, is the belief that it consumes great amounts of the little time available for teaching students what they need to know. We have argued the case for quality of understanding and feel that our position is supported in the standards documents that have recently been developed. Figure 8-3 is a lesson plan that we offer as proof of the economy of our madness.

The *value* added to student understanding of the concepts being taught makes worthwhile the time expended for the interdisciplinary exploration that provides context for the lesson. Figure 8–4 is our attempt to "flesh out" the benefits accrued from the context exploration provides.

We looked at a 1987 edition of *Addison-Wesley Mathematics* (Eicholz, O'Daffer, and Fleenor 1987) and found "cubic units" taught in sections titled "volume" and "capacity." Volume was defined as "measurement of a region of space. A unit for volume," says the text, "is a cube which has 1 unit on each edge. To find volume, we count the number of *cubic units*." This explanation is followed by a number of formulas and problems that ask for application of the formulas. The page on "capacity" has this explanation atop: "Mario has some mugs that each hold 200 milliliters (*mL*). Milliliters are units of liquid measure or *capacity*." These lines of text are followed by a box showing the relationship of units of volume to units of capacity. We ask that you consider and compare the kind of understandings students might attain from the different approaches, our thematic interdisciplinary approach and the text's approach.

InterMusing

Taking off from our last request, that you consider the qualitative difference between the thematic interdisciplinary approach we outline in Figures 8–3 and 8–4 and the approach taken by the text, play the role of instructional banker and add up the costs and benefits of each. Is the text's approach economical? Is ours? How are the understandings that are derived from the approaches different? Does the difference justify the extra cost of the thematic interdisciplinary approach? Beyond the mathematics learned, how might each contribute to an *economy of redundancy?* Are there understandings beyond mathematics that the approaches might offer? List what those may be and add them to your tally. Play the game of cost versus benefit and determine which of the approaches is more worthwhile.

Organizing

How classrooms are organized for thematic interdisciplinary teaching depends to a great extent on how schools are organized. Some reading this book will be teach-

Interdisciplinary Activity: In groups students will develop a well reasoned plan for the construction of a five-mile segment of highway between two given points. The plan is to serve as a contractor's bid.

Disciplinary Aspects
Mathematics

Concepts
Linear, square, and cubic measurements; formulas and algorithms for finding cost per given measure (cost per linear foot, cost per mile) and conversions such as feet to miles (if two cubic yards of material will cover X feet, how much is needed to cover X miles?). Graphing as another means of statistical reporting.

Structure: These measurements will be learned within the context of making determinations as to how much material is needed for completion of particular aspects of road construction.

Spontaneity: Students, within the structure of the activity and working toward the understood goal, will discover where and when particular computations, algorithms, and formulas are applicable.

Synthesis: Students will understand how several mathematical processes must be applied to derive the answers they need to achieve the understood goal of the project.

Resources
Students will make use of price lists from suppliers and regulatory documents that contain government specifications for road construction. These documents use the terminology of mathematics: linear, square, cubic inches, feet, and yards.

Benefits of Learning in ID Context
Each of these concepts is tied to concrete manifestations and shown in the context of its application to real-world problems. Computation, application of formulas and algorithms are not the end of the process. Knowledge derived from their calculations is then transferred to the decision-making process, thus linking mathematics to decision making. Because the problem is a complex one, students must not only compute and apply formulas and algorithms, they must also decide which are appropriate for answering the questions the project poses. Since the project's goal is to produce a persuasive document, students learn how numbers are used in persuasion. Graphing and other means for reporting of statistical data can be used. The project will provide a context of complexity not normally dealt with by students in mathematics courses. Cost must be considered in light of benefit: Less expensive materials might deteriorate more quickly, thus leading to greater cost over time. The human and ecological costs of routes will also have to be considered. In using documents such as suppliers' price lists and regulatory documents, students will see math as it exists outside the school.

FIG. 8–4 *Fragment of Fleshy Lesson Plan*

ing in multi-subject elementary classrooms, others in single-subject secondary classrooms. Some might be working on interdisciplinary teams with two, three, or four other teachers, and some may be working in pairs: an English teacher teamed with a social studies teacher, a science teacher teamed with a mathematics teacher. Our preference is for the team; more heads, varied expertise, more ideas. But teachers rarely get to select their situations and have to make do with what they have. Things can, of course, be changed, and if interdisciplinary teams provide the most economical means for moving students toward the goals at the top of the hierarchy of motives, then perhaps advocacy for change is something to consider.

Even if structural change is not on the agenda, interdisciplinary teaching can still take place in single-subject courses as well as multi-disciplinary classrooms. The highway mathematics illustrated in Figures 8–2 and 8–3 can be part of an *in-house* project dedicated solely to the teaching of mathematical concepts as they apply to a real-world endeavor, here, the building of a highway. This is one possibility, a disciplinary course utilizing a theme to teach the discipline.

Such a course is bound to have interdisciplinary benefits, but those benefits may be regarded as simply being ancillary to the real agenda. There is some waste here, we think, for the economy of redundancy is being ignored. There is also something rich about disciplinary concepts being taught within meaningful contexts.

Figure 8–5 offers a list of organizational possibilities for theme-based interdisciplinary programs. The first we've just described. Here a theme is simply a device for tying concepts to the world. The teacher explains percentages in terms

1. Subjects are taught independently of one another using thematic approaches. The use of the highway theme to teach concepts in mathematics would be an example. No attempt is made to move beyond disciplinary boundaries to understand the theme.

2. Subjects are taught independent of one another using thematic approaches. The focus is on using disciplinary knowledge and skill to solve theme-related problems but no effort is made to deal with the problems' implications for other disciplines.

3. Subjects are taught independently of one another, in single-subject classrooms or in discipline-specific units but integration of subjects is promoted to provide authentic situations for developing realistic understandings of the application of disciplinary concepts.

4. Interdisciplinary programs in which disciplinary divisions are maintained but integration of disciplines is promoted for solving problems that are interdisciplinary in nature.

5. Interdisciplinary programs in which disciplinary divisions are eradicated.

FIG. 8–5 *Organizational Possibilities for Interdisciplinary Study*

of how much of the total cost of Interstate 80 went to guardrails, or what portion of the population of Polaris left the town after U.S. 40 was bypassed. Students do not participate in thematic activities; their time is spent studying the discipline. The theme is used primarily to provide exemplars. The advantage of such programs is that they are relatively easy to put in place, rarely necessitate administrative approval, and require little restructuring of curriculum.

The second option differs from the first in that students are more actively engaged with the theme, solving problems generated by the theme to better understand disciplinary concepts. They might, for instance, build a model highway bridge to scale to solidify understanding of the concept of ratio. This type of program, like the first, requires little or no organizational restructuring. It does, however require curricular changes, mostly redesign of the materials used to reflect the theme and some restructuring of time to allow students to become engaged with the theme.

Option three moves closer to actual interdisciplinary study though the primary focus is still on the knowledge and procedures of a single discipline. Disciplines other than the primary discipline are recognized to give students an understanding of the nature of real-world problems to which the discipline might apply. The problem of building a highway bridge is compounded when regulatory statutes are introduced, when the geography of the area to be spanned must be considered, or when issues of aesthetics are raised. Instructional materials must be developed or found and, since some time will be dedicated to developing understandings outside the boundaries of the primary discipline, administrative approval may be necessary. The question of "Why spend time on social studies in the mathematics class?" is one that might have to be answered. We point to the hierarchy of motives as a tool for building the case. Using our beacon goal, we would argue that for mathematics or social studies to truly aid students in making real-world decisions, they must understand the complexity of the problems to which the disciplines pertain. Such understandings are naturally interdisciplinary.

The fourth option involves teams of teachers who retain their disciplinary affiliations but work together to design integrated thematic programs. In this category we also include elementary school teachers who continue to divide the curriculum into discrete subjects but utilize themes to connect these subjects to one another in significant ways. For example, we have observed teachers using materials from Project Ocean as a basis for teaching math, English, science, mathematics, art, and music. Locally, a group of teachers from Brown Elementary School in Reno created a more desert appropriate "land-locked" program titled *Teaching Nevada* (Dunton, Spencer, Taylor, Meibergen 1993). This kindergarten through sixth grade program utilized the desert community theme to study aspects of life in the region beginning with neighborhoods and expanding out to the ecosystems of Nevada. At each grade level a different aspect of life in the state became the focal point for all disciplinary studies.

At the secondary level, teachers from several disciplines teach their subjects using a common thematic base while involving students in projects that cause students to utilize skill and knowledge acquired through disciplinary studies. The theme and the projects create context for disciplinary studies, problems to which the disciplines can be applied, and exemplars for teaching disciplinary concepts.

Such programs do require changes in school structure, especially in scheduling configurations to allow teachers on interdisciplinary teams to share groups of students. Time must also be found for team planning sessions and for students to carry out project work. As with option three, complaints are sometimes heard that time is being drawn away from proper discipline-specific instruction. Again, we suggest that detractors be run up the hierarchy of motives to be shown the benefits of teamed and integrated approaches. Teaming can also be shown to be economical in allowing teachers to take better advantage of the economy of redundancy. To use a mining metaphor, the tailings of one discipline often provide rich ore for another.

In multi-subject elementary classes, individual teachers can work interdisciplinary magic. But even here, we recommend that teams be formed. There is synergy lost in being alone, the creative dynamic that comes into being when people with a common goal and different backgrounds come together to share ideas. Two or three elementary teachers joining forces for a single project also allows for greater flexibility in planning. On a given day, for instance, two teachers of a three-teacher team can take the bulk of the students the team shares while the third teacher supervises a local field trip for the remaining small group.

In secondary schools, pairs are better than singles, teams better than pairs. We have watched teachers at work with one another in schools and in our teacher education courses. Almost without exception, these sessions generate excitement and magnificent ideas for interdisciplinary instruction. The planning sessions create a synergy between teachers and this, we have seen, readily spills into the classroom. Students catch the excitement and feel the power of disciplines interacting as they as they are applied to make sense of the same phenomenon, used to find answers to a common set of problems.

The last organizational configuration is what we call *full bore* problem-based/project-based interdisciplinary instruction. This is the mode of instruction that best suits the questing model we have advocated throughout this book. Quests can take place in schools using option four, but they can really take off when the walls between the disciplines are torn down to the ground and students work where they need to work in order to contend with the problems their projects place before them. Option four has students working *occasionally* with projects, the greater portion of time dedicated directly to study in the particular disciplines; the curriculum revolves around discipline-specific studies.

Option five places the emphasis on projects; project work becomes the primary occupation of students. Disciplinary studies function to serve the needs of students as they develop during work on the projects. Teachers facilitate the development of projects, work to ensure that projects will indeed create a need for disciplinary knowledge and skill, and act as expert consultants to the projects. The disciplines are taught as a response to need through centers and seminars—students take advantage of the teachings when those teachings will help solve the problems generated by the projects.

We admit that this approach has a pie-in-the-sky feel to it and, at this point, we offer it as a radical alternative with great potential for helping educators to reconceptualize school programs. At this point in the history of schools, we recommend that teachers begin with one of the other options and make adaptations in the curriculum that move it increasingly toward the full bore model, dedicating increasingly larger portions of time to interdisciplinary questing, to students exploring those aspects of the world that become interesting to them as they try to make things happen through projects with real-world consequences. Our ultimate goal is schools in which students come to teachers requesting disciplinary skill and knowledge to accomplish tasks they, the students, understand to be meaningful, worthwhile, and necessary.

This goal, of students understanding the disciplines and teacher expertise as *resource* is achieved now, small scale, in some programs. The Lego-Logo project and RADD serve as examples. We know that students come to and appreciate expertise when there is desire or need. We have, for example, observed students reading computer manuals on their own and asking teachers for help in interpreting them without being assigned to do so when they have a strong desire to make computers do what they want them to do. We know of schools with lunchtime or after school programs that allow students to take courses on topics not addressed in the regular curriculum. Students ask for these courses. They know that there are things that they want to learn. Joan Lipsitz in *Successful Schools for Young Adolescents* describes schools in which one day each week is dedicated to student-elected courses (1991). The enthusiasm generated by these courses, the questions they cause students to want to have answered, could with relative ease be taken advantage of for teaching concepts that are a part of the standard curricula for the various disciplines taught within these schools. If students are brought to understand the *enabling power* of the disciplines they will come to the disciplines when that power is needed.

In a sense, we are calling for re-visioning that places greater emphasis on the building of attitudes appropriate for quality learning. We can begin to visualize kindergarten through college programs that grow students into the proper frame of mind for the independence of study programs of which we are speaking. These programs would, from the earliest days, introduce students to the purposefulness of their studies, focus on inculcating students in the wonders of a culture of knowing, help them feel the power that comes with knowledge and skill.

Instead of telling them what they need to know, the system would work to help them develop the knowledge and skill necessary for deciding what they need to know and where they can find it. If this is done properly, they would inevitably come to have sound understanding of the true basics underlying the disciplines and they would come to understand the concepts inherent in the disciplines in a deeper and far more meaningful way than they do now.

This is the vision. For now approximations will have to do and each of the options above this one on the list is an approximation with potential for improving the quality of instruction. The approximations may in themselves be developmental, in the sense of moving schools toward wholly new configurations, and in terms of moving students toward greater degrees of independence in their learning.

References

BROWN, H. 1991. *Inside Whole Language: A Classroom View*. Portsmouth, NH: Heinemann.

DUNTON, M., S. SPENCER, G. TAYLOR AND S. MEIBERGEN. 1993. *Teaching Nevada: An Interdisciplinary Approach*. Reno, NV: Nevada Humanities Committee and Nevada State Council of Teachers of English.

EICHOLZ, R., P. O'DAFFER AND C. FLEENOR. 1987. *Addison-Wesley Mathematics*. Menlo Park, CA: Addison-Wesley.

HIRSCH, E.D. 1987. *Cultural Literacy: What Every American Needs to Know*. Boston: Houghton Mifflin.

LEHR, S. 1991. *The Child's Developing Sense of Theme: Responses to Literature*. New York: Teachers College Press.

LIPSITZ, J. 1991. *Successful Schools for Young Adolescents*. New Brunswick, NJ: Transaction.

PAUL, R. 1994. "Overcoming the Addiction to Coverage: Less is More." *Educational Vision* 2(1): 11.

ROBINSON, F., J. ROSS AND F. WHITE. 1985. *Curriculum Development for Effective Instruction*. Toronto: OISE Press.

SARGIOUS, M. 1975. *Pavements and Surfacings for Highways and Airports*. New York: Wiley and Sons.

SCHON, D. 1983. *The Reflective Practitioner*. New York: Basic Books.

TYLER, R. 1949. *Basic Principles of Curriculum and Instruction*. Chicago: University of Chicago Press.

VYGOTSKY, L. 1989. *Thoughts and Language*. A. Kozulin, ed. Cambridge, MA: MIT Press.

WATSON, D., ed. 1987. *Ideas and Insights: Language Arts in the Elementary School*. Urbana, IL: National Council of Teachers of English.

PART 2

INTERDISCIPLINARY JUMPSTARTERS

The seven miniunits that follow are designed, as their title suggests, to give the reader some concrete examples of interdisciplinary units and some activities that may be helpful in the classroom. We hasten to add that these are not designed to be complete; they are not meant to be "installed" in your curriculum; they are not "teacherproof," and they are certainly not "student-proof." In other words, you should adapt these to your own circumstances or possibly just study them as models and examples that will trigger ideas for units of your own design.

These follow the S^2 planning model outlined in Chapter 4, giving you a brief rationale for the unit, some general ideas about the interdisciplinary concepts being covered, a bibliography (which will certainly need to be correlated and expanded drawing on materials available in your community), suggested classroom activities, and some ideas for performance and assessment.

1

The Loneliest Job
Weather Forecasting, Prediction, and Prophesy

Pity the poor weatherperson who is expected to get the predictions right, and attracts attention only when wrong.

This unit centers on exploring the specific topic of weather prediction, but it might well move on to examine the more general topic of prophesy and prediction in all areas of human life, from economics to horoscopes.

Central Concepts

Math/Science

- statistics and probability
- measurement and error
- climate and geography
- the precipitation cycle
- graphs, maps, and charts
- astronomy vs. astrology

Humanities/Arts

- weather as a theme in art, literature, and music
- historical prediction
- economic prediction
- futurism and science fiction

Community / Vocational

- local geography and climate
- career as a forecaster
- local/regional economic forecasting
- emergency preparedness

Resources

★ADLER, DAVID. *World of Weather*. 1983. Mahway, NJ: Troll Associates.

★BATTLES, ELIZABETH. 1973. *501 Balloons Sail East: The Story of a Schoolwide Weather Experiment*. Reading, MA: Young Scott Books.

★CARONA, PHILIP. 1974. *Finding Out About the Weather*. Winchester, IL: Benefic Press.

CASTI, JOHN AND ANDERS KARLQVIST, eds. 1991. *Beyond Belief: Randomness, Prediction, and Explanation in Science*. Boca Raton, FL: CRC Press.

DENNIS, JERRY. 1992. *It's Raining Frogs and Fishes: Four Seasons of Natural Phenomena and Oddities of the Sky*. New York: HarperCollins.

ELWELL, FRANK W. 1991. *The Evolution of the Future*. New York: Prager.

★FERAVOLO, ROCCO. 1963. *The Junior Science Book of Weather Experiments*. Champaign, IL: Garrard.

GANERI, ANITA. 1989. *The Usborne Book of Weather Facts*. London: Usborne.

LAFFERTY, PETER. 1992. *Weather*. Avenel, NJ: Crescent Books.

★LEHR, PAUL, WILL BURNETT, HERBERT SPENCER ZIM, AND HARRY MCNAUGHT. 1991. *Weather: Air Masses, Clouds, Rainfall, Storms, Weather Maps, Climate*. New York: Golden Press.

MCVEY, VICKI AND MARTHA WESTON. 1990. *The Sierra Club Book of Weatherwisdom*. San Francisco: Sierra Club. Boston: Little, Brown.

MILNE, ANTONY. 1989. *Earth's Changing Climate: Future Weather and the Greenhouse Effect*. Garden City Park, NY: Avery Publishing.

★ROGERS, DANIEL. 1989. *Weather*. New York: Marshall Cavendish.

★ROGERS, PAUL. 1990. *What Will the Weather Be Like Today?* New York: Greenwillow Books.

★TANNENBAUM, BEULAH. 1989. *Making and Using Your Own Weather Station*. New York: Franklin Watts.

Weather & Climate. 1992. Alexandria, VA: Time-Life Books.

WILLIAMS, JACK. 1992. *The Weather Book*. New York: Vintage.

Local resources: weatherpeople, water control and sewer management people, emergency services personnel, fortune tellers, prophets and predictors in business and industry.

★for younger readers

Classroom Activities

- Collect a week's worth of weather forecasts and study the language used by forecasters to hedge their bets or to build in a margin for error. Study the weather for your area for the same week. How often does the weatherperson get it right?

- Research average and record-setting weather in your area. What are the averages in terms of rainfall, snow, sunny days, cloudy days, windy days, warm days, cold days? What are the extremes?

- Get a book on how to create your own weather station. Build some of the instruments described in the book. Collect information and write your own weather forecasts. Compare them to those of the professionals.

- Interview a professional forecaster about his/her work. Write a profile of the person. Be sure to ask how the weatherperson feels when the forecast is *wrong*. What are the consequences of mistakes in the weather business?

- Is the world's weather changing? Is there a true "greenhouse effect"? If there is change, what are likely to be the consequences in your lifetime? What can we do to control the future of weather on our planet?

- Interview or invite a stockbroker to class to discuss prophesy in his/her business. How is a stockbroker like a weather forecaster? What does he/she predict? What are the consequences of whether or not those predictions are accurate?

- Do the balloon-launch activity (see Battles, resources list). Launch helium balloons into the wind with a request for the finder to send you a postcard. Use the postcards to track wind patterns from your region.

- Do research into predictors and prophets associated with your local government. Who are the planners for the community? What are they planning? What information do they collect, and how do they translate it into predictions?

- Learn about astronomy and astrology. How does an astrologist use the stars for predictive purposes? Collect horoscopes from the local paper and discuss the language they use and their accuracy.

- Find out what life insurance has to do with prophesy. What are mortality tables? How are they calculated? In what other ways is the insurance industry in the prophesy business?

- Who are the most famous prophets in history? What were their fates? What happens to false prophets? What happens to prophets whose success is not proven until after their deaths?

- Virtually all science fiction is, in its way, a prophesy of a possible future. Read sci fi books as predictions. What current issues, problems, or trends do science fiction writers choose to explore? What are their predictions for the future?

Performance/Assessment

- a school weather station that offers weather forecasts for the school, or possibly even for local radio stations

- a collection or reading of student science fiction pieces offering predictions of our future

- a bulletin board display tracking the accuracy of local weather forecasters

- a debate on the greenhouse effect and/or other climactic probabilities for the future

- a bulletin collection of class predictions and prophesies: for individuals, for the school, for the community, for the world, sealed in a time capsule, to be opened on, say, the students' twenty-fifth reunion

2

The *"Perfect" Langwidge?*
Exploring English

English is one of the world's most difficult and complicated languages, filled with ambiguities and trickeries, rules that have exceptions, inconsistent spellings, and inexplicable idioms. It drives even native speakers to irritation and proves especially difficult to learn as a second language. Yet because of the role of Great Britain and the United States in world affairs, it has also become "everybody's second language," learned all over the globe. Although one might think of it as the preserve of the teacher of the same title, English (or any language) proves to be a fascinating starting point for interdisciplinary studies.

Central Concepts

English

Start this unit with a definition for exploration: "Language is a set of verbal symbols by which people communicate." Be sure students understand the symbolic and systematic nature of language. Also of interest may be Robert Pooley's timeless description of "good English": "Good English is that form of the language that is comfortable for listener and speaker, true to the language as it is, and appropriate to the situation."

Math/Science

- linguistics as a science
- how language functions in science
- mathematical vs. ordinary or "real" languages
- the role of language in scientific truths

Humanities/Arts

- how symbols function
- art, music, and dance as languages
- the history of English
- the idiosyncrasies of English
- language in politics and advertising

Community/Vocational

- the nature and role of standard Englishes
- bilingualism in our community
- careers as a language teacher
- "job" English and practical discourse

Resources

COMRIE, BERNARD. 1987. *The World's Major Languages*. New York: Oxford University Press.

FARB, PETER. 1973. *Word Play: What Happens When People Talk*. New York: Alfred A. Knopf.

GORRELL, ROBERT. 1994. *Watch Your Language!* Reno: University of Nevada Press.

*GREEN, CAROLE. 1983. *Language*. Chicago: Children's Press.

HAYAKAWA, S.I. 1990. *Language in Thought and Action*. New York: Harcourt Brace.

*HOWARD, SAM. *Communications Machines*. Milwaukee: Raintree Children's Press.

ILLICH, IVAN. 1980. *ABC: The Alphabetization of the Popular Mind*. San Francisco: North Point Press.

LEDERER, RICHARD. 1992. *The Miracle of Language*. New York: Pocket Books.

ORWELL, GEORGE. 1983. *1984*. New York: NAL/Dutton.

POOLEY, ROBERT. 1946. *Teaching English Usage*. New York: National Council of Teachers of English.

RICHARDSON, DAVID. 1988. *Esperanto: Learning and Using the International Language*. Eastsound, WA: Orcas Publishing.

*STEWIG, JOHN WARREN. *Sending Messages*. Boston: Houghton Mifflin, 1978.

Local specialists: college linguists or language teachers, native speakers of other languages in your community, radio or television broadcasters, politicians, philosophers, immigration or voter registration officials, computer (language) specialists.

---

*for younger readers

Classroom Activities

- Imagine you have been invited to develop an international or even inter-galactic language—a "perfect" language without the problems of a natural language like English. Write the specifications or the outline for this new language. How would it work? What kinds of symbols would it use? What would its "grammar" be like? Create some samples of this language.

- Study the languages of science fiction. How do the earthlings and aliens talk to one another in books and on television? How often do writers solve the problem by having magical translating machines available?

- Study efforts to develop translating machines for real on earth. How do those pocket electronic translators for tourists work? What are some of the major efforts underway to develop machine translations? What are the pitfalls?

- Learn something of the history of English. (Especially good are the tapes of the PBS series, "The Story of English.") How did the history of English help to shape its weird grammar and spelling?

- Collect and analyze jokes, riddles, and puns in English. How does the imperfect nature of our language make things funny?

- Research issues in animal communication, beginning with the difficult question: "Does your pet know its own name?" Can dolphins and chimps actually learn a language? How does their communication differ from that of humans?

- Study the misuses of language: How do politicians use rhetoric to fog language and truth? How does advertising bend words and meanings to sell goods and services?

- Study how language functions in your particular (inter)discipline. What are the special uses of words within it? How does a person learn to speak the language of, say, science or history, or politics or mathematics?

- Learn some American sign language. How does it translate English into a whole new grammar and symbol system?

- Invite a teacher from the bilingual or English as a second language program to describe and discuss the English Only movement. What is it? What does it mean? Conduct research into bilingualism in the community. Invite bilingual speakers to class to discuss how they learned their second language.

- Find out if there is an Esperanto group in your community, people who have learned and are interested in this artificial world language. How does Esperanto work? What are the goals of the esperanto movement? How does it propose to solve some of the world's language problems and to be a (nearly) perfect language?

- Compare languages: whatever ones the kids or community residents know. How do symbol systems differ among English, Arabic, Hebrew, Amerindian, Japanese, Chinese, German, Italian, Russian?

Performance/Assessment

- a display of odd newspaper headlines

- a discussion, panel, or set of talks on the nature of "good," clarifying issues of what makes "proper" speech

- a "dialect fair," where students imitate (respectfully) various dialects of English, north and south, Appalachian and southern, German/English, Italian/English, etc.

- a video where people who have learned English as a second language discuss their problems

- individual folders created by students containing their troublesome spelling errors, usage items that give problems, samples of well written language

3

Water Water Everywhere
Clean Water for Your Community

The topic of water quality is natural for interdisciplinary inquiry at all levels of school. Not only is clean water a national priority, but the topic is as close as the nearest faucet. Although the library can supply resources for this project, here is a topic where a great many federal, state, and private agencies will send reams of material. We suggest that prior to the project you write (or have the students write) the various agencies listed asking for their materials.

Central Concepts

Math/Science

- statistics on all aspects of the drinking water supply
- the science of pollution: microorganisms, chemicals, etc.
- water purification
- contaminant levels: their measurement and accuracy
- mapping, charting, graphing

Humanities/Arts

- mapping, charting, graphing, illustrating
- responsibility and consequences
- weighing economic costs and consequences
- the language of law

Community/Vocational

- local history and demographics
- careers in environmentalism
- the politics of clean water
- relationship of federal, state, and local standards

Resources

*DeAngeleis, Lee, Stephen C. Basler and Loren E. Yeager, eds. 1989. *The Complete Guide to Environmental Careers.* Washington, DC: Island Press.

Drinking Water: A Community Action Guide. CONCERN, Inc., 1794 Columbia Rd., N.W., Washington, DC 20009.

*Earthworks Group, Inc. 1989. *50 Simple Things You Can Do to Save the Earth.* Berkeley, CA.

Environmental Protection Agency. Office of Ground Water and Drinking Water, 401 M. St. SW, Washington, DC 20460, or its Safe Drinking Water Hotline 1-800-426-4791. The following publications are especially useful:

Bottled Water: Helpful Facts & Information

Developing Criteria to Protect Our Nation's Waters

Ground Water Protection: A Citizen's Action Checklist

Home Water Testing

Home Water Treatment Units: Filtering Fact from Fiction

Is Your Drinking Water Safe?

Lead in School Drinking Water

Public Water Systems: Providing Our Nation's Drinking Water

Safe Drinking Water Act as Amended by the Safe Water Act Amendments of 1986

21 Water Conservation Measures for Everybody

Volatile Organic Chemicals: Are VOCs in Your Drinking Water?

"Geography: Reflections on Water." Teaching guide. National Geographic Association, Washington, DC 20036.

Heloise. 1990. *Hints for a Healthy Planet.* New York: Perigee.

International Bottled Water Association. 113 N. Henry Street, Alexandria, VA 22314. (Various leaflets on home or bottled water.)

Miles, Betty. 1990. *Save the Earth: An Action Handbook for Kids.* New York: Alfred Knopf.

National Drinking Water Week. 6666 W. Quincy Avenue, Denver, CO 80235. (Ask for "Water Trivia Facts" and the publicity packet for the "Blue Thumb Program.")

---

*for younger readers

NATIONAL SANITATION FOUNDATION. 3475 Plymouth Road, Box 1468, Ann
Arbor, MI 48106. (Ask for leaflets on home water units.)

★ROSSER, J.K. 1990. *The Teenage Mutant Children's ABCs for a Better Planet.* New
York: Random House.

Safety on Tap: A Citizen's Drinking Water Handbook. League of Women Voters, 1730
M. St., NW, Washington, DC 20036.

"Save Our Streams Adoption Kit." Izaak Walton League of America. 1401 Wilson
Boulevard, Arlington, VA 22209. ($8 for kit; $1 for teachers' guide.)

WATER QUALITY ASSOCIATION. Consumer Affairs Department, Box 606, Lisle, IL
60532. (Ask for information on home water units.)

Local and community experts: people from the water control board or municipal
water supply, doctors, sanitation engineers, biologists, water testers.

Classroom Activities

- Have students collect and compute a dazzling array of statistics on water—its
  omnipresence, its function in our lives, its consumption by people, animals,
  plants, and industry. See, in particular, "Water Trivia Facts" (See National
  Drinking Water Week, resources list) for statistics that range from how much
  of an elephant is water (70 percent) to the amount of the world's water that
  is actually suitable, with treatment, for drinking (1 percent).

- Compute statistics on water waste: If each person in your town wastes one gallon of water a day by running the tap while brushing his/her teeth, how
  much clean water goes down the drain? How much purified water is flushed
  down toilets in your community each day? How much is sent to the sewers
  as a byproduct of dishwashing or laundry?

- Review the federal MCLs (maximum contamination levels) as provided in
  the *Safe Drinking Water Act* (see EPA, resources list). Have students prepare
  graphs and charts showing the permissible levels of contaminants. Write out
  the permissible parts per millions as fractions, e.g., 1/1,000,000) to help students gain a sense of just how *few* bits of regulated chemicals or microorganisms can have negative effects on the human body. Write out 300 trillion with
  its string of zeros, the approximate number of gallons of water on the planet;
  then show what the 2/3 of the planet covered by water looks like; then show
  what the one percent of drinking water amounts to.

- Make contact with your local water supplier and your state water regulatory
  agency. Obtain water testing results from your local water supplier. Graph the
  relationship of your local drinking water to federal standards.

★for younger readers

- Study how the water cycle works in general and in your geographical area, in particular, whether you live in the desert, a mountain rain shadow, or the northern Midwest. What's your average rainfall? How is water stored naturally and artificially in your area? Where does any excess or waste water flow? Where does the water that evaporates from your region come down as precipitation?

- Create muddy, murky, or polluted water with a variety of ingredients: sand, scraps of paper, vegetable oil, gravel, salt, food coloring. Design a series of experiments with filters: sand, panty hose, cotton, coffee filters. Discover how easy or difficult it is to separate pollutants. (Thanks to Sheila Meibergen, Brown Elementary School, Reno, for suggesting this idea and the following one.)

- Create a solar still by stretching plastic wrap across a container of water, setting the container in the sun, and capturing the runoff. How effective is distillation in removing the sorts of pollutants described in the previous activity?

- Discuss the health science implications of clean water: What is the scientific mechanism of health problems created by bacteria and viruses, radium and radon, the heavy metals, and organic and inorganic products of landfills or agriculture?

- Study the geology and geography of ground water in your region. How does water get underground? How long does it stay there? What chemicals does your local ground water pick up? What is happening to the water table in your region due to rain or drought or human tapping of the aquifers? How much of your local water supply comes from ground water (as opposed to reservoirs)?

- Have students create a set of flash cards on science facts and figures about water and the water supply. Use these as the starting point for a "Jeopardy" game on water facts. (For more details, see the "Blue Thumb" materials of National Drinking Water Week.)

- Read a portion of the text of the Safe Drinking Water Act (see EPA, resources list) and have older students study its legal language. Why are there so many definitions, for example, "contaminant," "person," "Native American"? Why does the law use such complex language to say, "Don't mess up our drinking water?" Let students try to write a plain English law that they believe would control water quality.

- Research the history of the water supply in your community. Students may be surprised to learn that once upon a time the water was much, much cleaner, or shocked to discover that it once was much, much dirtier than it is now.

- Study the economics of your local drinking water. How much do people pay per gallon for their water? How much does it cost to treat water? What plans for expansion or renovation does your local water supplier have in mind? How much will that cost?

- The National Geographic Society (see resources list) suggests an excellent language arts activity: Have students make a list of all the words they can think of that have to do with water—mist, dew, rain, etc.—and water-based expressions—"drop in the bucket," "deep six," etc. What does the role of "water" in our language say about its role in our lives?

- Collect and analyze advertisements for water purification systems and bottled water. What tactics do advertisers use to persuade people to buy and use water other than that flowing from the tap? Have students interview water purchasers at a local supermarket to find out why they buy bottled water. (Also, for fun, do a survey to find out how many people buy bottled drinking water and then refill the bottle from the tap.)

- Encourage students to write science fiction or science fact scenarios about the future of water (e.g., the southwest runs out of water; global warming raises the world's sea levels; a villain figures out a way to contaminate the nation's drinking water supply; the earth becomes a desert, and water is more priceless than gold).

Performance/Assessment

- a "Water Facts" bulletin board showing statistics on water use in your community and displaying clippings of newspaper articles that relate to your community's clean water supply.

- a student-created map, chart, illustration, photograph, and/or videotape of the water supply and waste water systems of your community, illustrating graphically how safe drinking water gets to our homes and schools and how waste water is taken away.

- an audit of the school's drinking water for possible lead, done using materials supplied by the EPA.

- adopting a stream or pond (whether or not it is connected to the drinking water supply), with a group of students or the whole school taking responsibility for cleaning up and maintaining the stream (eliminating visible trash and pollutants, and even conducting scientific measurements of water quality).

- "Drinking Water Awareness Week" for the school or community, with displays, talks, and presentations on clean water. (See also the "Blue Thumb" materials of the National Drinking Water Week advisory board.) Other "products" of student learning can include: leaflets; demonstrations; displays on what citizens can do to conserve water, dispose of chemicals properly, and cut down on the consumption of products that require large amounts of clean water in their production. Students can also create posters, public service announcements, video or photographic displays, or even newspaper articles based on the research done in science, math, social studies, and humanities classes.

- a community forum where representatives of state, regional, or local water bureaus discuss programs presently in place and planned for the future to ensure a safe and clean water supply. Use your own students as panelists, moderators, and reporters.

**Interdisciplinary
Jumpstarter**

4

A Technological Wish List

Erich Fromm has observed that science and technology are value-free; that is, they are neither good nor bad in themselves. Humankind can choose to employ technology for good (e.g., to improve the human condition) or bad (e.g., ignoring human needs or simply killing people). The core activity of this unit asks students to write a *technological wish list* for a point in the future, say, twenty-five or fifty years from now, essentially a list of machines, devices, gizmos, that, as byproducts of scientific research, work for the good of humankind. Along the way, students might explore possible negative effects of future technology, including massively effective weaponry, undisposable nuclear wastes (see Jumpstarter #8), and the domination of the human intellect by cable television.

Central Concepts

Math / Science

- the distinctions between *science* and *technology*
- current directions in scientific research
- the processes of technology and invention
- mathematical projections

Humanities / Arts

- science and humanistic values
- balancing progress against side-effects
- futuristic literature
- current issues
- current human problems

Community / Vocational

- career and life projections
- the problems facing our town
- personal risk assessment
- human ingenuity in our town

Resources

ARENDT, HANNAH. 1958. *The Human Condition.* Chicago: University of Chicago Press.

*BRENNAN, RICHARD. 1990. *Levitating Trains and Kamikaze Genes: Technological Literacy for the '90s.* New York: John Wiley.

*GOLUB, RICHARD. 1990. *The Almanac of Technology: What's New and What's Known.* Orlando, FL: Harcourt Brace.

*McLUHAN, MARSHALL. 1965. *City as Classroom.* Agincourt, Ontario: Book Society of Canada, Ltd.

*NOBLE, HOLCOMB. 1987. *Next: The Coming Era in Science.* Boston: Little, Brown.

SIEDEN, LLOYD STEVEN. 1989. *Buckminster Fuller's Universe.* New York: Plenum.

*TAYLOR, PAULA. 1982. *The Kids' Whole Future Catalog.* New York: Random House, 1982.

Local resources: inventors (check to see if you have a local inventor's club), patent attorneys, research scientists at a nearby college or university, research scientists working for business or industry, handypeople—anybody who can fix things or figure out ways to jury-rig things so they work.

Classroom Activities

As noted above, the core activity for the unit is for students to prepare a technological wish list, a description/list of technological devices that would improve the lot of humankind. Some fun and games, some trivial inventions would be OK as a warmup: a machine that brushes your teeth while you sleep, a computer that can do homework. But the major thrust should be first toward understanding the impact of technology on the quality of life and second, figuring out ways to use technology to bring about broadly based improvements in human life. For example:

- Study and discuss the positive and negative effects of twentieth century technological innovation, for example, the harnessing of nuclear energy, the devel-

---

*for younger readers

opment of the computer, the invention of the automobile. What have been the advantages of innovation for humanity? What have been the negative side effects? Could the problems have been avoided?

- Marshall McLuhan argued that any technology is an extension of a human faculty: the wheel is an extension of the foot, clothing is an extension of the skin. Debate that assertion and explore the metaphor for modern technologies such as cars, light bulbs, or computers.

- Identify major problems that continue to plague humanity: hunger, disease, poverty, warfare. How can science and technology help to reduce or eliminate these problems? What will be required for this to happen?

- Victor Papanek argues that in western countries, invention and design have become slaves to the marketplace. That is, products are engineered to make money, leading to products that don't work, don't last, or are planned to be obsolete in a few years. Have your students research products to see whether this is true. How well do cars work? Coffee makers? Items of clothing? How easy is it to fix things that are broken? What do we throw away before it should have reached the limits of its usefulness?

- In America we have turned high technology into such amusements and entertainments as fast food, video games, MTV, flashy cars and clothes, and shopping malls. What needs are met by these applications of technology? How could the same technology be applied to the problems facing the world today?

- In the spirit of the Odyssey of the Mind, have students brainstorm new uses for familiar products or objects: a brick, a screw or screwdriver, a button. Also link this to brainstorming about recycling: What new useful products could we make from newspapers, aluminum, or glass? (Couple this with a visit to or from your local recycler. What's the current market for recycled goods?)

- For fun, study the inventions of Rube Goldberg (see resources list), the famous cartoonist who had elaborate devices and gizmos to perform ordinary tasks, from swatting a fly to fanning a sleeping baby. Have students design their own devices.

- Study a problem of unanticipated side effects from technology: increased use of fertilizer leads to poisoned streams and lakes, automobiles lead to air pollution, Styrofoam and air conditioner coolants lead to destruction of the ozone layer. Did the science/technologists who created these products anticipate the side effects? Could or should they have? Bottom line: Was the destruction worth it?

- From a patent attorney or inventor, learn about the process by which great ideas dreamed up in somebody's basement become marketable products. What does it cost to protect your invention? What are the odds of a great idea actually making it in the marketplace?

Performance/Assessment

- an Inventor's Fair where students display drawings, writeups, models, or even working prototypes of futuristic gizmos that would help humankind. Submissions should be serious in purpose, and within the range of imagination if not immediately practical.

- a bulletin board or notebook of newspaper and magazine clippings, with the theme "Technology at Work." Have students keep an eye out for any article or advertisement that claims to or demonstrates ways to put technology to work in new and interesting ways. With this display, keep a scoresheet or rating system: Is this a valuable use of technology?

- a "Museum of the Future" with collected information, writing, sketches, or models of technological innovations that will become a reality in the students' lifetimes. A prophesy for each device might be included as part of the labeling: Does the student think this gizmo will, in fact, produce beneficial effects for humankind?

- radio scripts for brief introductions to a segment titled, "New Directions in Science and Technology." Consider getting the scripts performed as a public service by a local radio station. Alternatively, have students write a series of short articles or fact sheets on these new directions, including both praise of science and technology and concerns about possible negative side effects.

5 *Ye Olde Kids' Almanac and Book of Facts*

*Being a Compendium of the Wit, Wisdom,
and Culture of Your Students*

A great many teachers have discovered the joy and value of having kids do informal research into folklore: remedies for common diseases; the arts and crafts mastered by elders; stories, myths, and legends from the region; local history; games and amusements; cookery; family and regional traditions. For this project, set your students to the task of creating an almanac. After studying some of the commercial almanacs that are available, simply set students to the task of writing an almanac of their own. There are no ground rules on what such a book should contain. The rule is this: answer the question, "What interesting information can we gather from our area?" A major purpose, of course, is to save and preserve ideas, materials, and stories that might otherwise be lost. We recommend doing the almanac as a looseleaf notebook pages can be added and inserted. However, it may be that it can lead to development for local publication on a small or large scale. (See performance and assessment).

Central Concepts

The concepts learned will vary with individual student projects. As students complete their work, you might even have them describe their learnings. Sample student learnings might be:

- Health science (from studying household remedies, cures for hiccups, the common cold, blisters, warts, etc.)
- Myth and legend (from collecting folktales about your region).
- Local history (from interviews and collecting stories)

- Computations and statistics (from compiling facts about the weather, sports, population, the economy, etc.)

Every student will likely learn:

- Research skills (from posing questions, seeking answers, weighing data or resources).

The almanac project is one of the most broadly based learning projects we know of.

Resources

ASSOCIATED PRESS. Annual. *The Official Associate Press Almanac*. New York: Almanac Publishing Company.

★★BETTELHEIM, BRUNO. 1976. *The Uses of Enchantment: The Meaning and Importance of Fairy Tales*. New York: Alfred A. Knopf.

★ELWOOD, ANN AND CAROL ORSAG MADIGAN. 1989. *The Macmillan Book of Fascinating Facts: An Almanac for Kids.* New York: Macmillan.

FELT, THOMAS EDWARD. 1976. *Researching, Writing, and Publishing Local History*. Nashville: American Association for State and Local History.

★*Foxfire*. Various editions and dates. Rabun Gap, Georgia: Foxfire Fund; New York: McGraw-Hill.

Hammond Almanac of a Million Facts, Records, Forecasts. Annual. Maplewood, NJ: Hammond Almanac.

Information Please Almanac, Atlas, and Yearbook. Annual. New York: McGraw-Hill.

★McLOONE-BASTA, MARGO, ALICE SIEGEL AND RICHARD ROSENBLUM. 1985. *The Kids' World Almanac of Records and Facts*. New York: Ballantine.

The Old Farmer's Almanac. Annual. Dublin, NH: Old Farmer's Almanac.

PAGE, LINDA GARLAND AND HILTON SMITH. 1985. *The Foxfire Book of Toys and Games: Reminiscences and Instructions from Appalachia*. New York: E.P. Dutton.

★★PUCKET, JOHN L. 1989. *Foxfire Reconsidered: A Twenty-Year Experiment in Progressive Education*. Urbana, IL: University of Illinois.

Reader's Digest Almanac and Yearbook. Annual. Pleasantville, NY: Reader's Digest Association.

SAGENDORPH, ROBB HANSELL. 1970. *America and Her Almanacs: Wit, Wisdom, & Weather, 1939–1970*. Dublin, NH: Yankee.

★★SIMONS, ELIZABETH RADIN. 1990. *Student Worlds, Student Words: Teaching Writing Through Folklore*. Portsmouth, NH: Boynton/Cook.

★for younger readers
★★teacher resource

**TATAR, MARIA M. 1992. *Off With Their Heads!: Fairy Tales and the Culture of Childhood*. Princeton: Princeton UP.

WEITZMAN, DAVID L. 1976. *Underfoot: An Everyday Guide to Exploring the American Past*. New York: Scribner's.

*WEITZMAN, DAVID L. AND JAMES ROBERTSON. 1975. *The Brown Paper School Presents My Backyard History Book*. Boston: Little, Brown.

WORLD RESOURCES INSTITUTE. 1992. *The Information Please Environmental Almanac*. Boston: Houghton-Mifflin.

Local resources: museum curators, historians, and just about anybody older than your students, especially senior citizens and people who have grown up in the region.

Classroom Activities

- Bring in a supply of almanacs, fact books, Foxfire books, local history and folklore gleaned from your library. Give students time to pore over these materials, perhaps pulling out tidbits of information to share with other students in the class. In short, promote the fascination of almanac browsing.

- Bring in several senior citizens whom you know to have stories to tell, people who have lived all their lives in your town; somebody who coached football or ran a business for forty years; a couple who have just celebrated their fiftieth or seventy-fifth wedding anniversary. Help the students learn to interview these people about their personal histories.

- Provide the students with a list of possible contents for the almanac and have them choose projects. Among the possibilities are:

  household remedies
  local trivia and quizzes
  great moments in childhood
  common riddles
  holiday traditions (home or school)
  childhood games
  legendary accidents, fires, and floods
  bad advice
  any student's family tree
  the town's history or "family" tree
  How-tos such as
  investment tips

---

*for younger readers
**teacher resource

canning

original poetry

sewing

horoscopes

woodbutchering

weather forecasts

car repair

great book nominations

family aphorisms and proverbs

school or town records

strange but true stories

let the truth be finally known

- Have each student work out a research plan for his/her project. What questions will be asked? Where will students go for information? If the project includes interviews, make the students include phone numbers of their contacts and write in dates of interviews. Also include due dates for students to submit notes, rough drafts, and polished copy.

Performance/Assessment

- The almanac itself is the most important final product. As noted, it could be a loose-leaf notebook, but it could also lead to a bulletin board display.

- Consider publishing the almanac. Conceivably, there will be enough community interest to warrant publication. (Talk to the Kiwanians or the Rotarians about sponsorship.) Alternatively, have each student reduce his/her contribution to one page and produce a class book through photocopying.

- Show or play video- or audiotapes of interviews.

- Create a performance of a "living almanac" where students, parents, and community members come together to talk about memories, arts, crafts, traditions, etc.

6

The Campaign
Exploring the Media of Persuasion

Most students have a general awareness of the role of media persuasion in their lives: the direct marketing of products, the indirect marketing of ideas, the examples of sports and music personalities on shaping tastes and values. Yet few people, adults as well as youngsters, fully understand the pervasiveness of the media of persuasion in their lives. This interdisciplinary unit takes a hands-on approach that helps students understand persuasion by *using it* (presumably to good ends). They promote an idea to which they are committed, using the full range of contemporary persuasion tools. This is a project that could be done within the microcosm of the school, but it might well be done "for real" to promote an idea in the community.

The General Assignment

Students are to choose an issue or problem that they feel strongly about. They then research the problem—its statistics, the opposing viewpoints, the proposed solutions—and develop materials to promote their beliefs as powerfully as they can.

Some representative issues or problems:

compulsory education	the quality of television
energy resources	materialism
the elderly	teaching and teachers
class size	discipline codes
the value of walking	public transportation
video games	music television
family values	realpolitiks
capitalism	reading
newspapers	pornography

The best source of topics is likely to be your daily newspaper; students might monitor it as a source of topics that invite exploration. Students might work as a whole class on a single idea (probably a bit too large for easy management), pursue a topic individually (possibly too few to produce a full-fledged media campaign), or work in small groups (in our experience, just the right size).

Once the students have researched their topics, they prepare their advertising campaign. Among the kinds of materials they might produce are:

buttons	essays
editorials	petitions
laws	bumper stickers
rebellion	debates
interviews	letters to editors
advertisements	PR "spots"
newspaper articles	radio documentaries
soap box oratory	threats
rumors	talk shows
lobbying	pressure groups
placards	leaflets
brochures	billboards
newspaper ads	television "infomercials"
press packet	

Central Concepts

These will vary with the projects—the big ideas—that students select. Any issue will likely have math/science, humanities/arts, and community/vocational components, and the learnings can easily be shaped to a particular discipline or field that may be your starting point. That is, if you are an English teacher, you can focus a bit more heavily on the *language* of persuasion; if you're in math or science, push the data-gathering and analysis aspects (not forgetting, of course, that our thrust is interdisciplinarity).

Overarching concepts for this unit will include:

- rhetoric and the art of persuasion
- research skills
- planning and organizing a presentation
- assessment: of public interest and need, of the effectiveness of one's campaign

Resources

BAKER, WAYNE E. 1994. *Networking Smart: How to Build Relationships for Personal and Organizational Success*. New York: McGraw-Hill.

CLARK, ERIC. 1989. *The Want Makers: The World of Advertising: How They Make You Buy*. New York: Viking.

DEAN, SANDRA LINVILLE. 1988. *Small Business Guide to Successful Advertising: A Handbook for Small Business*. Wilmington, DE: Enterprise Publications.

EDWARDS, PAUL, SARAH EDWARDS AND LAURA CLAMPITT DOUGLASS. 1991. *Getting Business to Come to You: Everything You Need to Know About Advertising, Public Relations, Direct Mail, and Sales Promotion to Attract All the Business You Can Handle*. Los Angeles: J.P. Tarcer.

HARRISON, E. BRUCE. 1992. *Environmental Communication and Public Relations Handbook*. Rockville, MD: Government Institutes.

HAYNES, COLIN. 1989. *Guide to Successful Public Relations*. Glenview, IL: Scott, Foresman.

HOWARD, CAROLE. 1985. *On Deadline: Managing Media Relations*. New York: Longman.

LEVINSON, JAY CONRAD. 1990. *Guerilla Marketing Weapons: 100 Affordable Marketing Methods*. New York: Plume.

LOIS, GEORGE, AND BILL PITTS. 1991. *What's the Big Idea?: How to Win with Outrageous Ideas (That Sell!)*. New York: Doubleday Currency.

SAFFIR, LEONARD AND HOWARD TARRANT. 1986. *Power Public Relations: How to Get PR to Work for You*. Lincolnwood, IL: NTC Business Books.

WEISS, ANNE E. 1980. *The School on Madison Avenue: Advertising and What It Teaches*. New York: Dutton.

YARRINGTON, ROGER. 1983. *Community Relations Handbook*. New York: Longman.

Classroom Activities

- As suggested above, conduct a newspaper (or other medium) canvass of important issues for a week or so prior to beginning the unit. Put potential topics on the chalkboard or a bulletin board so students have a chance to study and reflect on the list.

- Have students keep a diary or journal of the number of times they are bombarded by persuasive talk or literature in a period of time, say 12–24 hours. How many radio commercials do they hear? How often does somebody say or demonstrate "the right thing to do"?

- As part of their newspaper scan, have the students clip out *everything* that has a persuasive appeal in an issue or two. Include news stories (if, in fact, the students determine they are slanted), editorials, columns, advertisements, feature articles, letters to the editor, want ads, etc. Help the students develop a second list, supplementary to ours, of all the means of persuasion that are open to them.

- Get your small groups started researching their issues. (As we have suggested elsewhere [Chapter 5], make certain this is a full canvass: library, community resources, surveys, etc.)

- As the students become more knowledgeable about their topic, bring reference texts (see see resources list) to class and have them begin developing their persuasive campaign. We won't go into the full details here, but you can use the following as a checklist of possible activities:

clearly identifying the position to be taken
identifying the audience: Who needs to be persuaded?
selecting media/projects: Should we concentrate on newspaper editorials, billboards, TV ads, etc.? What would be most effective?
drafting and field-testing materials.
planning, rehearsing, polishing a presentation, leading to . . .

Performance/Assessment

Here, too, activities will be determined in large measure by the individual directions taken by groups in their campaign. This can lead to kids talking to the mayor, sending press releases to area media, developing ads for the school or local newspaper, preparing a variety of hand-crafted ads, placards, buttons, and bumper stickers for use around the school. The persuasive imagination is the only limit. We recommend that you build in assessment as well including:

- discussion of the effectiveness of various media: What works best—TV or writing, buttons or placards?

- the effectiveness of the students' own campaign—were people successfully persuaded?

- the ethics of persuasion: Were groups tempted to use any persuasive technique, no matter how crude or shabby, in the efforts to sway people to their side?

7 *Exploring the Quality of Life*

A traditional aim for the school curriculum is to prepare or educate students for life in a democracy, to help them become fully functioning articulate citizens. Too often these goals are vaguely taught during civics or social studies lessons, propagandized through the biases of history and literature texts, or practiced only in the pseudo-democracy of school elections. Interdisciplinary study provides an important way of giving students a sense of civic responsibility while helping them understand that one must work to become an informed citizen, that social/political/economic decisions must be based on a solid knowledge base. Each of the topics that follow has implications for that illusive concept "quality of life."

This last jumpstarter follows the S^2 model obliquely: It is an umbrella topic that really contains 101 possibilities for individual, small group, or class inquiry. It concludes the book by demonstrating one of our long-range goals for interdisciplinary inquiry, moving beyond the point where the teacher operates from a single theme or topic toward ways of engaging students in identifying and pursuing individualized topics for study. The final question, as you'll see, moves toward the student as lifelong interdisciplinary learner.

For each topic on the list, the teacher (or better, individual students) would likely do an S^2 planning sheet describing:

- The central issues or problems created by the question. This will help you identify the *central concepts* for each problem, possibly subdivided by math/science, humanities/arts, community/vocational.

- The *resources* in our class texts, the library, through networking, through research, and in the community.

- Individual or group *activities:* What can we actually do to extend our knowledge, collect data, etc.?

- Find the implications of findings for the quality of life in our community, our country, and our world. How can we share our findings with other people? What steps can an informed citizen take to improve the quality of life for people? Such topics encompass *performance and assessment.*

The Quality of Life: 101 Questions for Exploration

1. Do we still need capital punishment?

2. Is there a greenhouse effect?

3. Should we spend money to search for extraterrestrial life?

4. What is the Frankenstein myth and what does it have to do with research in science and technology?

5. Do people use their powers of observation to their fullest capacity?

6. Why are people in such an uproar about creationism vs. evolution?

7. What would be the best way to celebrate Arbor Day?

8. What are the ten most common forms of life on this planet and what do they have to do with people?

9. Will researchers ever be able to develop a computer that is able to think on its own?

10. What is the future of America's cities?

11. What does it mean to say that ours is an "oil-dependent" economy?

12. Will universal credit cards replace money?

13. How efficient are cows?

14. Should we continue to spend money to investigate UFOs?

15. Why don't we have more electric cars, buses, and trucks?

16. Should old, sick people be put to death?

17. Should we continue to put fluoride in our water?

18. Why are there so few famous women scientists?

19. Is it possible to live *too* long?

20. What should we do about nuclear energy and nuclear waste?

21. How did eating utensils evolve and how will they change in the future?

22. How did weapons evolve and how will they change in the future?

23. Should women be allowed to have abortions?

24. How much wealth is enough?

25. Do we need to build any more automobiles?

26. Should scientists be allowed to conduct experiments on live animals?

27. Is it possible to feed everybody now living on this planet?

28. What is "fabric," what does it do for people, and how has it changed over the years?

29. What's the best way to get things clean?

30. What does the sun have to do with it all?

31. What are hormones and why should we care?

32. Does eating right really make a difference?

33. Does gossip do more harm than good?

34. What is the usefulness of odors?

35. Is extrasensory perception for real?

36. What are the biggest birds, the biggest animals, the biggest fish, and what can we learn from them?

37. What does money have to do with the way we live our lives?

38. Does it make sense to irrigate dry lands?

39. What is the International Date Line and why is it there?

40. What would happen to us if everyone were naughty?

41. How can you get on the World Wide Web and what can you do there?

42. How does radio work and what has been its impact on people?

43. How many religions are there in the world and how many of them are found in our community?

44. What if there were no tomorrow?

45. Where did love come from, what good is it, and how is it changing?

46. How does a computer work?

47. Who invented boredom, and what are its causes and cures?

48. Who were the First Americans?

49. What are the most valuable jewels, why are they valuable, and what are they good for?

50. What makes uranium fiss?

51. Are sports a waste of our county's time, energy, and money?

52. How many wars will there be during our lifetime?

53. What is the importance of Japan to the future of our country?

54. How many senior citizens are there, how are they cared for or caring for themselves, and what will it be like for you to be an older person?

55. What is the history of MTV, what came before it, and how is it influencing the values of young people today?

56. What is acid rain, where does it come from, what damage does it do, and how can it be stopped?

57. How many earthquakes are there in the United States in a single year, how are they measured, and how are they predicted?

58. How many people in the world and in the United States have AIDS, what is their future, and what are the possibilities for finding a cure?

59. How do car phones affect ways in which people interact, and will car phones be replaced by wrist phones some day?

60. How many chickens and turkeys are in the United States and under what conditions do they live?

61. How many pets are there and how much does it cost to keep them fed and healthy?

62. When will our community run out of landfill space for trash, and then what?

63. How does our community recycle, and what improvements could be made in the system?

64. What's to prevent our town from banning automobiles and making everybody walk, ride a bicycle, or use a skateboard?

65. What is the history of artificial sweeteners, what tests are conducted to make certain they are safe, and how much artificial sugar is used every year in this country?

66. Does acupuncture work and is it a reliable form of medicine?

67. What's the difference between a chiropractor and a physician?

68. What's the newest in high-tech dentistry, and what shape, generally, are people's teeth in these days?

69. Does your horoscope make sense?

70. What is a "hidden agenda," and what hidden agendas can you find around school or town?

71. What is the history of our school and how have things changed?

72. If your class had three wishes for the betterment of humankind, what would they be?

73. If you had three wishes for yourself, what would they be?

74. Who determines the "top 40" and the "best-sellers," how do they do it, and what difference does it make?

75. What is domestic violence, how much of it exists, and what is being done about it?

76. Is it true that the "infrastructure" is falling apart?

77. Why does getting sick cost so much and what is being done about it?

78. Should suicide be legal?

79. Who are the most courageous people living today and how did they get that way?

80. If you were naming ten people to a Hero/Heroine Hall of Fame, whom would you nominate and why?

81. What are the "classes" in American society?

82. Are we a racial melting pot, a salad bowl, or neither?

83. How many languages are there in the world, which ones are spoken by the most people, and is there any hope that any single language will ever become a world language?

84. How does advertising shape your life?

85. Have you heard about microbes, worms, and other creatures that actually eat and recycle materials?

86. Should the world become vegetarian?

87. Are there spies anymore, and what do they do?

88. Could a comet or asteroid ever hit the earth, and should we worry?

89. How will Africa affect our future?

90. What are the best forms of exercise for people your age?

91. Is the universe running out of steam?

92. Which animals are most intelligent?

93. How and what does dancing "express"?

94. What is that tune you keep singing in your head, and where does it come from?

95. Where is the happiest place on earth?

96. What is the significance of your name, your school's name, and the names of places in your community?

97. How do stories of creation differ from one culture to another?

98. What is the function of tests, examinations, and grades in the world?

99. What makes things funny?

100. How will Europe affect your future?

101. What are the topics, ideas, and issues that most concern you, and how could we explore them in this class?

INDEX